LACROSSE
Fundamentals

by

G. Heberton Evans, III
and
Robert E. Anderson

New York: A. S. Barnes and Co., Inc.

London: Thomas Yoseloff Ltd

Library of Congress Catalogue Card Number: 66-12111

A. S. Barnes and Co., Inc.
Cranbury, New Jersey 08512

Thomas Yoseloff Ltd
108 New Bond Street
London W1Y OQX, England

First Printing, June, 1966
Second Printing, November, 1970

ISBN: 0-498-06371-2
Printed in the United States of America

To our
Governor Dummer Academy
lacrosse teams
who through their
determination, enthusiasm, skill, and successes
have brought
pleasure and pride
to their coaches

Acknowledgments

Fortunately there are no secrets in the lacrosse family, and we could never give due credit to all those who have contributed to our understanding of the game. We realize that many of our methods and tactics have been derived from our coaching friends and opponents. Some of their ideas we have incorporated into our own Governor Dummer program; some we have rejected as unsuited to our personnel; but we have drawn freely on their knowledge.

Specifically, George M. Chandlee, Jr. of Gilman School in Baltimore and Robert P. Hulburd of Phillips Academy, Andover, volunteered to read, criticize, and suggest improvements and additions to the manuscript. As highly successful and experienced prep school coaches, their assistance was invaluable. For similar contributions from the college point of view, we are indebted to Robert Scott of Johns Hopkins University.

We have relied on the advice and assistance of the rest of our Governor Dummer staff; and our Junior Varsity coaches, David M. Williams, John B. Ogden, Jr., and Douglas I. Smink, Jr., made vital contributions, not only through their experience in developing younger players, but also their command of the language as English teachers!

Our photographic illustrations were made possible by

the willingness of our Varsity Teams of 1964 and 1965 to demonstrate over and over various skills and situations. To name the contributors would be impossible, for almost everyone on both squads appears on these pages in one role or another.

While the actual photographing was undertaken by the authors, technical assistance was supplied by Lester Burndt of Cine Service Lab in Watertown and Douglas L. Miller of the Governor Dummer faculty. W. H. Brine Company of Boston generously contributed equipment for our contrasting uniforms and also markets our lacrosse scorebook in their line of lacrosse equipment.

Though this has been a joint production, Bob Anderson has been saddled with the bulk of the artistic work needed for the many diagrams. While we have collaborated on all descriptions, problems, and solutions, the final editorial decisions and the writing of the text have fallen to my lot, so that I must assume final responsibility for the material.

Our original objective was to lend assistance to the neophyte coach and player, but lacrosse is a fluid game, and we realize there are many different approaches to actual play. We have tried to include many different techniques, knowing that no single team or player is likely to employ all. But in so doing, we have gone farther than the limits dictated by "fundamentals" and have intended to incorporate material that would be helpful to more experienced persons.

While we hope this volume will assist others in further development of lacrosse, if it does nothing else, it has forced us to analyze and test our own coaching techniques.

G. Heberton Evans, III
South Byfield, Massachusetts
October, 1965

Foreword

Few athletic events have as colorful a history as does lacrosse. Its origin is lost in the unwritten histories of the Indian tribes of North America. When exploring Europeans arrived, the game was being played in one form or another by the Sauks, Sioux, Ojibwas, Dakotas, Six Nations, Chippewas, Cherokees, Creeks, Potawatomi, and others. Rules of the game, of which there were few, were local in nature. Sticks were about three feet long and had pockets considerably smaller than those of the modern crosse. In some tribal contests each player carried a single stick as today; while in others players carried a stick in each hand.

The Indian tribes had various names for their game. Frenchmen, on seeing the game, likened the appearance of the stick to that of a crosier, similar to a shepherd's crook, carried by bishops as a symbol of office. The Jesuit Pierre Francois Xavier de Charlevoix is generally credited with having drawn the first such parallel when he observed some Algonquins playing the game along the St. Lawrence in 1719. It was probably his description of the Indian sticks that led to the modern name of the game. Few of the

9

Indian names have survived, but the Ojibwa name of *baggattaway* is probably the most well remembered.

Distances between goals varied from 500 yards to several miles, and boundaries were normally nonexistent. The number of players on a side was equally indefinite, and whole villages could be engaged in a single game. Goals were improvised by using natural objects, such as rocks and poles, which the ball had to strike or between which the ball had to be thrown for a score. Games could go on for days.

The Indians played their game for recreation and used it as training for their young braves. Uniforms consisted of only the simple breech-cloth. The tribal medicine men were the game officials, and the squaws and children cheered on their warriors. No quarter was given or asked; and injuries were fairly frequent, either as a result of play for the ball or extraneous action.

Historically the most memorable game was reported to have been played in front of the British garrison at Fort Michilimackinac on June 4, 1763. The Ojibwas and Sacks who had camped nearby staged a game to celebrate the birthday of King George III, and the personnel of the garrison trooped out to watch the contest. In the course of play the ball was thrown near the gate of the fort, and as the braves dashed through the crowd chasing the ball, they were handed weapons previously concealed by the assembled Indian spectators. The fort fell quickly to the onslaught. Few if any of the British garrison survived, though the Frenchmen in the vicinity were spared.

Despite the game's bloody beginnings, the color and science of the game began to catch the fancy of the Canadians. A Montreal physician, Dr. W. George Beers, drew up rules and regulations for the game in 1859. It was played mostly by club teams in Canada. Dr. Beers earned the title of "father of lacrosse" for his pioneer work in spreading the game in Canada and his attempts to popularize it in England. To this date lacrosse is still the National Game of Canada although the game is probably now much more familiar in the United States.

Lacrosse clubs were organized in the North, East, and Midwest in the United States by 1875; but interest soon centered around New York, Boston, and Philadelphia. Baltimore was added to the list in 1879. Players from the club teams—from the Baltimore team in particular—were largely responsible for introducing the game into collegiate athletics. In the 'eighties teams sprang up at Johns Hopkins, Yale, Harvard, Lehigh, Stevens, and Princeton. Harvard had the honor of being the first Intercollegiate Champion in 1881.

The Intercollegiate Lacrosse Association was formed in 1888, and in 1894 the Inter-University League was formed. The two were combined in 1906, and twenty years later the present United States Intercollegiate Lacrosse Association came into being and continues to this date as the lacrosse governing body. Since 1936 The Wingate Trophy has been awarded to the national collegiate championship team.

International competition in lacrosse has been attempted at various times. Touring Canadian teams in the late 1800's introduced the game to England. On several occasions lacrosse has been played in the Olympic Games, but competition was never extensive. Recently touring American college teams have played in England and Australia, either against local opponents or in exhibition games.

Gradually the rules of the game have been refined. The size of the field has been defined and reduced to fit more

easily into the concept of a modern athletic plant. Early
Canadian rules specified a field 200 yards long and 150
yards wide, but these dimensions have been roughly halved.
Twelve players on each side was the rule until 1933, when
the number was reduced to ten. As coaches of the sport
appeared, the job of the "Field Captain" was assumed by
a non-playing man on the bench. Additional linings were
introduced on the field to define playing areas. In 1948
the rectangular crease area was replaced by the present
circle. The modern square goal soon replaced the poles
used by the early Canadian clubs. The brutal nature of
the Indian game was quickly altered by adding sensible
rules and requiring some protective equipment. The helmet and face mask came into general use in the 1930's and
are now required equipment. The present game resembles
the Indian sport only in that the crosse is used and that
the object of the game is to score goals. Science and skill
have taken the place of the rough and tumble of the Indian
contest, and injury to players as a result of abnormal contact or free swinging of the stick is most infrequent.

Lacrosse has always had "champions" of the game who
have given extensively of their time and money to pro-
mote the sport in various areas of the country through
sheer love of the game. With no professional overtones,
ex-collegiate players have banded together to form lacrosse clubs throughout the East, North, and Midwest in
particular, and despite their business commitments, club
players have endeavored to continue to play a fine brand
of lacrosse for many years after the conclusion of their
collegiate careers. Such players have acted as missionaries
of the game in many areas, and they have introduced the
game into many intercollegiate and interscholastic athletic
programs.

Early starts in the interscholastic area centered around Baltimore, Long Island, central New York, and New England. As experienced players were developed on the school level and then moved on to college, they provided an experienced nucleus for many colleges starting the game. The initial geographic areas of interscholastic strength continue today, but more schools throughout the country are adding lacrosse to their programs each year.

Contents

Symbols Used in Diagrams

◯ Offensive Player

△ Defensive Player (Shaded Area Indicates Direction
    Faced)

⊙ Player with Ball

⌒⌒ Preliminary Position of Offensive Player

⌃⌃ Preliminary Position of Defensive Player

⟶ Path of Player without the Ball

- - ➤ Path of Ball on Pass or Shot

〰➤ Path of Player Carrying the Ball

·······➤ Path of Ground Ball

⊢◯ Stationary Player Creating a Post

⊢ Position of Player at Time of Brush; Player Is in Motion

➝ Arrow Indicates Point of Release or Reception of Ball

▢ Coach

Lacrosse Fundamentals

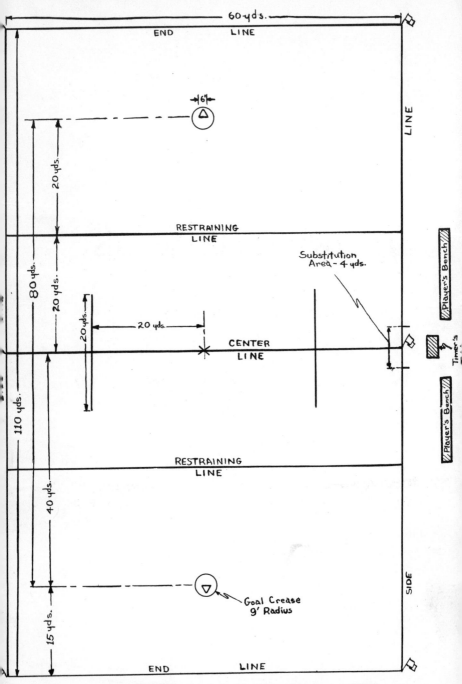

Figure 1. Major Markings and Dimensions of Lacrosse Field.

1. The Game

The modern game of lacrosse differs greatly from the ancient Indian sport. Basically the lacrosse stick remains the same, and the object of the game is still to outscore the opponent. Otherwise restrictions on the number of players, their movements on the field, and equipment involved have made the game one of the most colorful, exciting, and fastest moving of all field games.

THE FIELD

The lacrosse field approximates that used for either football or soccer, making it easy to adapt such areas for lacrosse play. The goals are 80 yards apart and centered on the field, leaving an area 15 yards deep behind each cage as part of the playing area. In this respect lacrosse play most resembles that of hockey, since in both contests it is possible to work from the rear of the goal.

PLAYERS

A lacrosse team consists of ten players plus any number

21

of substitutes. The players are grouped in units of three depending on their normal field position—attack, midfield, and defense. The tenth player of each team is the goalkeeper or goalie. A team must have four players in its defensive half of the field at all times—these are normally the goalie and his three close defense men. At the same time three players must stay in the attacking half of the field, and these are normally the members of the close attack. The three midfielders play the entire field concentrating on attack or defense depending on the position of the ball. They provide the link connecting play between the halves of the field. While it would not be unusual for an attack man or a defense man to play an entire game, a midfielder is normally rested at intervals because of the amount of running his position demands. Many teams organize their midfielders in units of three and alternate the units similar to the way in which hockey lines are alternated.

There are many ways in which the players may align themselves. In the attack group, however, there is usually a crease attack man assigned to play just in front of the circular crease with a 9-foot radius around the goal. A terminology that has recently gone out of style entitled him the First Attack. The other two attack men usually start playing in positions behind the goal, coming around in front of the cage to shoot, but oftentimes passing the ball to others in front of the goal. Informally they are labeled as feeders. Their older titles were In-Home and Out-Home.

If the defense covers their men on a man-to-man basis, the defense man playing against the crease attack man is called the crease defense man. Formerly he was called the First Defense. The other two close defense men who cover the feeders used to be called the Point and Cover Point.

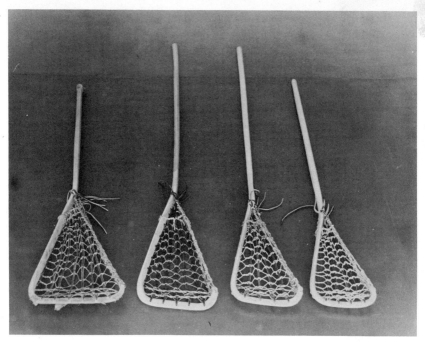

Figure 2. Four Sizes of Lacrosse Sticks. Goal, Defense, Midfield, and Attack (from left to right).

One of the midfielders, or middies, is the center and the other two are now wing midfielders. Their older titles were Second Defense and Second Attack.

THE CROSSE AND BALL

Lacrosse is played with a hard rubber ball about eight inches in circumference and weighing about five ounces. When dropped from a height of six feet onto a hardwood floor, the ball will bounce to a height of almost four feet.

It is permissible to propel the ball in any direction or manner provided it is not batted or thrown with the hand, but it is intended that the ball be passed from player to player and finally into the opponent's goal by using the crosse, or lacrosse stick. The stick varies in length from

40 to 72 inches; though that of the goalie has no minimum length. The width of the head of the stick varies from 7 inches to 12 inches, but only one 12-inch stick is allowed on the field at any one time, and the goalie by definition possesses this stick. Normally the attack players will use the smaller sticks of 7-inch width. A midfield stick measures 8 inches across the head and is likely to be longer, while the defense stick is 9 inches across the head, and the men using these sticks will probably play with sticks close to the six-foot maximum length. Figure 2 illustrates the four kinds of sticks, and Figure 3 gives the proper names for the parts of a stick.

The pocket of the stick is all-important for proper ball control. It may be woven from gut, rawhide, clock cord, linen cord, or nylon cord and is roughly triangular in shape. When new, the pocket is taut and unyielding, allowing the ball to bounce out of the crosse readily. As the player breaks in his stick, the material of the pocket becomes loose and supple having the give needed to soften the impact of the thrown ball and enabling the receiver to control the ball and retain it in his stick until ready to pass.

PERSONAL EQUIPMENT

The spread of the game has accelerated in recent years, but some athletic directors have been reluctant to initiate lacrosse both because of a lack of available, trained coaching personnel and a seemingly large initial investment in equipment. Actually the expense of equipping a player can be kept at a relatively small amount if some ingenuity is used. By regulation each player must have, in addition to his crosse, a helmet equipped with a face mask, and gloves. It is possible to fit football helmets with the necessary

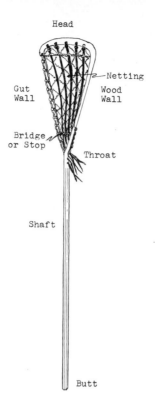

Figure 3. Parts of the Crosse.

face masks. However, lacrosse helmets, which are lighter and equipped with a visor to support the face mask, are more practical and more comfortable. Many players will go through their lacrosse careers playing with standard hockey gloves, but gloves with flexible thumbs are again more comfortable. Manufacturers are now beginning to offer a combination glove with the flexible thumb for both sports.

While shoulder and arm pads are not mandatory pieces of equipment and the rules prohibit striking a player with the crosse other than on the gloves, occasional blows are received on the arms. Although such blows are illegal and occasion penalties, they can nevertheless be momentarily painful, and it is wise to protect the players. Beginners actually need this protection more than experienced players, for the more skilled the opponent, the less likely is he to strike with his crosse in illegal ways. Shoulder and arm pads especially developed for lacrosse are best, although in an emergency hockey pads can be employed.

Otherwise lacrosse uniforms are probably already available in the school's uniform supplies for other sports. Football or soccer shoes are usually worn. Football jerseys and either soccer or basketball pants will fully equip the lacrosse player.

TEAM EQUIPMENT

The 6' by 6' goals are easily purchased or made locally from 1½-inch pipe painted orange. The *NCAA Lacrosse Guide* should be consulted for further dimensions. The goals are fitted with pyramidal nets that can be purchased at a nominal cost. The only other team equipment needed is a supply of lacrosse balls, which are quite inexpensive.

THE GAME

At the start of the game the players are aligned on the field as shown in Figure 4. The ball is placed between the crosses of the opposing centers as shown in Figure 5. On the referee's whistle the two centers battle for possession of the ball. (See Chapter 14 for methods of gaining the center draw.) The wing midfielders are released from their restraining lines to assist their centers, but the attack and defense players are restrained behind their lines until a midfielder gains possession of the ball or the ball

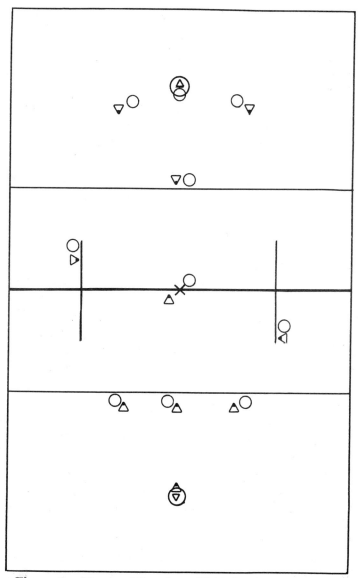

Figure 4. Players Aligned on Field for Start of Game.

Figure 5.   Opposing Centers Ready for Center Draw.

rolls over one of their restraining lines, at which time
the referee releases them.

The team gaining the ball moves forward on the attack,
while their opponents drop into defensive positions to
guard their goal and try to force the attacking team to lose
control. As play settles down after the center draw, the
various players take general positions as shown in Figure
6.

The attacking team tries to control the ball and work it
into scoring position by passing from one player to another.

Figure 6. General Alignment of Players with Ball Settled Down at One End of Field.

Obviously it is of paramount importance for the beginning player to learn to control the ball in his crosse. With inexperienced teams the ball is on the ground a good portion of the time as a result of erratic passes or faulty receptions; but as the players become more experienced, the ball stays in the air or in their sticks a greater percentage of the time. Another fundamental skill a player must learn is to scoop the ball from the ground with his crosse; many games are decided in favor of the team that consistently comes up with the ground ball.

Lacrosse is a wide open game with a good deal of body contact, for in trying to gain possession of the ball a defensive player may check an opponent in possession of the the ball with his stick and with his body. Generally speaking any block that would be legal in football can be thrown by a defensive player at an opponent in possession of the ball or within 5 yards of a loose ball. The *NCAA Lacrosse Guide* should be consulted for specific details. The defending player may use his crosse to check his opponent's stick or strike his gloves (if his opponent's hand is on the stick) in an attempt to dislodge the ball. In addition, should the attack player while carrying the ball come in contact with his defense man, the defender may use his hands, if on the stick, to push the attacking player back—although he may not reach out and strike his opponent.

Frequently spectators uninitiated in lacrosse gain the impression that the contest is rough since players are "swinging sticks at each other," but anyone who has played will quickly assure them that is far from true. The play is always wide open; and while there is frequent contact, serious lacrosse injuries are quite rare. Relatively little contact is generally the rule when skilled opponents meet. The stick itself looks like a dangerous weapon, but in reality, if the defensive player is skilled, his checks with the crosse are legal and non-injurious. Wild swinging is illegal, as is slashing or hitting other than on the opponent's stick or gloves. Occasionally blows are caught on the arms, but these are softened by the player's arm pads and do little damage.

Except for playing the man with the ball or an opponent within 5 yards of a loose ball, intentional contact between other players is prohibited. There may be minor collisions, for a player is allowed to occupy that section of the field on which he is standing, while at the same time another player is allowed to run a true course even if he does not have the ball. Thus the pick-off play to prevent a player from covering his man successfully is frequently used.

Players are penalized for illegal checks and other rules' infractions. For technical violations, such as off-sides, entering the crease on the attacking half of the field, interference, pushing, and the like, the penalty is loss of the ball if the offender's team had control, or expulsion from the game for 30 seconds if the offended team had the ball. For personal fouls such as tripping, illegal checks, slashing, hitting from the rear, and other offenses of this nature, the penalties vary from one to three minutes, with the one minute penalty being normal, and the longer periods reserved for flagrant infractions. These penalties provide the attacking team with one of its best chances to score. Lacrosse play is so fast that it is virtually impossible for five defensive players to keep six attacking players from getting at least one good shot at the goal during a one-minute period—provided the attack controls the ball. As a result a player who continually checks illegally and draws penalties soon finds himself relegated to the bench, for his team cannot consistently afford to play without a man as a result of penalties for his lack of control.

The goalie in lacrosse is unique among goalies. His first job, naturally, is to stop shots taken at the cage; but his almost equally important duty is to come out of his crease area when his defense gains possession and help them to clear the ball down to the attacking half of the field. As a result the good goalie frequently moves downfield close to the midfield line—40 yards from his goal—in the course of a "clear." While in his goal, he is protected from the attack by his circular crease, 9 feet in radius, and no attack man may enter the crease or strike the goalie while he is in this area.

If the ball goes out-of-bounds, it is awarded to the team opposed to that which last touched the ball, with one exception—which again makes the game of lacrosse unique. If a ball goes out-of-bounds as a result of a shot at the goal, the ball belongs to the player, on either team, closest to the spot where the ball crossed the side or back line when it went out. As a result the players behind the cage have a special responsibility for being sure that their team gains possession of the ball after a shot.

After a goal, and at the beginning of a period, the ball is brought back to the center of the field and faced off again as in the beginning of the game.

Lacrosse is a relatively high scoring game, and if the scores of the two teams are added after a game, the total will often run higher than 10 goals, with a total of 25 goals being not uncommon. The complexion of a game can change radically in a few minutes, and it is not unusual for a team suddenly to find a defensive weakness and to score several goals in a short period of time.

For the lacrosse novice, a fuller discussion of the rules of the game is necessary, and the current *NCAA Lacrosse Guide* should be consulted.

GETTING STARTED

Lacrosse has spread through many areas as a major spring sport because of the efforts and interest of those who have played the game. In new areas there is always the problem of sufficient interscholastic competition, but a good start can be made on an intramural basis. The game sells itself, once one school in the area starts to play. There is a natural fascination inherent in the stick itself which starts to draw players. In addition the contact nature of the game often appeals to the best of athletes.

The expense of initiating lacrosse causes reluctance in the offices of some athletic directors, but the lacrosse fraternity is such that it is easy to get assistance in starting a program from almost any neighboring institution where lacrosse is flourishing; from the United States Intercollegiate Lacrosse Association; or from the United States Lacrosse Coaches' Association.

Players will pick up basic stick work quickly provided they are given some instruction in proper technique. It would be better if a coach had played the game, but it is not vital. Often someone who has not played himself can better understand the difficulties his players are having in handling their sticks.

Any coach with a basic knowledge of a similar game can pick up the strategy of lacrosse and thus instruct his players in proper field position and maneuvers. Close parallels in technique can be drawn from soccer, basketball, and hockey, while the contact and evasive maneuvers of football are useful in lacrosse.

In like manner, it is easier to instruct a player who has some knowledge of another sport. The defensive play in particular has strong parallels in soccer, basketball, and hockey, and an athlete trained in one of these quickly picks up the field position and play patterns of lacrosse. All he needs now is the ability to handle the crosse!

2. Stick Work Fundamentals

Provide a stick and a ball, and a player will gradually discover how to handle them. Supply some instruction, however, and learning will be more rapid, and some pitfalls and poor habits can be avoided.

The first thing a beginner will want to do after he experiments with his stick for a day will be to cut it off to a minimum length. This practice should be strongly discouraged immediately. It is true that initially the beginner will find it easier to pass and catch with a small stick, since it will be quite maneuverable, but as soon as he starts to play the game as distinct from playing catch, there are serious disadvantages to a short stick. First, all players, no matter where they are on the field, must play some defense. With a long stick a check can be delivered while players are three to four feet away from physical contact. An opponent who is allowed to work in close to the defender poses a more serious threat than does one kept at a distance. Second, a stick of proper length insures proper leverage for power and accuracy in shooting and passing. Finally, a long stick enables a player to reach for high or wide passes and to make interceptions.

There is no ready formula for proper length of a stick. According to regulation it may not be less than 40 inches long—except for the goalie's stick, which may be of any length—and it may not be more than 6 feet long. Between these limits the proper length will depend partly on the position played. In general the defense men use the longest sticks, the midfielders ones of medium length, and the attack men the shortest ones. However, the stick should be as long as the player can handle. A stick can always be cut, but there is no satisfactory way to add length. As a general rule, the stick of a defense man, when standing in front of him, should reach to the bridge of his nose; that of a midfielder, to a spot about 2 inches below his chin; and that of an attack man, approximately to the breast bone.

Breaking in the Stick

The new stick will be tight and inflexible. Gradually, however, a pocket will develop as the rawhide and the material used for netting stretch and become more pliable. With the pocket it will be easier to control the ball both in passing and catching. A stick will be broken-in most satisfactorily by playing catch with it for several days. If the netting is linen or nylon cord or rawhide, the pocket will be pretty well developed in a day. A clock cord stick will take longer. The temptation to try to develop the pocket artificially should be resisted. Each player handles his stick slightly differently; any artificial method of creating the pocket does not take this into account.

Since the gut wall may have been compressed through

shipping or storage, it should be straightened and then kept erect. The thongs at the rear of the wall should be tightened before practice and loosened afterwards. If the wall is kept taut at all times, the constant pressure will gradually increase the bend in the head of the stick. The wall should stand erect when tightened and should be equal to or higher than the wood wall. Perhaps a player would like the gut wall to lean inward just slightly. More than a slight lean will appreciably cut down the surface available for catching. To have the wall lean outward allows some balls to roll over the wall. If the wall is warped, or leans the wrong way when tightened, it may easily be straightened by interweaving pencils or tongue depressors at intervals along the wall over night. If the wall is so out of shape that this procedure will not change it enough, the wall may be soaked in cold water for a short period of time—five or ten minutes —and then shaped as desired and allowed to dry in that shape.

The size of the pocket varies with the habits of a player. To be legal, it cannot be so deep that, when a ball is placed in the pocket, the top of the ball will show below the wood wall when the stick is held horizontally. This provision does not apply to the goalie's stick. However, the pocket should not be so deep as to create a "whip" in the stick. As the ball is thrown from the stick it should roll smoothly down the netting and out in the intended direction. If the pocket is too deep, as the ball rolls out the head of the stick it will strike the gut strands across the top of the pocket and its course will be altered downward. If it is observed that a player must always release the ball from the stick early in his throw or if his passes are always lower than should be the case, suspect the presence of a whip. A beginner may not realize what is wrong, so another player should try to throw with the stick. If a whip is present, the more experienced player will easily find it. The pocket should then be tightened by drawing in on the rawhide thongs that support the netting.

There is no general agreement as to what material is best for stringing the net of a stick, and it is difficult to advise a player on the choice of webbing material. Linen cord is the least expensive; it will break in quite easily in a short period of time. On the other hand, the cord continues to stretch as the stick is used, so that a whip is likely to appear fairly soon; thereafter the stick must be tightened often to prevent the whip and to insure that the pocket does not become illegal. Also on wet days the cord will tighten, changing the shape of the pocket, and will still be tight the next day, although it can be broken back in quickly.

Nylon cord also breaks in quickly, but makes a loose pocket and is subject to changes in wet weather similar to linen cord. Rawhide is used infrequently for the netting, though the supporting thongs on which the netting is strung are usually rawhide. It shrinks when wet even more quickly than cord.

The most expensive webbing is clock cord; but it has the advantage of reacting to wet weather slowly with the result that in spite of rain, the stick will probably not change appreciably in shape during a game. On the other hand it breaks in very slowly initially and takes longer to work back into shape after getting wet. In dry weather the stick will hold its shape for a much longer period of time than with other webbing, making it less likely that a whip will develop. Perhaps the netting that best combines the advantages of each material is the stick strung with half clock cord and half either linen or nylon cord, a combination that may be especially appreciated by the beginner.

With the assumption that a whip should not be present and that the pocket should be legal, the depth of the pocket is a matter of individual preference. A relatively deep pocket will make it harder to dislodge the ball and will give the player more control while catching and cradling. A shallow pocket will make it easier to "quick stick"—that is, to receive the ball and get it off for a shot quickly—and a shallow pocket will probably make passes harder and more accurate. A goalie probably wants a fairly deep pocket. A crease attack man probably wants a shallow one. A player who dodges a good deal wants a deep pocket; one who feeds others wants a relatively shallow one. The shape of the pocket depends on the position played and the skills the player uses most in a game.

Figure 7.   Holding the Stick Properly.

Holding the Stick

As the novice starts to learn to handle his stick, the first consideration is the proper grip. As shown in Figure 7 the player should start by holding the stick parallel to the ground with the left hand—if he is right-handed—at the butt of the stick. The right hand then grips the stick in a position on the shaft so that his arms hang down to his sides in a natural manner. This will be the proper spacing for his hands for all normal catching and throwing motions. The hand covering the butt of the stick will remain stationary as he throws and catches, while the top hand is allowed to slide up and down as needed, returning to this normal spacing after any maneuver.

THE OVERHAND THROW

The first method of passing to be taught should be the overhand throw. It is the most accurate of all methods. If a player is left on his own at this stage of development, it is easy for him to develop bad habits that will be hard to overcome. The throw is illustrated in the series of pictures for Figure 8. Preparing to throw, the player should raise his stick as shown in Figure 8a. The lower arm should be close to the body, but relaxed. The forearm should be parallel to the ground, and the hand of that arm several inches past the midline of the body. The upper, or throwing, hand should be raised approximately to the level of the ear. The lower arm is perpendicular to the ground with the hand of that arm 6 inches to a foot from the player's head. The passer should *not* face directly toward his target but should be turned 45° to 60° away toward his stick side. The face of the stick, however, should be rotated so that it faces the target. The shaft of the stick should be slanted backward

Figure 8a.   The Overhand Throw; Preparing to Throw.

about 15° from the vertical. The illustrations shown are for a right-handed player. A left-handed player should be positioned exactly opposite. Because a player is normally right- or left-handed in other activities does not necessarily determine his primary side for playing lacrosse. Do not try to influence him on which side to hold the stick, although he should throw and catch with the same primary side. Let him learn to throw from whichever side feels more comfortable.

In Figure 8b the throw is in progress. The player takes a short step toward his target with his left foot—if he is right-handed. The upper hand starts to propel the stick forward while the lower hand moves only slightly. The best way to

Figure 8b. The Overhand Throw; Throw in Progress.

describe the throwing action is, to use as an illustration, the motion used in passing a football or throwing a baseball. The ball should be released from the crosse when it reaches an angle of about 30° forward of being vertical. The face of the stick should at all times be directed at the target. The player then follows through as shown in Figure 8c. The weight comes off the rear foot and onto the lead foot. The upper hand may be allowed to slide down the shaft of the stick slightly if desired, although the throw will probably be better executed if this hand remains in place. After the ball is released from the stick, the stick continues to move in the same smooth arc until the head of the stick is pointed directly at the target. Meanwhile the lower hand moves up under the armpit of the upper arm.

Greater power is supplied by the upper arm and the speed with which it moves. Although the lower hand does not move a great deal, the snap of this hand provides greater leverage. The thrower wants to work on developing this power after he has the proper moves well in mind, but not until then.

The overhand throw is best to start with since it is most likely to be accurate. If the stick is faced toward the target as described and the follow through is carried out until the stick points at the target, there will be little lateral deviation from the direction in which the thrower intends the ball to travel. The variation will be vertical—for which the receiver can adjust more easily. At first the thrower will have trouble with the vertical placing of the ball if he is learning with a new stick, since the lack of a pocket makes it hard for him to judge when the ball is being released. If, after the stick is properly broken in, the ball is continually thrown above the target, the thrower is releasing the ball too soon as a result of either starting the throw with the

Figure 8c.   The Overhand Throw; Follow Through.

stick cocked too far back or by not moving the bottom
hand at all. If the ball is continually thrown low, the thrower may not be developing enough power; this can be seen
easily if the ball travels in a pronounced arc. If the ball is
still low, without a pronounced arc, the cause is either that
the ball is released too late or the lower hand is moved too
much. Some time spent working with each beginner at this
stage will pay great dividends.

CATCHING THE BALL

The receiver should first learn to catch a ball on his stick side, about six inches over his head and a foot to the stick side of his head. The stick work in receiving such a pass is almost exactly the reverse of the throwing maneuver. The receiver should stand almost squarely facing the passer. He should reach forward with his stick to the same position from which the ball would have been released had he been passing. That is, the lower forearm should be parallel to the ground and close to the body. The stick should be angled forward about 30° from the vertical. The upper part of the top arm should be roughly parallel to the ground, while the forearm of the top arm is inclined about 30° to the ground. The catch is started in Figure 9a. As the ball arrives the receiver gives with it, cushioning the force by the backward motion of the stick. The stick continues backward to about 30° at most.

Thus caught, the ball will come to rest in the pocket of the stick under full control of the receiver provided the ball was not thrown too hard. To control a ball which arrives more rapidly, the receiver will now need to initiate a gentle cradling motion—which, as the name implies, is a rocking of the stick—for to drop the stick farther back would allow the ball to roll out. The upper hand and wrist do the cradling; the lower hand remains stationary, but holds the stick loosely so that the shaft can rotate easily. By allowing the wrist of the upper hand to flex backwards and forwards the face of the stick is allowed to move in an arc of about 60°. The natural tendency of the beginner is to cradle furiuosly. Cradling helps to keep the ball in the pocket when done gently; but if done violently, the ball can be cradled right out of the stick. The emphasis should be on a gentle cradle rather than a rapid or violent cradle, and the player

Figure 9a. Catching; Ready to Receive.

Figure 9b.   Catching; Giving with Ball.

should limit his cradles to no more than necessary to control the ball.

Unfortunately all balls are not thrown directly on target. With a ball thrown on the stick side in some place other than the ideal location over the shoulder, the receiver should reach forward to meet the ball, give with it, and move the stick as smoothly as possible into a position where the face of the stick is turned so that the ball cannot fall to the ground. A position with the stick parallel to the ground will work, or, better still, the stick should be brought smoothly up to a position so that the throwing motion to return the ball is ready to begin. The gentle cradling motion used to control the ball will be particularly useful while bringing the stick up to the throwing position.

With a ball thrown directly at the body, all players but the goalie should try to sidestep so that the ball will arrive on the stick side. The goalie, however, should learn to catch balls thrown at his body without sidestepping. In order to do so it will probably be necessary for him to choke up on the stick by sliding the lower hand up toward the throat as much as is necessary to get the stick into position so that the face of the stick is in front of the ball. (Refer to Figure 76 in Chapter 5, Goalie Play.) This is one of the very few times when the lower hand is moved on the stick, and the proper hand spacing should be regained as soon as possible. The stick should then be moved into the throwing position.

With balls thrown far over the head, the receiver should try to extend the stick as far as necessary above the head— perhaps even jumping to gain greater height. For maximum reach the upper hand will have to slide down the stick; this brings the hands closer together, making it harder to control the ball, but making it possible to reach balls that would otherwise go by. Again the stick is brought as quickly as is practical to the throwing position. A good cradle will help to control such passes.

Balls thrown to the off-side are the most difficult for the beginner. The first day he is likely to try to change hands on the stick, but by the second day he will find this awkward. To catch balls on the off-side without changing hands the player should rotate his body to face the side on which the ball is arriving by either advancing the foot on his stick side or dropping his off-side foot back. The butt of the stick should be carried behind the receiver's back, as the upper hand near the throat of the stick draws the stick across the receiver's body and positions the face of the stick

Figure 10. Catching the Ball on Off-Side.

in the path of the ball. If the stick is then cradled with a strong wrist action, the receiver can draw the stick back across his body and face his passer; or better still he can continue to turn so that he rotates almost 360°, ending up facing the passer ready to return the ball.

Beginners should be encouraged to work on developing their basic throwing and catching motions as much as possible outside the regular team practice time. However, during regular practice there are many possible drills that can be employed to speed the development of good stick work. A few of the possible ones are listed at the end of this chapter. Drills 1-4 are particularly designed to develop fundamental stick work.

PASSING TO THE CORRECT SIDE

In a game passes should be thrown so that they will not be intercepted by an opponent. For this reason a player should be forced, at an early stage, to throw to his teammate on the side away from the defender, and the receiver should become accustomed to receiving passes so that his body will be between the ball and the defender. This means that players should practice catching the ball on the off-side. After making such a reception the player must be trained to turn so that he is ready to shoot without exposing his stick to a check by the defender. The footwork in making such a turn is important.

A player cutting directly at the cage and receiving a pass from the feeder directly behind the cage so that the ball is on his stick side has no difficulty in catching the ball, cradling to control, and then shooting as he continues to move toward the cage. However, if the ball arrives on the off-side, to catch, cradle, and then pull the stick across the body to the correct side for shooting invites loss of the ball, since it can roll out of the stick as a result of centrifugal force generated when the stick is drawn back across the body. The pass may have been thrown there intentionally because the defender was on the stick side. To turn back into this defender gives him an opportunity to check the stick.

If the ball arrives on the off-side of the receiver, he positions his stick to make the catch. Then, to turn correctly, he plants the foot of his stick side (right foot, if he is right-handed; left foot, if he is left-handed), allowing his other foot to swing behind the planted foot until it makes contact with the ground, transfers his weight to this foot, and continues his turn. As the turn is being made, the player should rotate his head as quickly as possible after making the catch so that his head and eyes will be faced toward his intended target even before the footwork of the turn is completed. If the next move after the turn is to be a shot at the cage, the player should move toward the cage after the turn is completed.

The turn is difficult to teach to a player with limited athletic experience, but relatively easy to teach to a player who has engaged in other field sports where he has encountered similar problems.

Figure 11.   Making Proper Turn after Off-Side Feed. Pivot is made by putting weight on stick side foot and allowing off-side foot to swing behind.

Once the skill of receiving the ball on the off-side and pivoting to keep the stick away from the defender is introduced it is possible to start cutting, feeding, and shooting drills on the goal. Some such drills are listed at the end of the chapter, and drills 5-14 are directed at practicing these skills. These drills should be run not only for the beginning player, but also as warm-up drills for experienced players. Under no circumstances should an inexperienced goalie be put in the cage while these drills are being run.

CATCHING WHILE GOING AWAY FROM PASSER

Frequently a player moving away from a teammate with the ball must catch a lead pass over his shoulder so that he can continue to move downfield. This maneuver occurs often on the defensive half of the field in the process of "clearing" the ball from the defense to the attack. Therefore it particularly concerns the defense men, goalie, and midfielders. But similar situations also occur on the attack.

The ball should be thrown so that the receiver will get it on his stick side at better than shoulder height. The receiver should look back over the shoulder of his stick side as he moves away from the passer. The ball should strike the stick held in the same plane as the receiver's body, as in Figure 12. By giving with the stick, the receiver gains control of the ball. The defense men in particular should practice throwing such long lead passes.

Drills 15 and 16 at the end of the chapter are specifically intended to emphasize this skill.

Figure 12.   Catching Over-Shoulder Lead Pass.

CRADLING

The ball bounces out of the beginner's stick frequently because the stick is new and he holds it too rigidly. As soon as he is told that cradling will help him retain possession, he cradles furiously. Such cradling usually results in throwing the ball out of the stick, further complicating his problem of possession; so only brief mention of the cradle has been made thus far in situations where it is absolutely necessary to cradle.

Cradling is a gentle rocking motion of the stick in a circular arc probably of not more than 60° except in unusual circumstances. The motion is provided by the wrist of the upper hand on the stick while the lower hand is loose on the butt of the stick allowing the stick to rotate slightly as the ball is cradled.

Figure 13. Cradling. Motion is supplied by wrist of upper hand.

Cradling will help control a ball just received, will help keep a ball in the crosse while a player runs, and will assist in retaining the ball when a defender tries to dislodge it by checking the stick. Gentle motion of the stick by a player preparing to feed or throw makes it harder for a defender to gauge when and where a pass is to be made. But in all cases the cradling motion is a gentle one. It is necessary to engage in an energetic cradle only when a ball arrives at a place where if the receiver did not do so the ball would roll out of the stick. Such is the case on very high or very low passes.

QUICK STICK

As the attack men and midfielders become more proficient in handling their sticks, they will want to get their shots off quickly and accurately. They are particularly interested in developing a "quick stick." They should receive the ball, give with it until it is under control, and then shoot immediately without having to cradle first. All the shooting drills listed at the end of the chapter can be repeated with the receiver quick sticking the ball for a shot—if the ball arrives on his stick side slightly above shoulder height. As the shooter gains greater control over his stick, he will learn to quick stick balls that arrive on the off-side, but drills aimed at teaching such proficiency have little value.

The natural tendency for beginners learning to quick stick is to drop the stick back too far in controlling the pass so that the ball rolls out of the stick before the shot is started. If such is the case, the receiver is either not reaching far enough ahead for the ball as it arrives, or he is starting to give with the ball too soon and too rapidly. To quick stick properly the stick should first be placed at about a

30° angle in front of the receiver and allowed to give with the ball until the stick is vertical or slightly to the rear of vertical. Since a crease man or an attacking player who has a lead on his defender will open his stick up for a check by the trailing defender if he drops it back, it is better for such players to quick stick with the stick and ball well in front of them. At the same time they should extend their elbows as widely apart as possible for better control.

Figure 14.   Quick Stick. Player gives with stick as ball arrives, controls ball, and shoots as soon as control is gained.

While all cutting and shooting drills can be used to teach the quick stick, any player can work on this skill alone against a high wall. Working 5 or 10 yards from the wall provides the best practice since the player's reactions must be fast enough to receive the ball as it comes off the wall, and he can keep the ball high enough so that it rebounds at shoulder height or better.

Another good exercise is to have players pair off so that

they quick stick the ball back and forth at a distance of about 10 yards. The procedure follows the pattern of Drill 1 at the end of the chapter. Quick sticking can also be practiced by 3 or 4 players working in a triangle or square; such a drill forces the player to change the direction of his pass because the next receiver is not directly in front of him.

PICKING UP THE GROUND BALL

The ability to scoop up a ground ball cannot be over-emphasized, since with beginners the ball frequently falls to the ground. Even with experienced teams, the ball is on the ground a good number of times. In competition the team that consistently controls the ground balls will control the game and will certainly have more chances to score.

Most teams spend some time every day working on ground balls either individually or in drills in which two or more men go for the same ball.

Proper form in scooping up the ball is essential. In the throwing and catching maneuvers discussed thus far, two hands were kept on the stick at all times. This is also true for all scooping operations and should be stressed. As the scooper approaches the ball, he should assume the stance shown in Figure 15. The head of the stick should contact the ground six inches to a foot in front of the ball. The body should be bent at the trunk so that the back is almost parallel to the ground, and the knees should be bent as the player approaches the ball. The player's body should be under control so that he is not falling forward—no weight should be placed on the stick while scooping. The player should have his weight on the balls of his feet as in normal running. The position of the hands on the stick should not be altered from normal. The front hand should be low, and

Figure 15. Scooping Position.

the rear hand should be at knee level so that the stick makes about a 30° angle with the ground. The scooper should reach forward with his stick so that the arm of his rear hand, which should be straight but relaxed, will be perpendicular to the ground; the butt end of the stick will thus be shielded by the body from a trailing defender.

Carrying the stick in this manner, the player will shovel or scoop the ball into the stick. As the ball enters the pocket, the player should start to raise the stick off the ground with hand on throat of stick, being sure to shield the stick with his body from the defender to the rear. He should be careful not to raise the stick too fast or too high, but should wait until it is under full control. After the head of the stick is perhaps a foot off the ground, a gentle cradling motion will assist in keeping the ball in the stick while raising it to a height where the ball can be passed.

If a player is scooping properly, he cannot pick up a ball right under his feet. To try to do so would expose the butt of the stick to a trailing defense man. Such a ball should be kicked in the direction in which the player wants to go and then picked up by scooping correctly.

There are occasions when the direction of the rolling ball should be changed or when the player will prefer to rake the ball back into his stick rather than scoop it up. Such game situations requiring these maneuvers would be when the ball would roll out-of-bounds if not stopped or when the player would run out-of-bounds if he scooped through. If a defense man is following closely, a player may want to stop the ball, let the defender rush by, and then pick up the ball after the defender has passed. To rake the ball the player assumes the same stance he would take if he were scooping, but instead of putting the head of the stick on the ground, he allows it to pass over the ball, brings it down on the ground, and draws back on the stick, pulling the ball along in the process. Then, quickly picking up the stick and returning it to proper scooping position, he scoops the ball up as it rolls back toward him. However, the rake should definitely not be taught until after the scoop is mastered. Players will try to use it in situations where it will get them into trouble. A majority of these situations occur as a result of the necessity of stopping and remaining still at least momentarily while raking, thereby allowing a trailing defender to catch up and have a crack at the ball also.

Drills 17-19 at the end of the chapter are intended to provide practice for individuals in picking up ground balls.

ONE-ON-ONE GROUND BALLS

Only occasionally in a game does a player have the chance to pick up a ground ball completely unchallenged by an opponent. Therefore, most teams work on one-on-one ground ball situations where two players from different teams are going after the same ball. In a game, rarely are the two players exactly even when they arrive at the ball, and so it should be in practice.

The man who arrives at the ball first has a definite advantage over his opponent which he should exploit. Speed is not the only factor that insures first arrival. Positioning on the field and anticipation of where the ball is going are most important. A straight line course should be run to intercept the rolling ball at the earliest possible moment. Too many players try to circle to get a better scooping angle and so are beaten to the ball. The ball should be taken by the player getting to it first.

For the player who arrives first, the problem is no more

complex than picking up the ball alone. All he must remember is not to slacken his pace and so lose his advantage as he approaches the ball; he also must keep his stick protected from the trailing defender not only while actually lifting the ball off the ground but also as he makes his move to get into position to pass off to a teammate. He must turn away in order not to let the defender have the chance to check his stick.

Figure 16. Checking Up on Head of Stick of Opponent Leading While Pursuing Ground Ball.

If the defender is close behind, the man arriving first will protect his stick better if he takes one step to right or left to get directly in front of the opponent. If it takes more than a one side-step move to get in front of the defender, the first man should not bother, for to do so would mean no longer running a straight course to the ball and losing valuable seconds trying to block out a defender who would otherwise arrive too late. Body contact is not the object of this maneuver; the scooper just plans to screen off the defender from the ball.

If the opponent is parallel to the player as both approach the ball, the opponent should be checked with a shoulder block to throw him off stride. However, a player should never lose sight of the objective of picking up the ball. If the defender is running out of control, the ball can be clamped with the stick and raked back to be picked up after the opponent has gone by. Or perhaps if the ball cannot be picked up immediately, it should be batted with the stick in another direction more to that player's advantage. For instance, if the defender is running on the player's left side, the ball might be tapped to the right so that on the new course, the player will be ahead of the defender. If the ball is suddenly under the feet of the two men, it should be kicked in such a direction that it can be picked up easily.

Even though beaten to the ground ball, skillful persistence on the part of the player pays dividends, especially when he is confronted with opponents who rely on body contact or uncontrolled speed. The first man may bungle his scoop without the defender doing more than providing pressure by his mere presence. To influence the first man to miss the ball, if at all possible, the second man should reach forward with his stick, place it under the stick of the first man and lift it up so that the first man rides over the ball.

Figure 17. Checking Butt of Stick on One-on-One Ground Ball.

The second man's stick is now in proper position to scoop up the ball. Beginners, and some experienced players also, frequently check down on the first man's stick. To do so clamps both sticks together making it impossible for either to pick up the ball, and the only advantage gained is that neither man has the ball, and the situation is still neutral. To check up on the stick not only makes the opponent miss the ball, but gives the second man the chance to use his stick to control it. If the second man is so far behind that he cannot reach the throat of the first man's stick, he should work on the butt end of the stick, which in all probability will be somewhat exposed. Again to check up on the back hand is better than to check down. To check down hard all too often results in a slashing or tripping penalty if the check is poorly delivered.

The second man should not quit even after the first man starts his scoop. The first may lose control even then, or he may well turn unwisely and offer the trailer a good chance to check the stick before the man in possession gets himself oriented after the pick up. The trailer has to judge for himself when the cause is lost, for he certainly does not want to overplay the first man, allowing himself to be dodged and left behind.

TWO-ON-ONE GROUND BALLS

A team should try to make all ground balls two-on-one situations. Even if no one from the other team contests possession, there should still be two men going after the ball, for the first man may miss. No player should wait to see if a teammate is going to get the ball; help should be rendered before it is absolutely necessary. This is particularly true of attack men and midfielders. Defense men must first decide if they should leave the men they are covering.

When two players on the same team are after the ball, the player in the lead should take the ball. So there will be no possible confusion, he should immediately call "Ball" or instruct his teammate by calling "Take the man." The second man should then check the opponent with his body and call "Man." A shoulder block is better than any other since the blocker never loses his footing and is immediately ready to take part in the next play. In most situations it is sufficient merely to screen the opponent off from the ball without trying to block him so completely that he goes to the ground. As the first man scoops up the ball, he should command his teammate to "Drop off," for there is danger that the second man may not see the successful scoop and continue to block or screen the opponent while the first man has possession. This would constitute interference, which is a technical foul.

If the second man is not close enough to the play to throw a legal block, he should not attempt to do so, but should call to his teammate for a quick pass to take the pressure off the scooper right away. Frequently this pass should be thrown underhand or side arm to get it off quickly. Or if the teammate cannot pick up the ball cleanly, he can often kick the ball over, bat it with his crosse, or "goose" the ball to his teammate (i.e. flick the ball with the stick without gaining sufficient control to pass).

Drills 20 and 21 at the end of the chapter are designed to provide practice on two-on-one and one-on-one ground ball situations.

UNDERHAND FLIP PASS

Particularly when working two-on-one ground balls there is a need for a quick underhand shovel-like flip of the ball from one player to a teammate. The pass is intended to cover only 10 to 15 yards at most and therefore does not have to be hard. The same flip is also useful for the defense in clearing. With more power the same move can be used by an attack man for a low back flip shot when close to the cage. Such a shot is useful when the attack man does not have time to pull his stick into overhand shooting position because there is a defense man right on him or because he is moving past the cage and will lose the angle he has if he delays.

The player holds his stick in front of him with the face of the stick about a foot off the ground. When passing to a teammate on his off-side, the pass is made across his body and involves the same motion used for the overhand pass—

Figure 18.   Underhand Flip Pass Across Body.

Figure 19.　Underhand Flip Pass to Stick Side.

that is, a push with the upper hand and a snap back with the lower hand while the face of the stick is turned toward the receiver.

If the ball is to be thrown to a teammate on the player's stick side, he should shovel the ball to his teammate by pulling back with the upper hand and pushing away with the lower hand. Most of the force of the pass or shot comes from a quick snap provided by the upper hand.

Drill 22 at the end of the chapter provides practice on the underhand flip.

SIDE ARM PASSING

After the overhand throw is mastered, and not before, it is worthwhile to work on the side arm. Frequently a shot has to be taken side arm because of the place where the ball was caught. Sometimes a side arm shot should be taken to get the ball around a defender who would otherwise block or be in the way of an overhand shot. If the feeder finds that a defense man is consistently blocking his overhand feeds, he should try the side arm.

The two difficulties of this pass are, first, that any deviation in the path of the ball will result in horizontal displacement, which is harder for the receiver to adjust to quickly than is a vertical error; therefore the side arm is not nearly as accurate as the overhand pass. Second, if this method is taught first, it is very difficult to get the beginner to unlearn his side arm motion and learn to throw overhand. The reverse is not true.

A side arm shot can be very hard. If controlled there is a tremendous amount of leverage that can be built up and then translated into speed. The body is turned 45° or so to the stick side of the target. The stick is held out to the side at a slight angle. As the throw is started the player steps forward onto his off-side foot, pushes hard with his upper arm, and snaps back with his lower one. His upper arm is almost straight as the throw is completed, and his upper hand may have to slide down the shaft of the stick slightly, but the movement should be slight if needed at all. The lower hand pushes the butt of the stick past the ribs of the thrower. As the throw is completed, the weight is abruptly shifted onto the lead foot, and the body is turned toward the target. The follow through is much like that of a baseball pitcher, as the back foot swings off the ground and ends up pointed in the direction of the target. The stick is allowed to carry through naturally in an arc until the shaft points directly at the target.

Figure 20.   Side Arm Shot.

UNDERHAND SHOT

This shot is used primarily by a midfielder 15 to 20 yards out from the cage and produces a shot that will, under normal field conditions, whistle along the ground without bouncing high. If the field is wet, the ball will skid; such a skid is extremely difficult for the goalie to judge accurately or stop decisively. The shot is started with the face of the stick held a foot above the ground as the player cradles to keep control of the ball. The footwork and throw are the same as for the side arm, except that the upper hand needs to slide down the shaft of the stick before the throw is started. The face of the stick is rotated toward the target just as the shot is about to leave the stick; while the head of the stick remains about a foot off the ground.

Figure 21.   Underhand Shot.

PLAYING WITH BOTH HANDS

A player should learn to pass and catch while holding the stick on whichever side feels more comfortable. Without influence he will find out for himself which feels more natural. If he claims that it is easier to catch one way and throw the other, then he should be advised to play by holding the stick on his primary side for other activities. Until he learns to play both ways, he should not try to switch sides for every throw and catch.

There is some debate as to when a player should start to learn to play with his off-side. Many coaches feel that he should concentrate on one side for several years before trying to play both. However, there are definite advantages to being able to play both ways, and the really top-notch players are skilled using either hand. When the player starts to play with his off-side, he will feel awkward at first. However, the sooner he starts to master the off-side, the easier will be the adjustment. After he becomes fairly proficient on his primary side, nothing will be lost by encouraging him to practice on his off-side.

A defense man who plays both ways finds he can always cover his opponent's stick. A midfielder who can switch will not be overplayed on his stick side and will find it easier to work into shooting territory. The pressure on an attack man is such that he must be able to protect his stick at all times and be able to feed at a moment's notice. This can best be done if he can play both ways.

DRILLS

Drill 1—Elementary Instruction in Throwing and Catching
To instruct players in proper form for both throwing and

catching, form parallel lines of players 10 to 15 yards apart. Pair the players so that a player in one line has a man directly opposite him. Give each pair a ball and have them pass back and forth. If the coach prefers to work slowly at teaching players to pass correctly, first have the throwers lay aside their sticks. Then have them throw the ball as they would a baseball. Then have them pick up their sticks and, remembering the arm position and foot work just used, throw the ball with their sticks. To work carefully on catching skills have the player receiving the ball catch properly with his crosse while the passer throws the ball with his hand. Initially this procedure will allow concentration on proper catching form, since the player throwing will be able to place the ball with much more accuracy.

Figure 22. Drill 1. Elementary Instruction in Throwing and Catching.

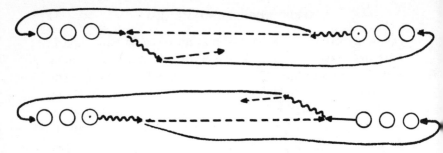

Figure 23. Drill 2. Passing and Catching While in Motion.

Drill 2—Passing and Catching While in Motion

Have two lines of players face each other—perhaps two or three players to a line—about 25 yards apart. Start the ball with a player in one of the lines. Have the first player in the opposite line run toward the ball, perhaps jogging when the drill is first introduced, and receive a pass thrown to his stick side by the man with the ball. After receiving the ball, he should stop immediately and throw accurately to the player in the other line who should now have started moving toward him. Concentrate on having the passer throw while his weight is on the proper foot—the one diagonally opposite from the side on which he carries the stick. As players become more proficient, have the passer throw while in motion. If this drill is used as a warm-up for experienced players, both the passer and the receiver should be moving at full speed toward each other.

Drill 3—Elementary Shooting

Start drills of shooting at a cage. Do *not* under any circumstances put an inexperienced goalie in the cage. To do so at this stage of his development would spell his doom as a goalie. Putting him in the goal when he is not yet able to catch the ball will in almost all cases make him unintentionally ball shy.

Place a feeder almost directly behind the cage and form a line of shooters directly in front of the cage. At first have them jog directly toward the cage, receive the pass from the feeder, control the ball, and shoot. At first, use as feeders those most likely to throw accurate passes to the cutter's stick side. Then rotate the feeders, giving all players a chance to feed. After the cutters begin to get the feel of the maneuver, have them increase their speed.

To influence them to place their shots, either put some kind of target in each corner of the cage at which they can aim or suspend a 4-by-4-foot sheet of plywood with ropes from the pipes of the cage so that only those shots near the pipes will go in.

Drill 4—Working Against a Backboard

If practical, a solid wooden backboard with surface larger than the goal mouth but with a 6-foot square to represent a goal painted on it, should be available for use near the practice field. Shooting drills can be run against it, or individuals can practice their stick work against it.

Drill 5—Receiving Feeds on Off-Side

With one line coming directly at the cage with a feeder placed behind or slightly to one side of the cage, feed the ball to the receiver intentionally on the wrong side and have him make the pivot needed to turn away from the defender on the stick side. The receiver must plant the foot of his stick side and make his pivot on that foot. It would be well to work this drill in slow motion at first since it is difficult to stop quickly and make the turn when primary attention is focused on catching the ball.

Drill 6—Feeds to Diagonally Opposite Receivers

Establish two lines starting at about the restraining line (20 yards from the cage), each about 5 to 10 yards off the center of the field. Locate feeders on either side of the rear of the cage and have them alternate in feeding cutters from the diagonally opposite lines. Have the cutters pretend there is a defender between them and the cage—or put a dummy

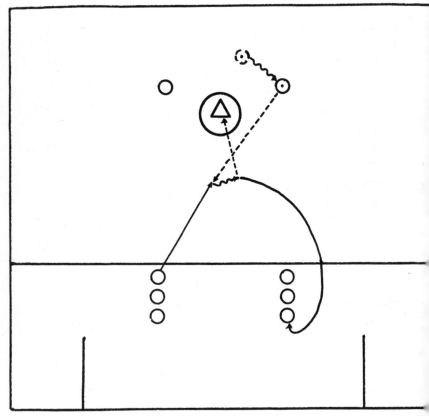

Figure 24.   Drill 6.   Feeds to Diagonally Opposite Receivers.

defender there—and have the feeders throw to the side of the cutter away from the simulated defender. This means that if a cutter is right-handed and is running from the line to the right front of the cage, he will receive the ball from the feeder to the left rear of the cage on his stick side. However, when he switches lines and cuts from the line to the left front of the goal, the ball will arrive on his off-side (away from the simulated defender who is between him and the cage), and he will have to pivot to shoot correctly.

Drill 7—Cutting off a Brush

One of the best ways for a player in front of the goal to free himself of close coverage by his defender is to run as close as possible past one of his teammates so that the man covering him will either collide with another player or be forced to sag off his man to avoid the collision. Such a "pick off" play or "brush" is an integral part of most attacking patterns.

Add a brush to Drill 6 by having players cut from both lines at the same time. The player going away from the feeder goes through the center first, and the cutter going toward the feeder passes behind him as closely as possible. Have the feeder time his pass so that it arrives just a step or two after the brush has occured.

Drill 8—Feeds to Receivers on Feeder's Side of Cage

Establish two lines at the restraining line as before, but feed each line from the same side of the cage with the feeders throwing the ball to the outside of the receiver— the side away from the center of the field. Since the receiver changes lines after each cut, half the time he will be getting the ball on his stick side and half the time he will be getting it on his off-side.

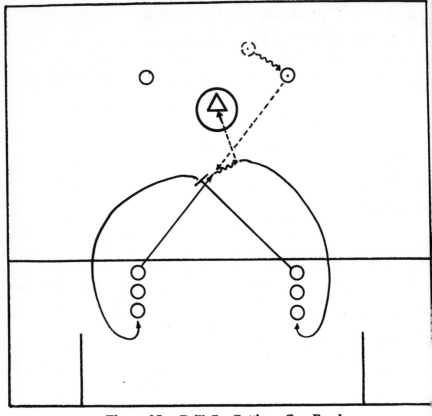

Figure 25. Drill 7. Cutting off a Brush.

Drill 9—Breaking Receivers

All drills outlined thus far have had the receiver running directly at the feeder. This was done so that the passes from the feeder would be most accurate. In actual game conditions, however, in order to get free, a receiver invariably must make at least one change of direction in the course of his cut. At the same time a feeder must learn to lead a receiver who is cutting for the cage and not directly toward him.

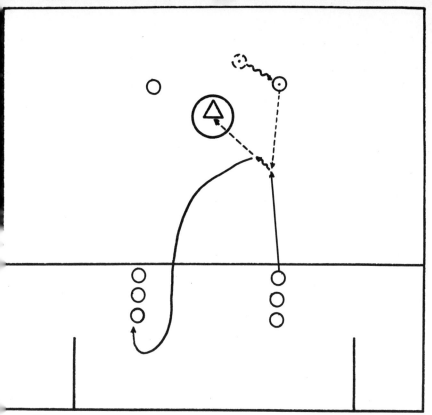

Figure 26. Drill 8. Feeds to Receivers on Feeder's Side of Cage.

Repeat Drill 6 so that the cutter starts in a path perpendicular to the back line of the field for about 10 yards and then breaks across the mouth of the goal about 10 yards from the goal in a path parallel to the mouth of the goal about 10 yards out. Have the feeder lead him as he comes across so that the feed will arrive when the receiver reaches a position opposite the pipe of the cage farthest from the feeder. By the time he has the ball under control and is ready to shoot he will be a few steps in advance of this position, but he will still have a good angle from which to shoot.

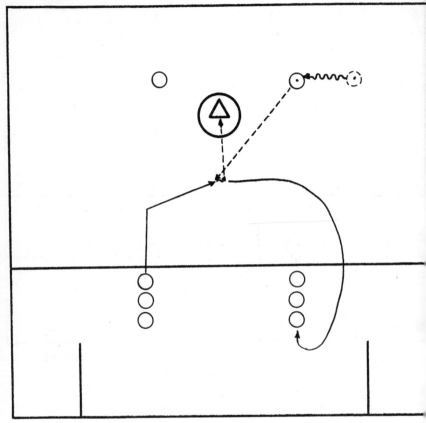

Figure 27.   Drill 9.   Breaking Receivers.

Drill 10—Breaking Receivers Using a Brush

Break the receivers as in Drill 9, but add a brush coming from the opposite line as in Drill 7. The receiver should time his cut so that the brush occurs at a point on the field 10 yards out from the goal and opposite the pipe of the cage most distant from the feeder.

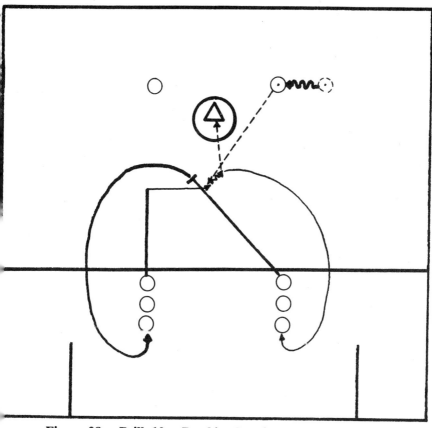

Figure 28. Drill 10. Breaking Receivers Using a Brush.

Drill 11—Breaking Receivers Fed from the Same Side
Have the receivers in Drill 8 first cut toward the center of the field. When they reach a position in front of the cage and about 10 yards out, have them then break sharply toward the feeder on their own side of the goal. Be sure that the break is made toward the feeder or toward the goal. There is a tendency on the part of some players on

this drill to break out wide of the cage giving them a poor shot when the feed is received.

Another breaking cut under the same conditions has the cutter start moving directly toward the feeder on his own side until he is about 15 yards in from the restraining line. He then breaks sharply across the mouth of the goal

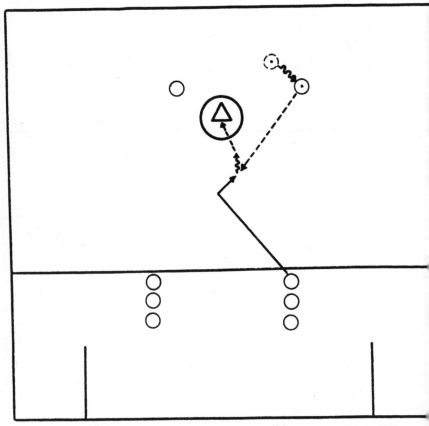

Figure 29. Drill 11. In-Out Cut by Receiver on Same Side of Cage as Feeder.

about 5 yards out. The feeder gives him a lead pass just before the cutter arrives opposite the cage. If the receiver gets the feed on his off-stick-side as a result of the lead pass, he should then pivot to make his shot—or he can continue running and shoot backhanded.

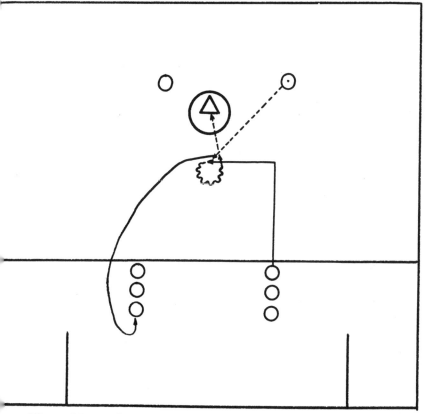

Figure 30. Drill 11. Cut Across Crease by Receivers on Same Side of Cage as Feeder.

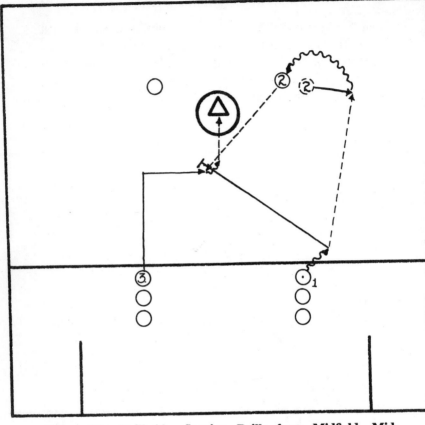

Figure 31. Drill 12. Starting Drills from Midfield. Midfielder No. 1 passes to feeder No. 2 and then breaks for opposite side of crease to set up brush for midfielder from opposite line (No. 3).

Drill 12—To Start Drills from Midfield

To add more stick work to any of the above cutting drills, start the ball with the cutter on the side of the field where the feeder will be throwing, and have him pass in to the feeder. The cut should not be started until the feeder has control of the ball. The pass to the feeder should be thrown to his outside, away from the cage, and should force the feeder to move a step or two to his outside to receive the ball. The feeder should then turn, keeping his stick away from a simulated defender to his inside, come back to the position from which he started, and get off his feed. This makes the feeder move as he would in a game. To add realism to his moves a defense man can be added to play the feeder, allowing him absolutely complete freedom to feed, but picking off erratic passes thrown incorrectly to the feeder. Feeding while standing still will invite interception by the defense man playing him, so the feeder should be trained to feed while moving. The feeder should be cautioned to throw off the correct foot as he first learns to move—the foot opposite the side on which he carries his stick. As he makes his feeds the feeder should step toward the receiver with that foot.

As the players involved in the above drills become more advanced, each cutting drill should have at least one change of direction during the cut. The cutter must learn that such a change of direction is much more likely to make it possible for him to get free in a game. The feeders must learn to anticipate such changes by the cutters and to adjust their passes.

Drill 13—Double Feeding the Midfield Brush

To maximize the shooting practice on a midfield brush drill several feeders are stationed to one side of the cage. With the midfielder in the line closer to the feeders' side setting a post for a midfielder breaking past him from the line nearer to the center of the field, one of the feeders passes to the cutter as in Drill 7. The man who acted as the post carries his cut past the point of the brush, and

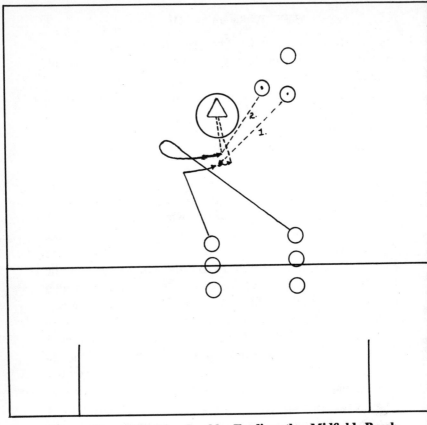

Figure 32. Drill 13. Double Feeding the Midfield Brush. First feeder hits midfielder coming off brush; second feeder hits post midfielder rolling back.

into the vicinity of the crease, stops, and then rolls back toward the feeders to receive a pass himself. The drill will work most expediently with a battery of more than two feeders working from the rear of the cage, but it is necessary for the feeder to call out to his cutter before the play starts so that the receiver will know from whom to expect the pass.

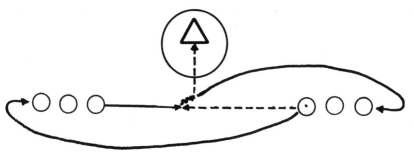

Figure 33.   Drill 14.   Close Shot Drill for Close Attack Men.

Drill 14—Close Shots for Attack Men

A good drill, particularly for the close attack men, is to establish two lines of players about 10 yards on either side of the cage, and about 5 yards out from the plane of the goal. Give a ball to a feeder in one line and have him feed the man in the other line coming directly toward him across the mouth of the cage; timing his feed so that the cutter receives the ball when he is opposite the pipe of the cage on the side where he started. The feed should be thrown so it arrives on the side of the cutter away from the goal. Half the time the cutter will have to turn to get off his shot; half the time he will be able to quick stick since the ball will be on his stick side. This drill should be run a few times with the feed coming from one side, and then several times with the feed coming from the other side.

Drill 15—Receiver Moving Away from Passer

Establish a line heading downfield. Give the ball to the second man in line and have him pass to the first man in line moving away from him. After he receives the ball, the first man should pretend that there is a trailing defender and turn so that his stick is protected until he is ready

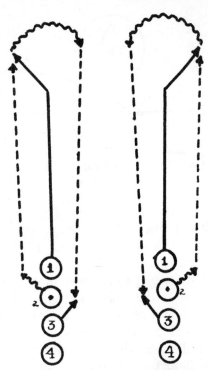

Figure 34. Drill 15. Lead Pass Drill for Receiver Moving Away from Ball. Left hand diagram illustrates proper manuever for a left-hander receiving ball over stick shoulder and turning correctly to his right after reception. Right hand diagram illustrates procedure for a right-handed player.

to throw back to the third man in line. The third man then passes to the second man going away from him, and so on. The turn by the receiver is important and should be stressed. Many beginners will turn so that their sticks are offered to the trailing defender. By turning this way they are also likely to roll the ball out of their sticks. A right-hander receiving the ball over his right shoulder should swing to his left after the catch. The left-hander should do just the opposite.

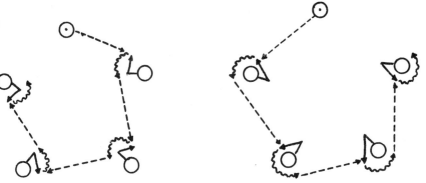

Figure 35. Drill 16. Circle Passing. Left hand diagram illustrates procedure for passing ball in counterclockwise direction around circle (where all players are right-handed). Right hand diagram illustrates procedure for passing ball around circle in clockwise direction (where all players are right-handed).

Drill 16—Circle Passing

Establish a circle of players who pass the ball around the outside of the circle in a given direction. (Vary the direction, clockwise or counterclockwise to give practice both ways.) The ball should always be thrown to the receiver's outside to keep it away from a simulated defender. As each receiver prepares for the ball he should move several steps toward the center of the circle and then break back out so that he is in motion as he makes the catch. He will then be moving toward the passer or away from him depending on the receiver's stick side.

Drill 17—Single Man Ground Ball Drills

Establish a line of players and roll the ball out gently for them to scoop up, paying particular attention to the form used. After the scoop be sure the players turn so that their bodies will protect the stick from a trailing defender. A right-hander should therefore turn left, while a left-hander circles right to return the ball to the starting point. Few balls in a game are completely stationary when picked up; therefore it is better to practice on a rolling ball. Vary the angle from which the ball is rolled so that a player gets practice on balls going away from him, coming toward him, and coming from the side. The best way to work this drill is in a group of four players. Have one player pick up the ball and pass it back to player No. 3, who in turn rolls the ball out for player No. 2, who returns it to player No. 4, and so on.

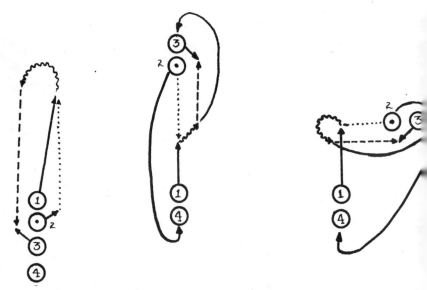

Figure 36. Drill 17. Ground Ball Drills for Groups of Four Players. Various diagrams illustrate procedure for rolling ball delivered from possible directions. In all diagrams player No. 2 rolls out ball for player No. 1 who scoops ball and returns it to player No. 3, who then rolls out ball for the next man in line.

For beginners, the ball should be rolled softly so that
it does not bounce, for a majority of ground balls in
a game are of this nature. A bouncing ball may be fielded
as though it were a low pass; obviously the player must
gauge the bounce correctly. As players gain skill and experience, the speed with which the ball is rolled or bounced
should be increased.

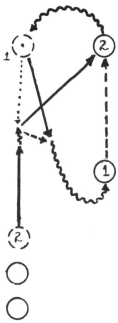

**Figure 37. Drill 18. "Scoop To" Ground Ball Drill. Player
No. 1 rolls ball for player No. 2 and then passes on stick side
of player No. 2. Player No. 2 flips ball to player No. 1. Player
No. 1 turns correctly and throws lead pass to player No. 2.
Player No. 2 then turns and rolls back for next man in line.
(Diagram is illustrated for right-handed players.)**

Drill 18—"Scoop To"

This ground ball drill combines the scoop with other elements of basic stick work. Player No. 1 starts about 15 yards in front of a line of players. He rolls the ball toward player No. 2 and then runs toward player No. 2 passing him on his stick side. Player No. 2 scoops up the ball and flips it underhand to player No. 1 as they pass. Player No. 1 turns correctly (direction depending on his stick side) and passes to player No. 2 who continues on his course after the flip and takes the return lead pass over his stick side shoulder. Player No. 2 then turns correctly and rolls the ball back for player No. 3.

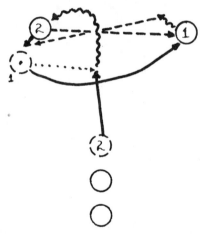

Figure 38. Drill 19. "Scoop From" Ground Ball Drill. Player No. 1 rolls ball for player No. 2 and then passes behind player No. 2. Player No. 2 turns correctly and passes to player No. 1 who returns ball immediately to player No. 2. Player No. 2 then rolls ball for next man in line. (Diagram is illustrated for right-handed players.)

Drill 19—"Scoop From"

This is another drill that combines ground balls with other elements of basic stick work. Player No. 1 starts to the side and ahead of the rest of the group. He rolls the ball for player No. 2 to scoop and then cuts so that he passes behind player No. 2. Player No. 2 turns correctly after scooping the ball and passes immediately to player No. 1. Player No. 1 receives the pass and immediately passes back to player No. 2 who continues toward the spot from which player No. 1 started the drill. After he receives the return pass, he rolls the ball out for player No. 3.

Drill 20—Two-on-One Ground Balls

Establish three lines of players. Either designate which lines are to be teammates before starting or so designate as the ball is rolled out in front of a group of three players. Alternate lines so that each player gets the chance to be the lone man. This drill teaches the fundamentals of teamwork on ground balls, but fails to train players to anticipate a game situation in which they will be called upon to go for the ground ball. In this respect it is an artificial situation, since three players are equally aware that the ball will be loose for them, and all three are starting on the same signal. Nevertheless, the skills stressed by the drill make it a valuable training routine. A contest can be made out of this drill by rewarding individuals or pairs that are successful in retrieving the ball and signalling out for extra practice those who are less successful. The drill unfortunately places a premium on fleetness of foot, whereas in a game the player who has quick reactions and good field position usually beats out the player who is merely fast.

The drill is best worked with the three lines parallel;

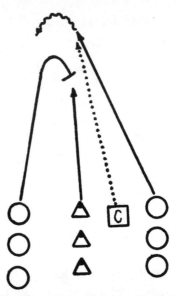

Figure 39. Drill 20. Two-on-One Ground Ball Drill. If one member of a pair of players operating as a team arrives first at ball, he takes ball while partner blocks or screens lone man.

there is some danger of injury in setting it up so that the lines converge. The ball should be rolled out gently. If one player on the two-man team retrieves the ball, he should be required to pass immediately to his partner. If the lone man gets the ball, he should be required to pass back to the coach who rolled out the ball. Possibly some boundaries should be established for the drill so that groups are not pursuing the ball all over the field in unrealistic situations that lose effect as ground ball drills.

The drill can also be used for two pairs of players on each side, rather than two-on-one. Naturally the drill is the same for a one-on-one situation, which actually should be introduced to the practice before the two-on-one is used.

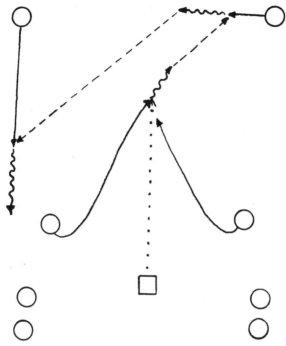

Figure 40. Drill 21. Additional One-on-One Ground Ball Drill. Man who recovers ball passes to either deep man, who throws lead pass to other deep man breaking back.

Drill 21—Additional One-on-One Ground Ball Drill

A coach or manager is positioned between two players selected to go for the ground ball so that they are approximately ten yards downfield from him. The players are spaced ten to fifteen yards apart. The ball is rolled between the players, who must remain stationary facing the coach, until a command is given to go for the ball. Each player then turns, locates the ball, and attempts to secure it off the ground. As the ball is scooped up, the player gaining possession is instructed to pass or flip the ball as soon as possible to either of two additional players stationed about 15 yards farther downfield, starting about 20 yards apart. As the pass is thrown to one of these players, the other breaks back toward the coach's position taking a lead pass from the player receiving the flip.

Drill 22—Underhand Flip Pass

Players should run up and down the field in pairs, flipping the ball back and forth as they go, while staying about 15 yards apart as they pass. When they go up the field, they must flip one way; when they turn to come back, they must reverse and flip the opposite way.

3. Close Attack Play

The close attack's first assignment is to score goals or set up such scores to be accomplished by a midfielder. Their second, and often just as important task, is to control the ball in the offensive half of the field. Since the opponents cannot score unless they have the ball, the best defense is a good offense. If a team's attack can control the ball for long periods of time, its midfields will not become exhausted by being forced to move up and down the field continuously.

An attack man is primarily a dodger, a feeder, or a crease man, but in order to be effective, he must be all three to some extent. Attack play is discussed first because the skills of an attack man are also prerequisites for a midfielder, though he need not be such a specialist.

THE DODGER

Some players develop greater skill than others in getting past their defense man with the ball, but all attack men must be able to dodge when the occasion demands. In normal play each attack man must pose enough of a dodging threat so that his defense man will not try to overplay him. However, it is possible to dodge only when a defense man commits himself or has been forced into a position where he cannot react quickly enough to prevent the attack man from going by. The dodging attack man must be alert to the mistakes that a defense man can make and must know how to lead the defense man into committing such errors.

Figure 41.   Attack Man Carrying Stick with Hand on Throat When Moving to Stick Side Ready to Dodge.

In all dodges, after the attack man moves past his defense man, the dodger must make sure that his body protects his stick from a check. He must head toward the cage in as straight a line as possible. (The necessity of remaining outside the crease may make it impossible for him to run a perfect straight line course.) If he runs even a slight arc while the defense man recovers and runs a straight line, the attack man will be intercepted before he can make a play. The attack man continues toward the cage either to shoot or, if another defense man comes to pick him up, to pass off to an uncovered teammate. In all dodges the trailing defense man has a good crack at the attacker's stick if the dodger cocks his stick back over his shoulder to shoot. Therefore the dodger must remember to cover his stick at all times. There are four basic dodges:

The Running Dodge

The attack man uses a running dodge on his defense man after getting his defender into such a position that with a burst of speed the attacker can run past and gain an inside position. The attack man should first isolate the defense man he is going to dodge so that when he does get by he will not be picked up by another defense man before he has time to see what should be done next. All the attack man needs is a step, or at most two steps, on the defender. He can get this advantage in several ways.

The easiest method is to outrun the defender, but because it is so simple it works best against an inexperienced defense man. The attack man starts a gentle circle of the cage running less than full speed. He works in close to the defender keeping his stick protected by his body. The easiest way to protect the stick is to carry it in one hand. If the attack man can play both hands, he should carry his stick in his upper hand leaving the lower hand off the butt of the stick until ready to pass. If he can play only one way, he should carry his stick with the upper hand, as shown in Figure 41, when running to his stick side. When going to his off-side, he should carry his stick in the hand normally on the butt of the stick, as shown in Figure 42.

Figure 42.   Attack Man Carrying Stick with Lower Hand When Moving to Off-Stick Side Ready to Dodge.

As the attack man starts to run, he should observe the position of his defense man with respect to the cage. The defender should keep himself directly between the attack man and the cage. As soon as the attack man observes that the defense man is getting out of line, the attacker should break past the defender by turning on the extra speed that he has held in reserve. While setting up the dodge, the attack man wants to be as close to his defense man as possible without making contact. To get closer will slow him down and give the defense man a chance to knock him off stride. Figure 43.

A second way to get the needed step on the defense man is to offer him a crack at the stick which looks so tempting that he is unable to resist throwing himself off stride trying to make a stick check. The attack man must make the offer realistic enough so that the defense man will take the bait, but in turn must not offer so much free stick that the defender checks successfully. While running along at less than full speed, the attack man lets his stick drag, or holds it in front; when the defense man bites, he turns on the steam. Figure 44.

A third way to lose the defense man is to change direction quickly. The attack man will have to gauge his change so that as little time as possible is lost in reversing his field. This is expediently done by planting the foot closest to the defense man, pushing off it, and making a 180° turn away from the defense man using as few steps as possible in the process. If the attack man can change hands, he will want to do so as he reverses his direction. If he can not play both ways, he will shift from carrying his stick in one of the manners illustrated in Figures 41 and 42 to the other. The attack man may have to reverse his direction several times in quick succession before he gets the step lead that he needs to go by. Figure 45.

A fourth way to run past the defense man is to block him momentarily on either another defense man or a fellow attack man. By running a course close to another player the attack man forces his defense man to alter course to avoid the collision. If the pick is to be worked using a teammate, the post man must be stationary when the pick occurs and must not lean into the defense man.

Figure 43. Running Dodge; Using a Change of Pace on the
Defender.

Figure 44. Running Dodge; Offering Part of Stick to Defender, and Then Pulling in "Bait" and Running by Before Defender Can Recover from a Stick Check.

Figure 45. Running Dodge; Changing Direction.

Often, in this play, the two defense men involved will switch men. If the dodger is covered successfully, there is a good chance that his teammate will not be picked up adequately; therefore the player who formed the post should head for the cage immediately. He may be open for a feed.

Figure 46. Running Dodge; Using Another Attack Man or Player on Whom to Brush the Defense Man.

The Roll Dodge

As the attack man runs toward the cage, the defense man will be stationed ready to play him. As soon as the two players are close together the defense man will have to make some move to stop the attack man. Usually the defense man will try first to check the attack man's stick. As soon as he commits himself, the attack man plants the foot diagonally opposite his stick, pivots almost 360° on that foot, and rolls by the defense man to the opposite side.

Figure 47. The Roll Dodge.

The attack man does not want to make violent contact with the defense man—he may lose his stride or bounce off, but he does want to roll on the defense man thereby freezing the defense man's stick. The attack man must hold his own stick as perpendicular as possible while rolling, for the centrifugal force generated by the roll can throw the ball out of the stick if it is held parallel to the ground. After the roll is started, it is probably easier to hold the stick with one hand rather than two.

The Face Dodge

There is no dodge more graceful than the face dodge, and none that makes the defense man feel more foolish. However, the attack man can not completely dictate the situation in which it is going to be used. In order to work, the defense man must raise his stick as though to block the attack man's pass, and the defense man must be moving forward to meet the attack man. Unless the defense man makes these two moves, the face dodge should never be attempted. The attack man fakes an overhand pass and then pulls his stick across in front of his face to the opposite side as shown in Figure 48. As he pulls the stick across, he moves forward going past the defense man with only a slight change in direction. The dodge depends on correct timing—if started too early, the defense man will not have committed himself enough; if too late, the check will connect.

Figure 48. The Face Dodge.

The Dip Dodge

The dip dodge is similar to the face dodge. It is used primarily by a feeder; however, the defense man need not be charging him. The attack man fakes a pass causing the defense man to raise his stick to try to block. Instead of passing, the attack man draws his stick diagonally across the front of his body, from the point where he had the stick ready to pass to a position on the opposite side and several feet off the ground. Holding the stick with only the hand on the butt of the stick, the attack man then goes by the defense man, holding his now free upper arm in position to receive a check directed at his stick. The free arm may be used only to receive the check, and the attack man may not push off the defense man's stick with that free arm.

Dodging Drills—Drill 23—One-on-One

Pair off defense men and attack men. Start an attack man with a ball near one of the out-of-bounds lines and let him try to dodge. He will usually have to run or roll under these conditions. For added variation, place a crease man and a crease defense man in position so that there will be a defender available to pick up the dodger and an attacker to whom the dodger can pass when he is picked up.

Drill 24—Three-on-Three

Work three attack men against three defense men with the provision that the two attack men behind the cage are to dodge, if possible. This allows them to brush on each other and also leaves the defense man guessing as to which attack man is going to be the dodger.

Figure 49.   The Dip Dodge.

THE FEEDER

A feeder should be primarily interested in passing off to others who will score. His primary position is to the rear of the goal, and while he should not be reluctant to come to the front when he has the ball, he should watch closely for open teammates in scoring position.

It is up to the feeder to decide when a teammate is open enough to receive a pass. The feeder must recognize situations when a man is about to become open and must be prepared to pass the ball so that it arrives at the optimum time. This skill can be partly acquired through practice, but there seems to be an ingrown sense of timing which some athletes have that makes them good, prospective feeders.

In addition the feeder must have good stick work. He must be able to throw accurate, hard passes, for a teammate cutting for the cage cannot adjust easily to an inaccurate, soft, or lob pass. It would be advantageous for the feeders to have good speed and reasonable size so that they could not be overpowered by their defense men, but these qualifications are secondary when compared to timing and stick work.

The feeder should be ready to pass whenever he gets within 10 or 15 yards of the cage, although he would prefer to work about five yards off the crease. Occasionally a feed can be thrown from farther than 15 yards out, but the chances are that it will be intercepted unless the receiver is wide open. Still, the feeder should always be aware of what is going on in front of the goal. His best feeding territory is slightly to the side of the cage. A position directly to the rear looks promising until it is remembered that feeds from this area must pass close to the

Figure 50. Flip Pass Between Closely Covered Feeders to Rear of Cage.

goalie, allowing him the chance to intercept. The feeder
should carry his stick so that he is able to feed at a moment's
notice. The closer he works to the cage, the more intensive
the defensive pressure on him becomes. The feeder should
keep moving to prevent the defense man from getting a
good check on him with stick or body. However, he does
not want to fight the defense man for a particular spot
on the field. To do so will take his concentration off his
primary job of feeding. He should be willing to ride with
the check, always moving laterally across the field, but not
giving ground if it can be helped.

To feed he must have two hands on the stick, and he
should play that way as much as possible. He should
take his lower hand off to block a check and then put it
right back in place. If the feeder carries his stick in one
hand as illustrated earlier in Figures 41 and 42, the defense man is alterted to the dodge. He will not be concerned with the feed until the second hand is put on the
stick. If the feeder only gets the second hand in place when
he is going to throw, the defense man is alerted to the feed
and is ready to block it. The attack man should fake passes

frequently so that the defender does not know when the actual feed is to be made. He usually has his back to the play in front of the cage and cannot tell what is going on in front except by the call of his goalie or the movements that the feeder makes to give away what is about to happen.

A defense man will try to block the feed as it leaves the stick, so the feeder must vary his pattern of throwing. His basic feed is overhand, since it is most accurate, but he wants to be able to feed side arm at various angles. Once he decides to throw, he should step toward his target with the foot on his off-side and get his feed off quickly. If under great pressure, the attack man should move back away from the defender two steps quickly and then step forward to make the pass.

More than any other player on the field, the feeder is much more of a threat if he can throw with either hand. If he can not, half his time in feeding territory is wasted going in a direction from which he cannot feed without stopping and rolling back to get the right direction. He should roll back, however, rather than pulling the stick across his body, for to do so invites a stick check and will be dangerous unless he is trying to face dodge or dip dodge.

Until the feeder is skilled with both hands, he must be particularly alert to the situation in front of the goal. When there is little chance of a receiver being open, he should be moving toward his off-side; but as soon as a play develops where a feed might be thrown, he must roll back to his stick side and be ready to throw. There is nothing more frustrating for the midfielders than to set up a good play, execute it perfectly, shake a man clear in scoring territory, and then discover that the feeder was so far out of position that no pass could be thrown.

The best feeding opportunities occur in situations where the assigned defender is unable to pressure the attack man. Immediately after the feeder receives the ball from a teammate is one such opportunity. A second opportunity that is frequently available occurs as the feeder brings the ball in from the back line after an out-of-bounds, for if he moves into feeding territory immediately, he will be unmolested for a few moments.

When a feeder is not playing the ball, he should pull in close to the rear of the cage, for the feeders are responsible for backing up the cage to retrieve erratic shots. An out-of-bounds ball, as the result of a shot, belongs to the player on either team who was closest to the ball when it crossed a boundary. The feeder closest to the ball should be sure that such a ball is his.

The feeder without the ball may try to break past his defense man to receive a feed himself, but he should always be ready to help his partner. Part of the feeder's job is just keeping his own defense man so busy that he cannot be of any help to a teammate if the player with the ball were to dodge. All the feeder without the ball has to do is keep moving without getting in the way of his partner. To keep himself ready for a pass, he should position himself fairly close to the cage so that when a pass is thrown, he has the chance to break toward the ball and toward the back line away from his own defense man who might otherwise intercept the pass or check the stick. One good position for the player without the ball is just to the rear of the point of the cage. Here his partner may use him as a post for a brush if he wishes, as shown previously in Figure 46. If the defense man plays so closely that it is hard to get the pass from the partner, the feeder should break past the defender toward the cage a few times to make him respect the attack man's scoring potential more. If the pass is still hard to complete, the player should run toward his partner, pass him to the outside, and then take a flip pass from him.

THE CREASE MAN

In most offensive patterns there is one member of the attack stationed directly in front of the crease. This man plays in a rectangular area from the crease to about 5 yards out and about 10 yards either side of the center of the goal. A player in this area is a very serious scoring threat, and therefore is usually closely covered.

Although the crease man may pick up an occasional assist and may retrieve a lot of ground balls, he is not valuable as a crease man unless he scores. Because he is normally so closely covered, it is of prime importance that he be able to quick stick accurately. Only infrequently will he have the chance to cradle, control the ball, and look for his spot. At all times he should be aware of the position of the cage. As second nature he should study the moves of the goalie, and he should be able to decide in a fraction of a second where he will aim a particular shot. In general he should shoot for one of the corners since these are the most difficult parts of the cage for a goalie to cover. It is easier to quick stick to the top corners, but if he can pull his shot down to the bottom corners, it is even harder to stop.

Since the crease man operates in a relatively small area, his movements have to be quick and not extended. A long cut such as that run by a midfielder will take him off the angle by the time the ball arrives and he gets off the shot. Therefore the crease man operates to position himself so that his stick is free, and then with a step or two expects to be able to receive a pass without having his stick checked. His movement before the ball is thrown is directed at this kind of position. After the ball is thrown, he moves toward it so that the defense man cannot cover the already free stick.

The basic starting position for a crease man is on the part of the crease farthest from the ball. This gives him room to move toward the ball and still have a shot when the pass arrives. The moves that the crease man uses to get his stick free depend on where and how closely the defense man plays him. The defense man, if he plays correctly, will try to play between the crease man and the goal and will try to cover the crease man's stick with his own. The crease man tries to free himself of this coverage.

By moving around the crease, seemingly at random, the crease man may well get the defense man to relax his guard and may be able to "walk" into a position where the defense man cannot cover his stick. The ideal situation is one in which the defense man is caught on the crease man's off-side while the crease man is between the defense man and the feeder. He is now free, even though the defense man is standing right next to him. The feeder must be able to realize this; if the crease man moves toward the feeder to emphasize that he is free, he will have taken himself so far off center that the angle available to him for a successful shot is so small that the goalie fills the possible scoring area quite easily. The crease man now has no "angle" on the cage. To prevent this the feeder throws as soon as he recognizes the situation, and the crease man moves away from the defense man and toward the ball while it is in the air. The feed to the the crease man can come from any teammate; it does not have to come from behind the cage, and the crease man should move to free himself while the ball is in the midfield as well as when one of the feeders has possession.

There are two basic moves to use on an alert defense man:

(1) Fake going one way making it look as though a pass is expected momentarily to force the defense man, who may well have his back to the ball, to move to cover the stick. Stop, and come back the other way.

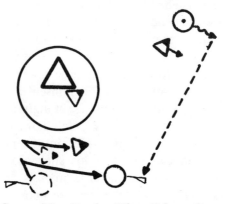

Figure 51. Crease Man Freeing Himself from Coverage by an Alert Crease Defense Man. Crease man fakes away from ball as though a pass were expected. When man moves to counter, crease attack cuts back toward ball.

(2) Start in one direction, stop as though expecting a pass, plant the foot closest to the defense man, and turn back almost 180°, rolling on the defense man as the move is made, to trap his stick and keep him from following.

The timing of a move by the crease man also helps. The defense man will look for the ball occasionally. When he looks away, the crease man moves.

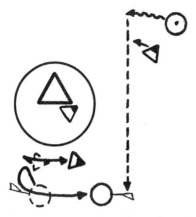

Figure 52. Crease Man Freeing Himself From Coverage by an Alert Crease Defense Man. Crease man fakes away from ball as though a pass were expected. When defense man moves to counter, crease attack rolls against defense man, pinning defense man's stick, and cuts back toward ball.

Crease Play as a Dodger Approaches

Sometimes one of the crease man's teammates gets by his defense man and comes in on the cage unguarded. Many teams instruct the crease defense man to move out to take the dodger as he approaches. Therefore the crease man moves away from the dodger and positions himself so that the dodger, the crease defense man, and he form a triangle rather than a straight line. If the defense man picks up the dodger before he can shoot, the dodger should pass to the crease man. The crease man should be careful never to take himself out of shooting range. Assuming the crease defense man does not pick up the dodger, the crease attack man should still move as directed, taking his defense man with him. The dodger will now be able to get close enough for his own shot. After the shot the crease attack closes in on the cage looking for a possible rebound.

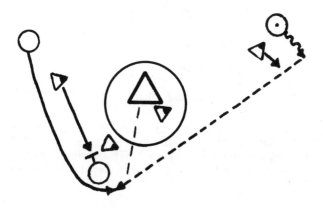

Figure 53.   Brush on Crease Man by Off-Side Feeder.

Crease Brushes

The crease man can also position himself to set up a post on which his teammates can brush. One of the simplest attack plays is to give the ball to one feeder, as in Figure 53, have the crease attack station himself on the side of the goal away from the ball, looking at the ball, and have the other feeder brush on him. The cutting feeder may be free, or the crease attack may be free if the defense tries to concentrate on the cutter. (The same play may be made with a cutting midfielder.) If the man with the ball feeds the cutter, the crease attack should look for the rebound or be ready to back up the cage if the shot misses. If the feeder decides to hold the ball, the cutter continues on past the mouth of the cage and takes a feeder's position to the rear of the cage on the side where the ball was originally located, while the man with the ball just slides across the back of the goal to take the side from which the cutter came.

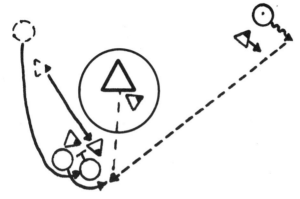

Figure 54.   Off-Side Feeder Brushing on Crease Man, Stopping, and Creating a Post on Which Crease Attack Can Re-Brush.

As a variation, when the cutter sees that no one is free, he should stop just after he has gone past the crease attack, and let him rebrush on the now stationary cutter. Having one attack man cut to the crease and then either continue or stay leads into the possibility of creating a rotating attack where the crease attack trades positions frequently with the feeders. This is difficult for the defense to play because the close attack is constantly in motion continuously forcing all defense men to play the more specialized and difficult crease defense position.

Screening Shots from the Front

Often a midfielder will find himself free enough in front

Figure 55. Backhand Shot by Crease Attack Man. Taken because an overhand shot would be checked by defense man, or (as in illustration) because an overhand shot would allow him no angle on the cage.

of the cage to shoot from about 15 or more yards out. It is the job of the crease attack to do his best to screen the goalie. He wants the ball to pass as close to him as possible. If the ball is thrown on the ground, he wants it to pass under him. If the crease defense looks as though he might get his stick on such a shot, his stick should be checked vigorously away from the ball as he reaches for it. As soon as the shot goes by, the crease attack should turn and get as close to the cage as the crease will allow to cover a rebound. An attack man may reach over the crease line with his stick so long as no part of his body touches the line or the ground inside the line. He may bat or scoop any ball in the crease which is not in the goalie's possession, but he may not interfere with the goalie.

If it seems to the crease attack as though the ball is going to miss the cage or be stopped easily by the goalie, he should intercept the shot and shoot immediately himself. The crease attack will be more dangerous on such shots—or feeds from the front—if he develops a backhand shot, for he may well not be able to turn to shoot without being checked. (A backhand shot is also useful if he receives a feed so far to the side of the cage that if he shot overhand on his stick side, he would have no angle.)

SOME POINTERS FOR THE INDIVIDUAL ATTACK MAN

(1) Get to know the defense man as soon as possible in the game. Test his strengths and weaknesses.

(2) A feeder in particular should work his defense man into a dodging situation early in the game to see how he plays and to see if it is possible to go by him. Such a

maneuver, even if not succesful, makes the defense man cautious about overplaying.

(3) Keep the defense man occupied even if the attack man does not have the ball and is not ready to break into scoring territory. The constant movement keeps the defense man's attention on his man, preventing him from backing up his teammates.

(4) Try to move the defense man so that he cannot watch both the ball and his man and still stay in position. Every time he looks at the ball, make a move of some sort so that he has to find the attack man again.

(5) When in possession of the ball, carry the stick so that an immediate feed, shot, or pass can be delivered. Fake passes constantly to keep the defense man confused. Keep passes and feeds short, hard, and accurate. Do not hold the ball for an extended period unless in the process of dodging. Keep it moving with quick, short passes around the outside of the attacking pattern, keeping the ball to the outside away from the defense men.

(6) Always move toward the ball as a pass is received. Look immediately to the crease area for a quick opening. Then look back to the man who just passed the ball; he may have been able to work a "give-and-go."

(7) Shoot frequently, but only when there is a chance of scoring. If by the time the ball is under control, a reasonable angle on the cage has been lost, hold the ball and look for another opportunity.

(8) At least one of the feeders should direct play on the attacking half of the field. It is better if both would share this responsibility equally.

(9) Make sure that at least one attack man is prepared to back up a shot.

(10) The attack is responsible for loose balls in their

half of the field, and there should be at least one attack man on every loose ball unless there are already two mid-fielders much closer.

(11) Help the other attack men and midfielders by providing an outlet for them for a pass to take pressure off themselves. In such a situation the attack man should move his defense man in close to the cage and then break to the outside toward the person throwing the pass.

(12) In a dodging situation, if the attack man's defense man has gone to pick up the dodger, that attack man should move in front of the cage and position himself to receive a pass from the dodger without lining himself up so that he, the dodger, and the defense man form a straight line.

So far the attack man's play has been discussed as though his only task was to score. He is also charged with controlling the ball in his half of the field. As such his job does not end when the attack loses the ball; he wants to keep the defense from moving the ball out of the area. He is now charged with playing defense to keep the ball in the attacking area. These duties are discussed in Chapter 10, Rides Against Clears.

4. Close Defense Play

How does a coach select the close defense men? It is easy to look over the prospective players and pick the largest, and give them defense sticks. But size is not everything. In general the defense men are likely to be heavier than other players, for it is vital that they not be pushed around by attack men. They must be able to stand their ground and give harder checks than they receive. More important than sheer size, though, is having quick reflexes. The attack man starts with the ball; all the initiative belongs to him; he knows what he is going to do; the defense man must react to his moves. Therefore the best defense man is not necessarily the biggest man on the team, but the one with the quickest reflexes. A defense man can be taught to react in a certain way to a particular play, but one of the beauties of lacrosse is that no two plays are exactly alike. The defense must make instant adjustments to counter what the attack does.

Endurance and speed are also very important assets. The attack man with the ball can afford to loaf to catch his breath. The defense man, however, must move when the attack moves, no matter how tired he may be. If a squad has only a limited number of skilled stick handlers, these players are probably best used on the attack and in the goal, but the stick work of the defense should not be neglected. Without reasonably good stick work the defense will have great difficulty clearing the ball, and the game will be played in the defensive half of the field.

Stick work for the defense is further complicated by the size of a defense stick. It is much easier for beginners to manipulate an attack stick. However, the defense wants larger sticks so that (1) they will have the reach to make stick contact with opponents without allowing them to get close; (2) they will have the reach to intercept passes; (3) they will have the leverage to throw long clearing passes to fellow defense men, midfielders, or even their own attack men; and (4) they will have a large head on the stick so that they will be able to block passes and feeds thrown by the men they cover. With the large defense stick it is difficult to dodge and difficult to hold the ball in the stick against a pressing opponent; so the defense tries to avoid such situations. Perhaps some of these difficulties can be alleviated by equipping the defense men with midfield sticks—which are an inch narrower—instead of defense sticks. There is merit in this idea, especially for beginners, provided the length of the stick is maintained. The smaller head of the stick will help improve ball control while only slightly decreasing the defense man's ability to block passes and make interceptions.

PLAYING THE MAN WITH THE BALL

The method of playing the man with the ball depends a great deal on his position on the field and how serious a

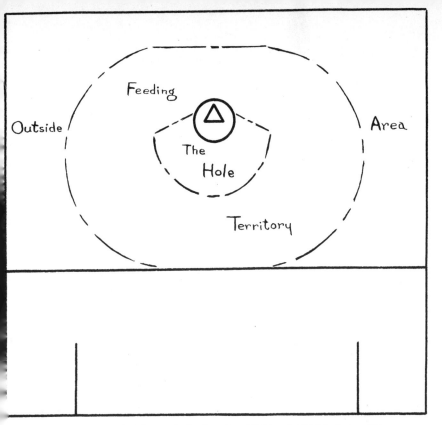

Figure 56. Division of Defensive Half of Field into Three Areas of Danger.

scoring threat he poses. Referring to Figure 56, the defensive half of the field can be divided into three areas. The "hole" is the area of extreme danger where the man with the ball has a good scoring shot. The area is roughly semi-circular in shape extending in an arc from the center of the goal with a radius of about 10 yards. The "feeding" territory is an area of medium danger where a player with the ball will become a very serious threat if he dodges his man or passes to a teammate in the hole. It is roughly rectangular in shape, with arced corners, extending from the restraining line 20 yards in front of the cage to a line 5 yards in from the back line. Laterally the boundaries would be 20 yards on either side of the goal. The "outside" area of less danger encompasses the rest of the defensive half of the field.

Playing the Man with the Ball in the Outside Area

The objective of the defense man is to hold a player in the outside area without pressing him so hard that he can dodge. The defense man wants to force the attack man to pass the ball.

The first rule of good defensive play is field position. The beginning defense man should be told to play on a direct line between his attack man and the mouth of the goal. As he becomes skilled he should then be told to play between the ball and the goal, which will cause him to play slightly to the stick side of his attack man. The defense man should move laterally with his attack man trying not to cross his feet in the process, for to do so makes it difficult to change direction should the attack man alter his course. If the attack man starts to move rapidly, the defense man will have to turn and run with him going back to a side step as soon as the attack man slows down enough. The stick should be held face down so that the head of the stick is held forward aimed at the attack man's waist or lower hand. The defense man must not reach so far forward that he is off balance; he should maintain a position in which his lower hand on the butt of his own stick is in the vicinity of his own hip and the upper hand is reaching forward to a comfortable position. The defense man in the outside area is willing to give ground if necessary to keep the attack man at stick's length. As the attack man starts to force, if the defense man is moving with a side step, he should use

Figure 57. Defense Man Maintaining Proper Position on His Attack Man. He moves laterally with a side step when possible and carries his stick face down aimed at the attack man's lower hand or hip.

the "poke check" or "chop" to try to dislodge the ball. If the attack man is moving enough so that the defense man must run with him, the defender should run without trying to stick check maintaining his position squared up on the man-goal line until the attack man slows down.

The poke check is similar to a billiard shot. The defense man aims his stick at the lower hand or butt of the attack man's stick, pokes his own stick forward with his lower arm, and allows the stick to slide through the glove of the upper hand. The poke should be sharp, quick, and recovered immediately. The poke should be about 6 inches or at most a foot. To poke farther throws the defense man off balance.

As the name would indicate, the chop is performed by taking short chopping blows at the butt of the attack man's stick or the glove of his lower hand. The chop is executed by moving the defense man's upper hand while using the lower hand as a fulcrum. The head of the stick moves 6 to 9 inches at most in the chop. It must not become a slash or wild swing. Even if a penalty is not drawn, the defense man throws himself off balance giving the attack man a chance to go by. The hope is to jar the attack man's stick enough to dislodge the ball.

Figure 58. Poke Check. Defense man pokes his stick forward aimed at the attack man's lower hand using his lower hand to move the stick allowing the stick to slide through the glove of his upper hand. Poke is 6 inches to a foot at most.

If the attack man carries his stick in one hand, it will probably be hard to poke or chop, so the defense man should bide his time in this area. If the attack man offers a very tempting target, the defense man might risk a harder stick check, but he should be wary of bait intentionally offered by a skilled attack man. To be dodged in this area

Figure 59. Chop. The defense man aims his stick at the attack man's lower hand, delivering a 6-9 inch chop stroke.

is senseless. The attack man is not dangerous, either as a scorer or feeder, and to lose him this far from the cage puts unnecessary pressure on the other defense men.

Early in the game a defense man should discover what his attack man can and cannot do. While the first rule of defensive play is to maintain a line between the ball and the goal, if the attack man can play only one hand, the defense man should play slightly to his stick side when the man carries his stick on his strong side and should play him head on when he goes back to his weak side. If the attack man can play both ways, the defense man plays slightly to his stick side depending on which is his stick side at the moment. If he is a dodger, the defense man's stick should be held opposite the attack man's waist. If he is a feeder, the defender can afford to play to block his feeds. To block a feed, as the attack man starts his throw, the defense man raises his stick trying to cover the attack man's stick exactly with his own. The defender must be careful never to charge the passer, for to do so opens up the chances of a face dodge. When playing an attack man in the outside area, the defender should be able to try to block passes without over committing himself since the attack man is at stick's length, and if the throwing motion is just a fake, the defender should be able to get his stick back down to waist level before any damage is done.

Playing the Man with the Ball in Feeding Territory

When the attack man moves into feeding territory, he poses more of a threat. He must not be allowed to advance into the hole. The defense man, therefore, now gives ground grudgingly. He still uses the poke check and the chop to bother the attack man, and he will still try to intercept feeds. There are now several other moves that the defense man should use.

When the attack man keeps boring toward the cage, his progress must be stopped. As he drives past the poke check and chop coming in closer to the defender, the defense man cannot afford to give ground to maintain his position at stick's length. His next move is to start applying a stick check against the attack man by covering the attack man's stick with his own and then checking down on the shaft of the attack stick with force.

Figure 60. Blocking Feeds. As the attack man starts to throw, the defense man raises his stick, matching the attack man's stick with his own.

It is preferred to stick check across the front of the attack man, but if he drags his stick, sometimes it can be reached by checking behind him. Care must be exercised, for the attacker may just be offering a bait, and if the check behind him misses, he is likely free to go by.

Another effective stick check to be used on an attack man can be the over-the-head check, *but it should be attempted only by an experienced player.* The timing is of great importance, for again, if the check misses, the attack man will go by. The defense man raises his upper hand just enough so that his stick will clear the attack man's helmet. He raises his lower hand higher, so that after his stick passes over the attack man's helmet, the head of his stick will strike the throat of the attack stick (he should not aim for the head of the attack stick) and dislodge the ball. Some defenders when using this check release the upper hand from the stick as it passes over the attack man's helmet and make the check with only the hand on the butt of the stick doing the swinging. More control is exercised if both hands are left on the stick, but the defense man must be careful not to hook or hold the attack man with his stick or arms.

If these stick checks still do not stop the attack man, or if he rolls back while being checked, the defender should now start to use his hands or forearms to play the attack man. The defender is allowed to use his hands and forearms to push a player with the ball (or within 5 yards of a loose ball) as hard as he wants provided the push (not a blow) is delivered from the front or side of the opponent while both hands of the defender are on his own crosse.

The methods of delivering the push will depend on how the defender's stick is being held with respect to his attack man. Ideally a defense man should be able to play equally well both right-and left-handed. If he could switch he would prefer to play a right-handed attack man holding his own stick left-handed. He would play a left-handed attack man right-handed. As a result the attack man's stick is always covered by the defense man's stick, and the defender's stick is always ahead of the man being played. However, if the defense man cannot play both hands equally well, he should not bother to switch to his weaker side, but should play the attack man using his stronger side all the time. As a result, if for instance the attack man is playing right-handed and the defense man is also primarily right-handed, the defender will be playing backhanded against his man. If the attack man then switches back to left-handed, the defender will be playing forehanded against him. While a defense man who can play either hand should try to play the attack man's primary side forehanded, if the attack man changes hands back and forth with ease, the defense man will have difficulty switching hands with every change his attack man makes, and he should probably not try to do so while in close contact with his attack man.

Playing the attack man forehanded, if the attacker continues to bore forward past the stick check, he runs into the defender's top hand on the throat of his stick. If the attacker rolls back, the defender plays him with his lower hand on the butt of the stick. With either hand the defender pushes the attack man back. After delivering a push hard enough to drive the attack man back, the defender should immediately break contact, draw back the hand that was doing the pushing and advance his trailing hand to preserve balance should the attack man recover quickly and possibly roll back the other way.

Alternately using his hands to push the attack man, the defender must be very careful not to crosse-check his opponent (i.e. check him with that part of the shaft of the crosse

Figure 61. Over-the-Head Stick Check. Should be attempted only by an experienced player.

Figure 62. Playing an Attack Man with the Hands. (a) Defense man and attack man both playing same hand (both right in illustration); defense man uses forearm of upper hand. (b) Defense man and attack man playing opposite hands; defense man uses hand on throat of stick. (c) Should either hand check fail, or attack man roll back, defense man uses hand on butt of stick.

which is between his hands). To avoid this foul, he should be careful to make contact with only one hand at a time positioning his other hand very close to his own hip so that the pushing hand is advanced well in the lead. He should also be aware that if the attack man rolls back onto the shaft of the stick, the foul is still the fault of the defender even though the crosse-check was unintentional.

If the defender was playing backhanded against the driving attacker, his push would be delivered with the forearm of the hand on the throat of his stick. This check with the forearm is delivered in the same manner as the push with the hand previously described. There is no danger of being trapped into a crosse-check because of the position of the stick, but should the attack man roll back in the opposite direction, the defender must break contact quickly, for he will have to catch the attacker with his upper hand for the push if the opponent continues to bore. While delivering the forearm push, the defender should take care not to hook or hold the attack man with the head of his stick.

If the attack man succeeds in boring in past the hand or forearm push, the defense man should throw a shoulder block, keeping his head in front of the attack man. He should be careful to keep his feet, for he does not want to take himself out of subsequent play with a violent check that misses.

Despite all the good intentions of the defense man, an attack man will occasionally get past. The defense man must recover as quickly as possible and attempt to get back in front of his man. The attack man is supposed to run a straight line to the front of the cage, but he will often curve, allowing the defender to run the chord of his arc and catch up. This will be particularly true if the crease gets in the way, for the attack man must run outside the crease while a defense man, not in possession of the ball, may run through.

Even if the defender cannot succeed in getting back in front of his man, there is still the chance that the defender will be able to prevent a feed or shot trailing his man. Though the attack man should continue to move as fast as

Figure 63. Defender Turns in Direction Opposite to That of Opponent to Recover When Attacker Dodges.

possible when he loses his man, and though he should keep his stick in front of his body shielding it from the trailing defender, there is still a good chance that he will make one or both errors allowing the defense man one last crack at the stick.

In recovering quickly once he had been dodged, the defender may have been moving in the opposite direction from his attack man when he was dodged. This is likely to be the case when the attack man executes a roll, dip, or face dodge. Under these conditions the defender will have to reverse direction prior to moving in order to cut off the attack man. Rather than trying to make this change, the defender will recover more quickly if he pivots in exactly the opposite direction to meet the attack man at the end of the turn.

As the defense man loses his man, he should not only try to recover but should also call immediately "Pick up the dodger" to the other defense men. The closest defender should then move off his own man to intercept the dodger. The defense man who was dodged, seeing his teammate in the process of picking up the loose man, should automatically switch men and pick up the player his teammate had to leave.

In feeding territory, attack men frequently work together to set up a brush. The post attack man must stand still while the brush is worked; as a result the defender covering him can see the pick coming and should call to his teammate playing the ball "Watch the pick" to warn him that he is about to be blocked. If absolutely necessary, the two defense men can switch men, but there will be less chance of error if each can stay with his own man. Alerted to the pick, the defense man covering the ball should try to force his attack man to run wide enough of the pick so that he can also pass to the outside of the pick. As a second choice, if he can not stay tightly on his man, the defender playing the stationary attack man should sag off his man far enough so that the defense man playing the ball can drop off his man momentarily, pass to the inside of the stationary attack man, and pick up his own man on the other side of the brush. The first method is preferred, however, for while the defense man is sagged off, the attack man is free to get off a good feed.

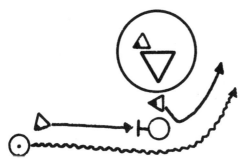

Figure 64. Switching Men When Defender on Man with the Ball Is About to Be Brushed on a Post. Defense man covering the post should call "Get ready to switch" as the brush situation approaches. At the moment of exchange he should call "Switch."

If the two defense men prefer to switch, either man may call the switch, but if one so calls, the other must execute the exchange even though he may think it unnecessary. To fail to do so would leave two defense men on one attack man and none on the other. The switch must be performed so that neither attack man is free. Either can reverse direction, so neither can be overplayed. While either defender may call the switch, the defender covering the post attack man is in better position to decide if the move is necessary.

As the brush approaches he should call "Get ready to switch." At the moment of exchange he should call "Switch." As the exchange is made the defense man coming off the ball carrier should take a step back so that his new man does not break by him immediately.

Playing the Man with the Ball in the Hole

From the defensive point of view no attack man should ever be allowed in the hole with the ball. But when the situation does occur, instructions are simple. *Body check the player immediately*. If the player's own defense man is still in position to throw the check, he must do so without hesitation. His block should be a shoulder block keeping his head in front of the attack man. If at the same time he can cover the attack man's stick with his own, he should do so. Under no circumstances, however, should he rely on the stick check alone to do the job. It is all too easy for the attack man to face dodge.

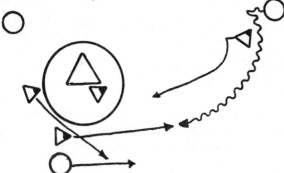

Figure 65.   Shift by Close Defense to Pick Up a Dodger. Crease defense man picks up dodger and body checks him. Off-side defense man shifts in to cover the crease attack man. Defense man who was dodged heads for the goal to pick up any open man in front of the cage.

If the attack man with the ball enters the hole unguarded, the nearest defender should move immediately to play
him with the body. This assignment frequently falls to the
crease defense man, and he should be prepared to leave his
man without hesitation in such a situation. The goalie can

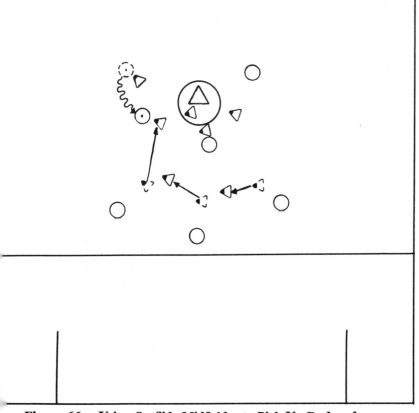

**Figure 66.   Using On-Side Midfielder to Pick Up Dodger from
Rear of Cage. Leave close defense in position; rotate midfield
to meet the dodge.**

be of tremendous help in meeting the emergency by alerting the crease defense man to the dodge and calling for the shift. With a dangerous crease man, however, the shift of the crease defense man should be avoided if possible.

On the dodge from the rear of the cage, the safer shift comes from the midfield. Some serious practice time must be devoted to the play, however, for any one of the midfielders might find himself in the situation where, as the closest man to the dodge, he will be responsible for making the shift. Therefore all midfielders must be aware of their responsibility. It is easier to coach a single crease defense man to make the shift, but to avoid the additional problem of picking up the crease attack, the midfield shift is preferred.

PLAYING THE MAN WITHOUT THE BALL

Paradoxically, playing the man with the ball is a cinch compared to playing a man without the ball. In playing the ball, all the defense man need worry about is his position on the field and the skills of his single man. When playing the man without the ball, the defense man must not only consider the same factors with regard to his own man, but must also consider where the ball is on the field, who has it, what shifts might be needed to help teammates, and naturally what the game situation might be.

Playing Man without the Ball Outside the Hole

The rules for playing an attack man without the ball outside the hole are quite simple, but in their execution mistakes are easy to make. (1) Play between the attack man and the goal, on the man-goal line in most cases. (2) Face in such a direction that both the man being covered and the ball can be seen with split vision. In the event that this is impossible, which will be true if the ball, goal, and man being covered lie in a straight line in that order, glance back and forth between man and ball. (3) Play the man at a depth such that if a pass were thrown to him, the defender would arrive on his man just before or just as the ball arrived. In the event that the attack man being covered is so far from the cage that he poses absolutely no threat, the coverage should be somewhat looser. (4) If the ball is located in front of the goal, and the attack man being covered is behind the goal, play either slightly in front of the goal favoring the side where the man is located or play level with the goal on the same side as the man being covered. (5) If the defense man is the player adjacent to the teammate playing the ball, he should be prepared to back up his teammate in the event of a dodge. He should announce his presence by calling "I've got you backed on right (or left)." (6) Play closer to the goal than the distance that the ball is removed from the goal. By so doing, if there is an emergency and more defense men are needed in the hole, there will be help nearby.

There are a few special situations where adjustments must be made to provide tighter coverage of a man even though he does not have the ball. (1) If the attack man being covered is the opposition's star feeder, he should be covered more tightly when he does not have the ball to make it more difficult for the opposition to get the ball to him. The decision to use this strategy should be known to the entire defensive team. (2) If the defense has an extra man as the result of a penalty, players without the ball should be covered tightly making it very difficult for the attack to move the ball. (3) If the defensive team is down a goal or two in the latter stages of the game, the attack will probably be quite deliberate in their movements. Since it is imperative for the defense to gain control of the ball, each man must tighten up on his man to reduce the attack's freedom to move the ball.

The defensive strategy might call for looser coverage of one feeder. Assuming that the opposition has one good dodger, the defense man covering the other feeder should sag off near the cage when the ball is in possession of the dodger so that he will be available to pick up the dodger if needed or will be able to shift onto the crease attack should the crease defense man be forced to take the dodger.

Other than staying alert so that the attack man being covered does not break past the defender to the inside, there are two favorite attack plays for which the defense should be prepared. One is the pick-off play often worked on the back of the cage.

The other is the "give-and-go." This play is worked by an attack man just after he passes the ball off to a teammate. When the pass is made, the defender who was playing him must immediately make the transition from playing the man with the ball to playing an attack man without the ball. As the pass is made, the defense man must move back two or three yards to establish the proper sag on his man. If he does not make the adjustment quickly, the attack man breaks by him looking for an immediate return feed from his teammate.

Playing Man in the Hole

Most of the defensive play thus far concerns the play of the defenders on the feeders. The attack man normally in the hole is the crease attack, and this section, therefore, concerns the crease defense man in particular. However, as soon as one of the feeders makes a cut to the front of the cage, his defense man must be alert to his new responsibilities.

The crease defense man plays between his man and the goal with one important exception. Were he to continue to follow this normal defensive positioning when the ball is in front of the goal, his attack man could receive a feed by holding his stick in front of his face and moving toward the pass. Playing behind the attack man, the defender will find it almost impossible to counter the play without fouling. Therefore, with the ball in the midfield, the crease defense man plays to the side of his man—on the side toward the center of the field. If the crease attack is playing directly in the center of the field, the crease defense should play the attack man's stick side. (The crease defense should learn as soon as possible whether the crease attack plays both ways or only one. Some crease attack men will carry their sticks on their weak side to try to confuse the defense man.)

If the crease attack man is within three or four yards of the crease and there is any danger of a pass being thrown to him, he should be covered so closely that the defense man is actually in physical contact. Farther from the crease, the defense man should be able to reach him with no more than one step. The defender is allowed to stand as close to his attack man as he wishes, but may not interfere with his free movement unless the ball is loose within 5 yards—and a pass is a loose ball—or the attack man actually has the ball. But the attack man cannot interfere with the defense man either. To maintain contact, the defense man should place his stick across the front of the attack man and maintain contact with his stick and upper hand. If he can change hands, he should switch so that this contact will be main-

Figure 67. Crease Defense Man Maintains Physical Contact with the Crease Attack. He prefers to cover with his stick in front of the attacker. However, if he can not play both hands, when faced one way his contact will have to be maintained with the hand on the butt of his stick.

tained. If he cannot switch, he should maintain contact this way when facing one direction, but establish contact with his lower hand when facing the opposite direction. With such contact the defense man can take his eyes off his man to watch the ball and still be alert to any move made by the attacker.

A crease attack man needs only to get his stick free to take a feed. If he gets his body between the defense man

and his stick, it is quite difficult to keep him from getting the ball—if he moves into the pass as he should. It might appear as though the defense man should turn to face his man at all times since he is so dangerous. However, by so doing the defense man takes himself out of all other play. Furthermore his coverage of his own man is not improved for he will not be alerted to a feed being thrown to his man except by the calls of his goalie.

The crease defender must strike a happy medium between too close and too loose coverage. He should maintain contact with his man and still watch the ball. If he cannot do both simultaneously, he should glance back and forth between the ball and the man.

When the ball is fed to the crease attack, the defense man should check the attack stick, aiming for the throat of the stick, just as soon as the ball gets within 15 feet. To check too soon constitutes interference. The defense man may see the ball thrown, or he may be warned to check by the goalie who should yell "Check" when there is a feed coming into the hole area. Finally, the actions of the crease attack man may telegraph that a feed is being thrown to him.

If the check is too late or cannot be made, the defense man should now body check his man vigorously. To try a stick check now that the attack man has the ball invites the face dodge. As the shoulder block is thrown, the defense man should try to cover the attack man's stick simultaneously, but the body check comes first.

The crease defense man's play is further complicated when more players come into the area. A second attack man means that he can brush on the crease attack. There should be another defender with him, so if each can stay with his own man, the coverage will be satisfactory, though the traffic gets heavy. If the two attack men brush well, it may be necessary to switch men, as on a brush by the feeders (see pp. 156-8) The attack man going toward the ball is the more dangerous of the two and should get primary attention. If the second attack man is just passing through the hole, his own man should stay with him. To switch leaves a player unfamiliar with covering a crease man in the center. If the second attack man is a relatively permanent fixture, as on one of the double crease attacking patterns described in Chapter 7, the defense man playing this additional crease man will have to learn quickly how to cope with his man, or someone will have to be substituted who is familiar with crease play. With two defense men playing the crease it is possible to zone successfully and have each cover part of the crease area. There are dangers to this tactic as shown when the patterns are discussed in Chapter 7, but it may still be the best method.

Of great concern to the crease defense man is the attack man dodging into the hole. Though a midfielder may be assigned the primary duty of backing up such a dodge from the rear of the cage (see Figure 66), the crease defender may well find himself the last player, other than the goalie, between the dodger and a score. To leave his man too soon to pick up the dodger invites the feed to his own man. To leave too late, allows the dodger to shoot. He should leave so as to arrive just before the dodger has a shot. As the crease defense man goes he should warn his teammates that he is making the move so that the off-side defense man will be alerted to move into the hole to pick up the crease attack. In making his move on the dodger, he should aim to body check the dodger—to try to stick check invites the face dodge. If at the same time he can cover the dodger's stick, so much the better. The nearest defensive player should be coming in to pick up the crease attack in the emergency. This is one of the hardest of all defensive plays, but if all members of the defense are ready to react, it can be made, even if the attack handles the ball correctly. Refer to Figure 65.

5. Goalie Play

More is expected of a lacrosse goalie than a similar player in any other sport. Naturally he is the last man responsible for keeping the ball out of the goal. He should also be the director, or field general, of his defensive midfield as well as his close defense. In addition a lacrosse goalie is expected to play a major role in the clearing pattern of his team. In so doing, it is not unusual for him to move as far from his goal as the midline. In fact, a good clearing goalie is quite likely to be down in his attacking half of the field on occasions. The goalie's role in clearing makes his job complex, and differentiates him from goalies in other sports, but at the same time makes his job both interesting and challenging.

A good goalie probably cannot win a game. His attack still has to produce goals for victory, but he can go a long way toward keeping his team from losing. Even the greatest goalie cannot be expected to stop everything. Shutouts in lacrosse do occur, but they are rare and are usually the result of excellent ball control on the attack rather than a superior defensive job by the goalie and his close defense. Even a team controlling the ball as little as 25 to 30 per cent of a game would be expected to score at least once. So, to be realistic, both the goalie and his teammates must expect to be scored on.

There are certain characteristics which successful players in this position are likely to possess. The goalie must have courage to stand up and face the attack man and his shot without flinching. It is possible to ruin a good prospect early in his career by handling him in such a manner that he becomes ball shy. There are many players who do superior jobs in other positions who will inadvertently flinch if put in the goal.

Lacrosse rules permit the goalie to bat or deflect the ball with his hand provided his other hand is holding the stick, but the better goalies make little use of this rule's provision because they can handle their sticks skillfully and quickly. The second attribute of a good goalie should therefore be good stick work. He must, of course, stop the ball, but he must also control it or he will be shelled with rebounds by an alert crease attack. Even after he has learned to catch the ball skillfully, he must learn to throw as well, for if he cannot clear the ball out to teammates downfield, he will have a busy afternoon, since the opposition will control the ball.

A successful goalie must have quick reflexes. He can be coached in the fastest way to move his stick, but he must have the reflexes needed to start the move he has learned soon enough to get in front of the ball.

A goalie must be "cocky." He must, in his own mind at least, dare the attack man to shoot. He must have enough self-confidence in his own ability to feel that one of the quickest and easiest ways for his team to gain possession of the ball is to have the opposition shoot at him.

Finally, the goalie must be willing to direct his defense. He must direct play in the defensive half of the field when the opposing team is attacking and also during his team's clearing procedure. For this he needs a thorough knowledge of the duties and capabilities of each of his teammates and the ability to see, describe, and counter offensive and defensive patterns as they develop in front of him.

Much as a goalie needs (1) courage, (2) stickwork, (3) quick reflexes, (4) a cocky attitude, and (5) leadership, it is impossible to predict that a beginner does or does not have the makings of a goalie before trying him at the position. It takes some time and careful coaching to develop a consistently effective goalie. However, after a player has tried the position for a season, it will probably become clear what his prospects are as a goalie. Conversely, it should not be assumed that a good player in some other position would make a good goalie. However, one key to a good defense is a good goalie; and one must be found, even if strength at some other point on the field must be sacrificed. Maybe the player who volunteers for the job will develop—he is more likely to make the grade than anyone else since he had the interest to volunteer—but if he cannot do the job, someone must be found who can.

GOALIE EQUIPMENT

Since the goalie must be able to move out of the cage on the clear, it is best not to weigh him down with large amounts of additional equipment not carried by other players. The best goalies stop 95 per cent of the shots with their sticks, so heavy pads are relatively useless. The goalie's helmet should be equipped with a full face mask, for there is enough opening in the mask designed for a normal player for the ball to enter if it hits exactly right. He should definitely wear a chest protector, since an occasional ball will get past the stick. A chest protector specifically designed for lacrosse is only slightly smaller than that worn by a baseball catcher. A few experienced goalies use only a piece of shock absorbing plastic foam pad to protect the chest. A cup supporter completes the goalie's minimum equipment.

Most goalies wear sweat pants. A few wear shin pads, but these are only extra weight. The beginning goalie must be mentally prepared to block some shots with his legs and body. As he gains experience and skill, he will learn to take more shots with his stick and less with his body. Some goalies prefer not to wear arm or shoulder pads because their stick movements are slightly slowed. However, this consideration should be weighed against the possibility that he may want such pads while clearing. The goalie has his crease to protect him from the slash or body check while stopping the shot. But as soon as he leaves this protection while clearing, he is subject to the same sort of coverage as any other player. The goalie does not usually want to take the risk of dodging, for if he loses the ball, the attack can often get off a shot at an open cage before the goalie gets back. However, there are occasions when he might be slashed or body checked. Since a team usually has only a few competent goalies on its roster, the arm and shoulder pads may well prevent serious team problems which could result were the goalie to sustain injury.

STARTING THE BEGINNER IN THE GOAL

Chapter 2, Stick Work Fundamentals, stressed instructing beginners carefully in throwing and catching. The prospective goalie should get all the stick work practice possible before he even looks at the cage. His problem is greater than that of others because of the size of his stick. If it is new, it takes longer to break in than does a smaller attack stick. After the goalie develops a sufficiently deep pocket in the stick in order to maintain control after the catch, he will discover that he has more trouble throwing the ball than any other player. He does not want a whip, but because of his deep pocket, he will probably have to release the ball earlier than any other player to avoid it. The wide stick will be cumbersome at first, and the beginning goalie will want to cut off his stick immediately, particularly since the 40-inch minimum length does not apply to him. This initial reaction should be resisted, for a goalie with a short stick cannot pass the ball far or accurately, and a good part of a goalie's value is determined by his skill on the clear.

Start the prospective goalie off just as any other player and have him engage in any and all drills, including ground ball drills. After a couple of sessions it is probably safe to introduce him to his goal. This is the crucial moment in his development. More prospective goalies are ruined in a few moments during the first week of practice than at any other time. An eager beginner wants to get in his goal right away, and if he has a goalie's natural temperament, he will dare people to shoot to test himself. To have equally unskilled players shoot at him at this stage is sheer suicide. In the first place, the goalie himself does not have the stick work to stop the ball correctly and as a result will be taking a lot of balls on his body, if he stops them at all; and a lacrosse ball is by no means soft! As a result he will unconsciously flinch, and the prospective goalie is ball shy before he even starts! It is possible to correct all sorts of mistakes in position play and stick work, but to make a gun-shy goalie over again is almost impossible.

At the same time, other beginners who are shooting feel frustrated if they do not score. On long shots they miss the cage; soon they move right in on top of the goalie. Even the best goalie stops only a portion of such shots; so immediately the new goalie is faced with an impossible situation. If he is trained correctly, he will make the impossible saves later on, but not during the first few days of practice. Since the inaccurate beginning shooter does not know himself where the ball is headed, the new goalie will find it almost impossible to judge the shot as it leaves the shooter's stick.

Introduce the goalie to the cage slowly. After he has some idea of proper coverage of the goal, have him start by stopping easy 20-yard shots in the air. Work at teaching him the correct moves as the shots get more difficult. After he has the idea of how to stop the ball in the air, start him on bounce shots. Then change the shooting angle. Gradually work in closer, still shooting softly so that if he takes the shot on the body, it will not bother him. He should be allowed several days to familiarize himself with the basic movements and patterns of coverage. Then start shooting harder; and when he is ready, start putting him in scrimmages. After he has become quite proficient, perhaps allow him to work in shooting drills, but certainly not until that time. *Up to this point only a coach or an experienced player who has been carefully instructed should be allowed to shoot at the goalie.* To let the bulk of the players have a crack at him in these early stages invites trouble.

GOALIE POSITION

The goal is 6 feet by 6 feet, and the goalie wants to occupy as much of that space as he can. His position is taken with respect to the location of the ball at any given moment. First, assuming that the ball is in front of the cage, the goalie moves so that he creates a straight line between the ball, himself, and the center of the goal. Perhaps it will help at first to stand on the goal line in the center of the cage and with the head of his stick trace a semi-circle on the ground. The radius of his semi-circle is about 3 feet, while the goal line of his cage will be the diameter. As he main-

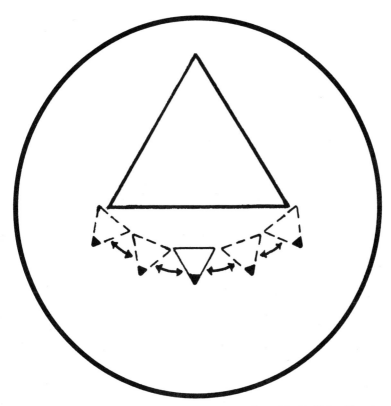

Figure 68. Path Followed by the Goalie with Ball in Front of Goal. Goalie should move in a semi-circular path, or a slightly elliptical version thereof.

tains his position in line with the ball, he should move on this semi-circle, or a slightly elliptical version of it. To move straight across the mouth of the goal would of course be shorter, but he would then run the risk of scoring on himself if the shot taken were hard enough to force his stick back past the plane of the goal.

The goalie should keep his eye on the ball at all times. With split vision he can also watch opponents who are in front of the crease and therefore are dangerous receivers, but his sight should be centered on the ball. As a result he often cannot see the goal itself. To make sure of his position, he should form the habit of tapping the pipes with his stick when he has the opportunity, to be sure of his location with respect to the goal. An experienced goalie needs to do this less than a beginner, but it soon becomes second nature to him.

If the ball is to the side of the cage, the goalie should hug the pipe on that side, still keeping his body in line with the ball and the center of the goal.

A somewhat different situation is created if the ball is behind the cage. The goalie still faces the ball squarely. He would like to intercept any pass thrown over his goal. He should hold his stick 6 to 9 inches from the top of the goal with the head of the stick higher than the bar. As he moves the stick forward to make the interception he must be careful to control the ball and not just deflect it into the goal. If the ball is merely deflected, the stick should be close enough to the top pipe so that the rebound will roll down the back of the net. Therefore he moves across the mouth of the goal as shown in Figure 70, in a straight line staying close enough to the cage to position his stick less than a foot from the top pipe.

Figure 69. Goalie's Position with Ball to Rear of Goal. Stick starts less than foot from top pipe of cage so that if ball is merely deflected while attempting interception, free ball will roll down back of net.

STOPPING THE SHOT

The mechanics of stopping the shot are no different than playing catch. All the goalie does is position his stick in front of the ball, give with it as it enters the stick, and control the ball so that it does not rebound.

Assuming that the shot will be taken from a reasonable distance—say ten yards or more—the goalie should be positioned in his cage correctly, be watching the ball, and be carrying his stick at the most comfortable position, keeping the face of the stick open at all times. In general, the stick should be held about waist high in a natural man-

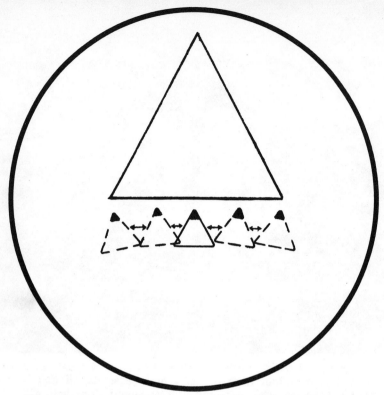

Figure 70. Path Followed by Goalie with Ball in Rear of Goal.

ner and parallel to the ground. Now with his feet a comfortable distance apart—about a foot—his weight on the balls of his feet, and his knees slightly bent, the goalie stands erect ready to move.

The first consideration is to get the stick in the way of the ball. The second is to get the body behind the stick, for even if the stick misses, the shot will still hit the body. The experienced goalie does not think of his moves in two parts. His stick moves, and his body naturally follows, or moves simultaneously. In moving to intercept the ball, the goalie should move to meet the ball or move perpendicular

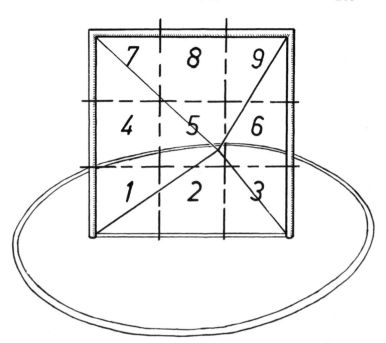

Figure 71. Division of Goal into 9 Small Squares for Description of Goalie Coverage.

to the path of the ball. Under no circumstances should he retreat as the ball approaches. On a low shot he might want to reach his stick farther forward to catch a ball before it bounces on the ground, but on all other shots, including most ground balls, the goalie does not want to move his stick forward more than about a foot in front of the plane of his body.

In explaining the proper moves necessary to stop various shots, the following procedure can be conveniently used. Draw on an imaginary diagram of the goal two lines parallel to the ground, equally spaced, and two more lines parallel to the side pipes also equally spaced, thus dividing the goal into nine smaller squares. Each presents a different problem for the goalie. For purposes of description the moves are discussed for a right-handed goalie. A left-handed one merely reverses the sides of the cage.

Figure 72.   Area 1.   Lower Corner; Stick Side.

Area 1—Lower Corner; Stick Side

Shots from about 20 yards out are frequently taken on the ground, for the bounce makes the shot trickier. To cover the lower corner on the stick side the goalie rotates the stick 90° downward so that the head of the stick swings in an arc an inch or two above the ground. At the same time the goalie steps off with his right foot toward the ball and pulls up his left foot so that his feet are together backing up the stick with his legs. The shaft of the stick should be almost perpendicular to the ground and should be in front of him. As the rotation of the stick is made, the hand on the butt of the stick slides down near the hand on the throat, which remains stationary. If the ball bounces a little higher, the goalie can lift the stick higher, but he should start with the head of the stick near the ground so there is no danger of the ball passing underneath. He allows the ball to bounce into the stick without reaching for it, unless he can catch the ball before it bounces.

Area 2—Low Shot; Center

A shot directly at the goalie's feet is easier since he does not have to move his body to get in front of the ball. He steps forward to meet the ball, draws his feet together, but otherwise the motions of the stick and its position are exactly as for Area 1.

Area 3—Lower Corner; Off-Stick Side

Normally this is the toughest of the low shots for the beginner since the stick must move farther to get in front of the ball. The stick is rotated downward in a plane parallel to the plane of the body so that the head of the stick swings in an arc a couple of inches above the ground again. The shaft of the stick will be perpendicular to the ground;

Figure 73. Area 2. Low Shot; Center.

parallel to the goalie on his off-stick side. In order to get the head of the stick near the ground, the goalie will have to crouch a little, or move the hand on the throat of the stick. The crouch is preferable since the position of the upper hand on the throat of the stick gives better control. The goalie then moves diagonally forward or perpendicular to the path of the ball to get his body behind the stick. *As always the goalie keeps his eye on the ball all the way in.*

Figure 74. Area 3. Lower Corner; Off-Stick Side.

Area 4—Middle; Stick Side

Balls into the middle area on the stick side come as a result of either a direct shot in the air or a high bounce. The goalie should react to either as though he were playing catch with the shooter, though he moves his body in behind the shot. The bounce shot is the more difficult. The goalie should have watched the ball, thus knowing how the shot was thrown. The ball will come off the ground at roughly the same angle at which it hit. A shot taken overhand is likely to bounce high. An underhand shot will probably bounce low. The distance of the point of impact from the mouth of the cage has an effect on where the ball should arrive; a ball close to the goalie's feet is the hardest to gauge, but it has less chance of bouncing high than does one that hits farther out. The field condition also affects the bounce. On hard, dry ground the ball will naturally bounce higher than it will on wet, slippery turf, where it is most likely to skid.

Area 5—Middle; Directly at the Goalie

A ball thrown directly at the goalie can easily be stopped with the body, but the goalie would rather catch the ball; for a save with the body allows a rebound. On a shot at his midsection the goalie moves as if the ball were directly at his feet, but he picks up the head of the stick to catch the ball. His hands will come together on the throat of the stick. The shaft of the stick will not be perpendicular to the ground except on very low shots in this area. Although the goalie wants his body behind the ball, he may find it easier to control this shot if he moves a little to his off-side so that the shot comes in slightly to the stick side of the center of his body. He still has his body partially behind the stick, but the ball will be on the stick side of his body.

Figure 75. Area 4. Middle; Stick Side.

Figure 76. Area 5. Middle; Directly at the Goalie.

Area 6—Middle; Off-Stick Side

To cover this area the goalie should move almost exactly the way he would for a shot to the lower corner on the off-stick side. He rotates the face of the stick downward to his off-stick side so that the head of the stick is parallel to the ground while the shaft of the stick is perpendicular to the ground. He then raises the stick to the proper height to stop the ball. He will find this move more comfortable if he slides his lower hand toward the throat of the stick so that his hands are quite close together. The goalie then moves his body in behind the stick as he makes the stop.

The coverage of this area may be difficult for a player who has previously played some other position on the field. Only the goalie wants to be able to move his body behind such a shot. Another player would rotate his body and allow the butt of his stick to pass behind his back when catching a ball in this area, but were the goalie to follow this procedure, he would not be able to move behind the shot.

Figure 77.   Area 6. Middle; Off-Stick Side.

Area 7—Top Corner; Stick Side

Any shot to the top area of the cage is difficult to cover, particularly since most such shots are taken from close to the goal, allowing the goalie very little reaction time. There are two methods that might be used to get the stick in proper position. The coach should select one method and instruct his beginner in this method. After the goalie learns to make the stop one way, he can be shown the second way, if he has trouble with this shot. To present the goalie immediately with both methods will leave him confused and shaky on such shots for a long time until he resolves the best way for himself.

Figure 78.   Area 7. Top Corner; Stick Side. Method 1.

Figure 79.   Area 7.   Top Corner; Stick Side.   Method 2.

Method (1) The stick is rotated upward so that the top corner is covered by the face of the stick. The shaft of the stick will end up at about a 45° angle to the ground as the body is moved in behind the stick. The hand on the butt of the stick slides slightly toward the throat if the goalie feels more secure that way. A goalie will also rise as tall as possible so that as he moves over behind the shot his shoulder will block as much of the cage as possible.

Method (2) From the normal relaxed position, with the head of the stick to the side and the shaft held parallel to the ground and waist high, the goalie lifts the stick keeping the shaft parallel to the ground as he makes the move. He then moves the body behind the shot.

Area 8—Top Center

There are two methods again for shots taken more or less at the goalie's head. (1) The goalie continues to rotate his stick past the point at which he would stop a shot in the top corner, stick side, until the face of the stick is roughly in front of his head. He may want to move slightly to the off-side to have his head to one side of the stick so that it does not block his vision.

(2) The goalie moves the shaft of the stick so that it is parallel to the ground, as in Method 2 for the top corner of the stick side; but he pulls the stick across his face to cover the area where the shot is arriving. He may move slightly to the off-side as in (1) to keep the stick from blocking his vision.

Figure 80.   Area 8.   Top Center.   Method 1.

Figure 81. Area 8. Top Center. Method 2.

Area 9—Top Corner; Off-Stick Side

The off-side high corner is the hardest of all to cover accurately. Again there are two methods. (1) The goalie rotates his stick so that its face is always open in a plane about 6 inches to a foot in front of his body. He takes the shortest route to this corner, rotating the stick across his face and covering the corner. The one disadvantage to this method is that it is difficult to move behind the shot.

(2) The goalie draws the face of the stick diagonally across his body to the top corner off-side. When the corner is covered, the shaft of the stick is roughly perpendicular to the ground, and the head of the stick is parallel to the

ground. The movement is similar to that for all off-side shots, but there will be little rotation of the stick if he knows the ball is headed for that top corner. He will draw the head of the stick directly across his body to the corner rather than moving it in an arc. The goalie moves his body quickly behind the stick partially blocking the top corner with his off-shoulder—jumping to get the shoulder up that high if necessary. This method has that obvious advantage; but there is also the disadvantage of the move being un-natural for any player converted to the goal.

Figure 82.   Area 9.   Top Corner; Off-Stick Side.   Method 1.

Figure 83. Area 9. Top Corner; Off-Stick Side. Method 2.

GOALIE POSITION ON CLOSE SHOTS

If an opponent with the ball gets to the area just on the edge of the crease after a dodge or a pass, the goalie obviously has little time to react to a shot. The attack man should, therefore, score. But in reality the goalie stops a good number of such shots, or covers so well that the attack man tries to be too exact and misses the goal. The goalie should move his body to give the attack man as little of the cage as possible. He should raise himself to his full height. For some reason his chest acts as a natural magnet, and if he fills as much area as possible, a rushed attack man often inadvertently shoots at the goalie's chest. If the attack

Figure 84. Goalie Covering Attack Man's Stick As He Shoots from Close to Crease.

man is coming around the cage—probably as the result of a dodge—the goalie should hug the post on that side and force the attack man to shoot for the far side of the goal. If the shot is more from the front, the goalie will leave the post and travel in his normal curved path as for any shot. Instead of holding the stick at waist level as usual, the goalie should cover the shooter's stick as best he can trying to match the position of the head and shaft of his stick exactly with the shooter's. The goalie should not make the mistake of looking at the eyes of an experienced attack man. A skillful man will not tip off where he is going to shoot. Instead, the goalie must watch the ball. The attack man is more likely to shoot high than low, although if he has time, the low shot will be harder to stop.

Many goalies feel the impulsive urge to come out of the goal to meet an attack man about to take such a close shot. To come out too far against a good attack man can be a serious mistake. He will easily shoot around the goalie who is advancing toward him. The goalie should move forward so that he is 3 or 4 feet in front of the goal. Sometimes even as much as 5 or 6 feet in front. Under no circumstances should he retreat into the goal. Only if an open man on the crease is waiting for a feed should the goalie consider coming out to meet him. If the goalie feels that he will reach the attack man after the ball arrives, he should stay in his goal. If he feels that he can arrive before or at the same instant as the ball, he should come out to meet the attack man. If he does so, he should body check the attacker with his shoulder and try to cover the attack stick with his own at the same time—just as a defense man picking up a dodger would try to do.

PLAYING A SCREENED SHOT

With the ball in the midfield the crease attack man is usually instructed to screen the goalie from having clear sight of a shot. The crease defense while playing his man should be careful not to act as an additional screen. If he cannot intercept the shot, there are frequent cases where he should body check the crease attack man out of his screening position so the goalie will have an unobstructed view of the ball. If the crease defense inadvertently obscures the goalie's vision, the goalie should instruct him to move.

However, the goalie must always be prepared for the shot. He should position himself so as to reduce the area of the cage left open and keep his stick ready, for he will have little reaction time once the ball passes the screen. If the shooter can be seen, the goalie can often predict the course of the ball as it leaves the shooter's stick, even though the ball is screened for part of its flight. Most screened shots are taken on the ground, so the goalie should be prepared for such a shot. He can rotate his stick slightly in anticipation of the bounce shot, but he must be sure that his body is behind the stick. A screened shot of this type often hits the ground near the feet of the crease attack man who is a good distance from the cage. Having little time left in which to position his stick when he finally sees the ball, the goalie will often have to take the probable high bounce with his body.

The screened shot is never easy to play. There is always the chance that the crease attack may deflect the ball, making the play even more difficult. The major danger in the shot lies in the goalie's not being ready for the shot. For at best the goalie's reaction time will be short. Therefore it is important that in every screening position, the goalie must be more alert than ever.

DIRECTING THE DEFENSE FROM THE GOAL

The goalie should constantly inform his defense in a loud, but calm voice of the position of the ball with respect to the goal. He may use any method to relay this information, but working in a clockwise direction from directly in front of him, the usual vocabulary is "Ball in the center; Ball on the right front; right; right rear; center rear; left rear; left; left center." At the same time he should give instructions to the defense man playing the man with the ball such as: "Drop in" (you are too far out, let your man come closer), "Square up" (you are out of line with your man and the goal), "Hold" (don't let your man come in any more). He also instructs the other defense men who are not playing the ball in the same manner. His usual command, in addition to those mentioned, is "Pick up" (play the man who is near you).

As a defense man picks up a man with the ball, the defense man should call out "Got the ball" more as a point of information for his teammates as to where the ball is located than anything else. His nearest teammates should then call "I've got you backed" or "I've got you backed on the right (or left)" to let the man playing the ball know where his nearest teammates are and how close help is if he gets dodged. If the defense men do not call to each other, the goalie should ask "Who's got the ball?" "Who's got him backed?"

As a feed comes in toward the front of the cage, the goalie should call "Check" loudly, and perhaps in a different tone of voice than that used for routine instructions; this call should signal all defensive players, especially the crease defense, in the hole that the feed is coming to their areas and they should check their attack men's sticks immediately and vigorously. The ball will be within 15 feet of them when the checks connect.

If a dodge succeeds, the goalie should send the nearest player out to pick up the dodger. Communication with the crease defense man in this situation is vital. There should be a signal arranged so that the defense man will go; a signal such as "Dodger on right (or left)."

As the goalie makes a stop and controls the ball, or a teammate picks up the ball, he should yell "Clear" and start into the clearing pattern. The goalie can then throw to an open teammate so alerted from the protection of his crease, or he may carry the ball out himself. In either event he has four seconds to get the ball out of the crease after he gains possession.

GOALIE'S ROLE IN THE CLEAR

The goalie's third major function is to play a leading role in the clearing pattern; this aspect of his play will be covered in Chapter 9.

Goalie Drills
Drill 25—Warm-Up

Either a coach or a designated experienced player should warm up the goalie before every practice and game. There are many possible procedures to follow. Here are two: (1) Start by shooting at top corners a couple of times softly from 20 yards out. Shoot several soft bounce shots to the lower corners from the same area. Change the angle from which the long shots come and repeat, still with soft shots. Then fire a few hard ones from a distance. Shoot some over-handed and some side arm. Shoot both right- and left-handed if possible. Move in to about 10 yards and repeat. Move about 3 yards off the crease and repeat shooting softly. If convenient shoot several after taking a feed from someone behind the cage (maybe the spare goalie who might be backing up the cage). Make the goalie return each shot with a good pass. If the warm-up is accomplished before a game, try to end with some long hard shots which the goalie is able to stop in order to make him feel confident.

(2) Start shooting close, moving in an arc in front of the cage, playing catch with the goalie. Gradually move out, shooting harder, but still in the air. Move back in close and repeat the same pattern with bounce

shots. Then repeat the pattern again mixing up bounce shots and shots in the air. End up fairly far out, moving in an arc, shooting hard but still mixing them up.

Drill 26—Scoring Game

After the goalie becomes proficient, make a game out of the number of shots he stops from far out as opposed to the number scored on him.

Drill 27—Stopping Shots after Feed from Rear

Work two coaches or experienced players around the cage moving so the goalie must react to their passes and movement. Have them pass the ball back and forth taking shots at frequent intervals. Let the goalie intercept occasionally.

Drill 28—Long Shot Shooting Drill

Have the squad take long shots at him only after the goalie gains confidence. This is best worked with two lines 20 yards deep. Each shooter should first receive a feed from the rear, the side, or from another deep midfield position. Make the long shot a practice for both the goalie and the shooter by making the shooter get his shot off as soon as possible after receiving the feed. Do not let him shoot if he drops the feed. With an experienced goalie a crease attack man can be added to screen shots and capitalize on rebounds.

Drill 29—Goalie Taking Part in Shooting Drills

If desired an experienced goalie can take his place in the cage on shooting drills outlined in Chapter 2 (but definitely *not* those drills in which the shot is taken right on the crease). Instruct the shooters to shoot as soon as they get the ball. Do not let them carry it in to the crease and then fire the ball. Do not run such a drill for any extended period of time. Be very careful when the goalie is first introduced to these drills. *If there is the slightest chance of making him ball shy, do not run the risk of putting him in the goal under these conditions.*

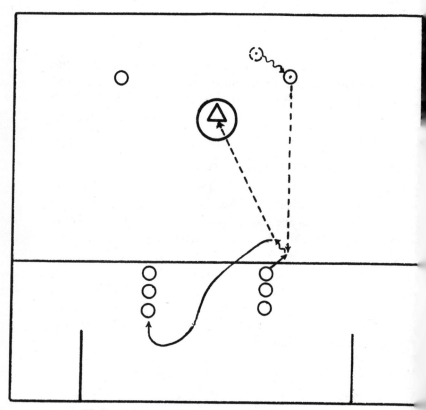

Figure 85.   Drill 28.   Long Shot Shooting Drill.

6. Midfield Play

While defense men and attack men are specialists of a sort, the midfielders must be jacks-of-all-trades. Any advice given to either attack men or defense men applies to the midfielders as well. They must be completely at home on both ends of the field. Midfield sticks, in size, are halfway between those of attack men and defense men in order to make them better able to play both roles. The beginning midfielder, though, may prefer to play with an attack stick for better ball control. If the midfielder chooses to play with an attack stick, it should be shortened very slightly, if at all.

In many respects the strength of a team depends on the midfield. Without adequate midfielders it is difficult to move the ball from defense to attack and then control the ball in that area.

After the center draw all midfield play is similar, so there is no need for special instruction for the center and wing midfielders. The draw and immediate play are covered in Chapter 14.

A midfielder needs only the talents of a top-notch defense man and a top-notch attack man—plus endurance and speed. However, in deciding which players are the best midfielders, it is of paramount importance to consider their defensive ability. Midfielders have been described as "defense men who are allowed to play a little on offense." Even a good offensive midfielder who fails on defense will cost his team more goals than he can possibly contribute.

Midfielders are often organized in units so that three men play together and are substituted, as a hockey line, as one unit. This is not necessary, but it does give the unit the considerable advantage of familiarity with each other's play. Certainly if a team has less than six adequate midfielders, it may be wiser to substitute individually rather than weaken the midfield. But if definite units are to be established, it is often best to form them of nearly equal strength. In so doing it is sometimes worthwhile to consider the side on which each player handles his stick. The center will have to face off right-handed, although if necessary a left-handed player can be trained to use his off-side. Otherwise it is best to have two midfielders in a unit who play one way and the third play the opposite, that is, two right-handers and one left, or two lefts and a right. Of course, it would be better if they could all play both ways!

MIDFIELD DEFENSIVE PLAY

Some of the glory in attacking often convinces new midfielders that their attacking responsibilities are greater than their defensive ones. Nothing is farther from the truth. A midfielder who does not check back on defense, pick up his man, and play the ball correctly is a detriment to the unit. After the opposition settles the ball down in their attacking half of the field, there is really very little difference in the play of the midfield from that of the close defense. Under normal attacking patterns, the ball is worked behind the cage to the feeders who then pass to the players in front. In this situation the midfield is more likely to be guarding players cutting toward the cage to receive passes than they are to be covering dodgers, though the latter occurs frequently enough. Midfield cuts are likely to be longer than attack cuts, but otherwise there is little difference.

Playing the Man without the Ball

The midfielder takes position on his man without the ball much as does the defense man. He plays inside his man and slightly to the ball side of a direct line between his man and the mouth of the goal, facing in such a direction that he can see both the ball and his man at the same time. With some split vision he should be able to accomplish this with a minimum of head turning, except in the situation where the ball, the goal, and his man are all in a straight line. Here he will have to glance back and forth. If the midfielder's man is so active that it is imperative to devote full attention to him, the goalie's calls on the location of the ball are invaluable. At the same time the midfielder should sag off his man toward the cage, as would a defense man playing a man behind the cage who is not in scoring territory. The distance of the sag will vary with the location of the ball; but in general, the midfielder sags to such a depth that were the ball to be thrown to his man, he would arrive back on his man a fraction of a second before the ball. If this injunction were followed perfectly, the defensive midfielder would intercept all passes thrown to the inside of his man or would check his man's stick on every pass where the man was not moving away from the cage to get the ball. A pass to the outside of his man would be completed, but such passes merely move the ball around the outside of the attacking pattern and do not normally constitute direct scoring threats.

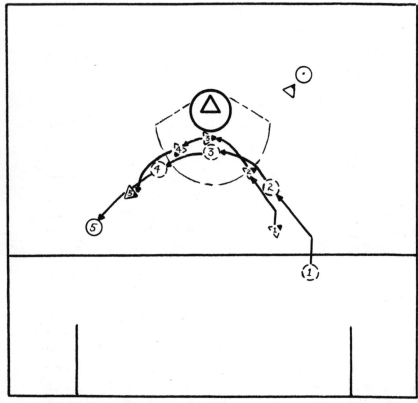

Figure 86. Defensive Midfielder Covering Cutter Passing Through the Hole. As play starts, defender is sagged off his man in position No. 1. As cutter makes his move and approaches the hole, coverage tightens. As he passes through the hole and assumes position No. 5, the defensive midfielder resumes his sag.

Attacking midfielders will do a great deal of cutting through the center of the attacking area to try to get free. If the defensive midfielder is on his toes, a single cut by his man should pose no real threat. As the cut starts, the defensive midfielder gives ground, keeping between his man and the cage as he does so. As the cutter gets closer to the hole, the coverage gets closer. As he continues with his man through this territory, he should be playing the cutter almost shoulder to shoulder. He cannot force the cutter to change course by shouldering him out, unless the ball is free within 15 feet, but he can run close to him. If at the same time he keeps a half step ahead of his midfielder, he will have just as much chance at the feed as does the cutter, or at least he will be able to check the stick of his man as the ball approaches. Most of his attention will have to be devoted to his man. Since the cutter can change course any time, to try to watch the ball with equal attention probably means the cutter will be lost when he alters course. Thus the defender must listen carefully for the goalie's calls on the location of the ball. He should pay particular attention to a call of "Check" by the goalie when the cutter is in close to the crease. He should check his man's stick as soon as the goalie calls; the ball will be close enough. As the cutter passes through the hole, the midfielder resumes his sagging pattern. If the cutter stops in front of the goal and remains on the crease, the midfielder then plays similar to a crease defense man.

Since single cuts can be covered easily by even a mediocre midfielder, the attacking team usually plans to make its cuts in pairs, or on a stationary post, so that the defensive midfielder will collide with his teammates or an opposing player—or at least be slowed by having to avoid the collision. Of the two attacking players trying to set up a brush, the one headed toward the ball is more dangerous. However, neither can be left unguarded, for the feed can be thrown to either. The defender covering the midfielder cutting toward the ball may not be aware that he is about to be picked off since his attention is focused on his man, but the defender on the other man should be able to see what is going on and verbally alert his teammate by calling, "Watch the brush." Other teammates can also see the play developing and help out with similar warnings. So alerted, the midfielder tries to avoid the pick by forcing his way between the pick and his man if he thinks he can fit. Or he can sag off his man as the pick nears, go around the pick, and get back on his man as soon as he comes off the brush. The feed should hit the attacking midfielder just as he comes off the pick, and here the defender must be ready to make his check.

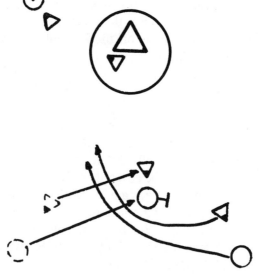

Figure 87. Defensive Midfielder Should Try to Force Between His Man and a Brush if He Can Do So.

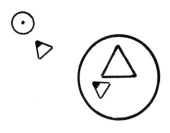

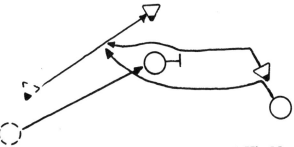

Figure 88. Defensive Midfielder May Sag Off His Man, Go Behind the Pick, and Meet His Man after the Brush. Pickup should be made immediately after brush, for the feed will be thrown to arrive at this point.

The two defenders involved in the play can also switch men. The defender on the man who is setting up the pick should be the one to make such a call, but either can call it. Once one man calls the switch, both must make the move even though one midfielder may have thought it unnecessary. If a switch is to be made, the midfielder making the call should announce "Get ready to switch" as the situation approaches. At the point of exchange, he should call, "Switch." If the two defenders are midfielders, the switch is logical; but if one is a defense man, it would be better not to switch, since they should not trade back until there is a lull in the play. The switch should be made just as the brush starts. If begun too soon, one of the attackers will be free for a few moments at least, and if made too late, probably both will be uncovered. Of course, the attack men can alter their courses; so they should be picked up smoothly and completely on the shift so that neither can gain an advantage of a step or two by altering course.

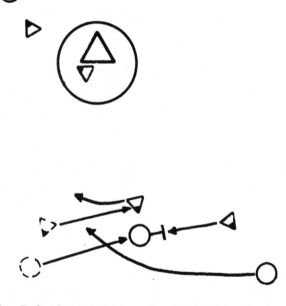

Figure 89. Defensive Midfielders Can Switch Men. Exchange must be smooth, for either man can be the target of a feed.

When the offensive midfielder is in feeding territory or on the outside and is not actively cutting, the defensive midfielder should sag off his man and be ready to assist his teammates as much as possible. If he is the neighboring defender to the man playing the ball, he should be ready to help out if his teammate is dodged. He should let his teammate know he is ready to help by announcing, "I've got you backed on right (or left)." He can then pick up the dodger if necessary. Of course, while backing his teammate, he has to continue his coverage of his own man, and so should not take himself too far off the line between his man and the goal.

Not only must the defensive midfielder be prepared to assist by backing fellow midfielders, but he must learn to back his close defense men. Many teams pick up a dodger coming from the rear of the cage by sagging off the nearest wing midfielder (see page 160 and Figure 66). If a team plans to assign this responsibility to the wing midfielders, some practice must be devoted to the maneuver, for at the moment of the dodge any one of a number of midfielders might find himself in the wing position where he must make the play.

Sometimes switches in midfield are needed to pick up players closer to the cage who have been left free because some other teammate had to leave his own man to make a play. For instance, on the play previously described, the remaining midfielders must slide toward the side of the dodge to cover the man left open when the wing midfielder picks up the dodging feeder. Some teams cover the dodging feeder by sending the crease defense man to make the play (see page 159 and Figure 65). In this case the center midfielder might help to cover the open crease attack man. Or if the off-side close defense man covers the crease attack, the wing midfielder on the off-side may have to sag toward the crease to cover the off-side feeder should he make a move to round the cage.

An alert defensive midfielder is invaluable in breaking up such plays even when his man is not involved. He must think ahead and figure out how he can be of greatest help. Of course, he must not allow himself to be so carried away with his "backing" responsibilities that he forgets his man and lets him cut into the play uncovered.

Playing the Man with the Ball

Defensive midfield play against the man with the ball varies only slightly from close defense play against attack men. The one difference is that offensive midfielders are normally in front of the cage and therefore always in position to shoot. An offensive midfielder, to have a good scoring chance, should probably be within 15 yards of the goal; but he does not have to dodge his defender to reach this spot. He may pursue a zig-zag course, boring in closer to the goal with each zig or zag, ending up 15 yards, or closer, from the goal where he can shoot even though his man is on him. Therefore, the defender must make a determined stand before the offensive man gets this close. This is hard to do alone against a midfielder who has good ball control; but if nearby teammates have the defender backed properly, the offensive midfielder can be confined.

The offensive man can of course be a feeder rather than a dodger and should be played as a close defense man would play a feeder behind the goal. A midfield feeder can pass to fellow midfielders, the crease attack, or to an attack man cutting in front of the cage.

All defense men should be alert to the "give-and-go" offensive maneuver, but it is most frequently practiced by midfielders. The man with the ball passes off and then immediately breaks past his defense man toward the cage to take a return pass. To counter this play each defense man should be trained to retreat toward the goal 2 or 3 yards as soon as his man passes off the ball, but again the move should be emphasized for the midfielders. It is all too easy to watch the offensive man pass off, turn to follow the flight of the ball and thereby allow the offensive man to break past.

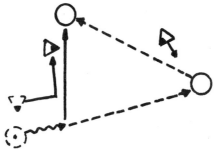

Figure 90. Midfield Give-and-Go. Center midfielder passes off to wing midfielder and then breaks immediately for the cage to take a return pass.

Playing Loose Balls in the Defensive Half of the Field

Any time the offensive team drops the ball, there should be one defensive player right on the ground ball. Then, if it appears to his nearest teammate, that there is a better than an even chance of getting the ball, that player should go over to help out. He should approach the play from the defensive side so that if the attack gains possession before he can get there, the defensive player will be in a position to pick up the man with the ball. The third mid-fielder (or the other two, if one of the players on the ball is a defense man) should sag in toward the goal even more than before to prevent the attack from coming up with the ball and heading toward an open goal. No more than two defenders should be committed to a ground ball fight at one time (they will just get in each other's way and leave the middle wide open should the attack get the ball). If three attack men go after the ground ball, it is permissible to commit another defense man to that area; but he should position himself on the goal side of the scramble and await developments. With four or more men fighting for the ball, there is a good chance that it will not be picked up immediately by any of them, and the ball will roll out of the pile to be picked up by someone on the outside of the scramble.

As soon as a defensive player has control of the ball, he should either head downfield, toward the sidelines, or back behind the cage; he must keep the ball out of the middle. His midfield teammates should break downfield to the clearing pattern which will be discussed in Chapter 9. There is a period of transition as the midfielders move from defense to offense, and vice versa, but this transition can better be discussed in reference to the clearing and ride patterns.

ATTACKING MIDFIELD PLAY

Once the ball is settled down on the attacking half of the field, the midfield fits itself into whatever attacking pattern is being played, but certain basic midfield moves are involved in these patterns.

Midfield Play with Ball behind the Cage

In general most patterns are set up so that the ball starts with the feeders behind the cage (though there is no requirement that this be the case). If the midfielder with the ball wants to get it back to the feeders, he should work the ball toward that area either by carrying it in to a point where he can pass to the feeder or throw the ball to a teammate who will get it in. In making such passes the ball should be kept to the outside of such a teammate or feeder so that the defense cannot intercept. The receiver should start toward the cage, taking his defense man with him; stop, and cut back to the outside taking an angle to the outside slightly toward the passer. The passer should be moving toward the man to whom he is going to throw, and perhaps moving to the outside at the same time, if the defense man is pressuring him.

With the ball now in the hands of the feeders, the midfielders can start to free themselves to receive a feed and score on the pass coming from the rear of the cage. As they do so, they should remember that they are also responsible for backing up any feed that goes through the area and into the midfield.

A single midfielder can cut to receive a pass anytime he thinks he can lose his defense man. Occasionally a midfielder may find that he is able to break straight past his defender and head for the cage leaving his defense man behind. However, against a reasonably alert defender the straight cut will not often work. Any midfielder expecting to free himself should plan to start his defender moving one way and then break sharply in a different direction to lose

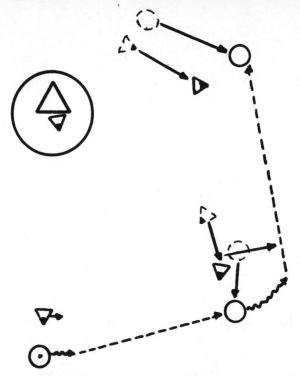

Figure 91. Moving Ball from Midfield into Close Attack. Man with ball should move toward his receiver and slightly to the outside. Each receiver should first move toward the cage and then break back to the outside and slightly toward the passer.

his man. There are several patterns that can be used, but the cutter should not make too many complex moves; the feeder is likely to throw the ball to the wrong spot if he can not fully anticipate where the midfielder is going to be to receive the ball. For the midfielder on the same side of the goal as the ball there are three good options. The first is an in-and-out pattern in which he takes his defense man toward the center of the field, stops, and breaks back toward the feeder. The second is a roll, essentially done the same way but requiring a roll in order to change direction rather than just breaking back sharply.

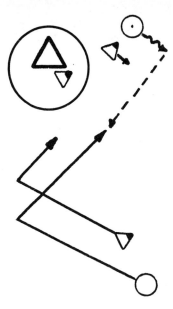

Figure 92. In-and-Out Cut by Midfielder on Same Side of Field as Feeder.

Or the midfielder can start his cut toward the feeder on his side and then break sharply toward the goal. Infrequently, if overplayed by the defender when cutting toward his on-side feeder, the midfielder may be able to break across the mouth of the cage taking a lead pass going away from the feeder.

The basic cut for the midfielder on the opposite side of the field, the one farthest from the feeder, is to start toward the feeder on his own side. About 7 yards in front of the crease, he breaks toward the feeder on the opposite side coming across the front of the cage far enough out so that the crease defense man cannot make a play on him. He can also roll to make the turn rather than breaking. The center midfielder can cut from his position using the same moves as either wing man. None of these moves is very difficult for the feeder to follow. Each involves a single change of direction, and if executed with speed, the attacker

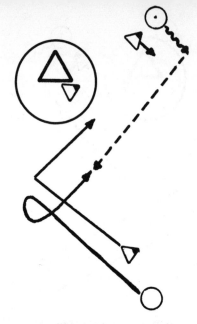

Figure 93. In-and-Out Roll by Midfielder on Same Side of Field as Feeder.

Figure 94. Break Across Front of Goal by Midfielder on Same Side of Field as Feeder.

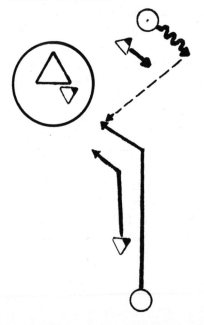

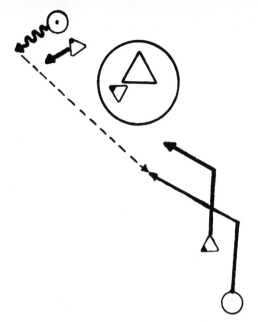

Figure 95. Breaking Cut Across Front of Cage by Off-Side Midfielder.

may well find himself at least a step ahead of the defender.

Two midfielders may work together by brushing on each other. The midfielder going away from the ball initiates the move, and the one coming toward the feeder with the ball cuts just behind him trying to force his defender to collide with another player. While either man may receive the feed, the primary target is the man going toward the feeder. The brush, therefore, should occur approximately opposite the pipe of the cage farthest from the feeder with the ball, so that the receiver gets the ball in front of the goal while he has a good angle on the cage. The man closest to the ball, the one who started the play, should run a relatively straight course. It is up to the second man, the primary target who started farther from the feeder, to come close enough to the first cutter to lose his man. Therefore, he should start his man going in one direction and then alter course to pass close to the first cutter. This change of direction should be calculated so that his defender will be forced to run into the first cutter.

It makes little difference which two midfielders work together. Probably the midfielder on the side where the ball is located and the center make the most logical combination, but the two wing men or the off-side midfielder and the center can also team to brush.

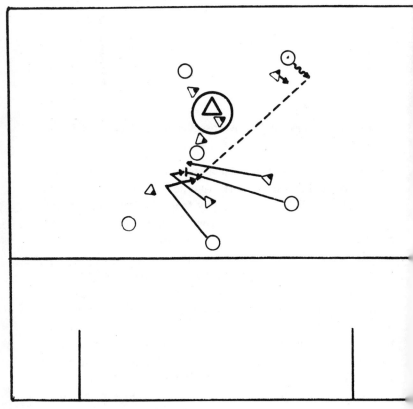

Figure 96. Two Man Midfield Brush.

All three midfielders can work a brush together by having the two men closest to the ball cut away from the ball headed toward the off-side feeder. The third midfielder starts his man toward the same spot and then breaks toward the feeder with the ball, passing just behind his two teammates as they go through the hole almost shoulder to shoulder. After the brush, one of the pair that formed the brush should return to the midfield center as

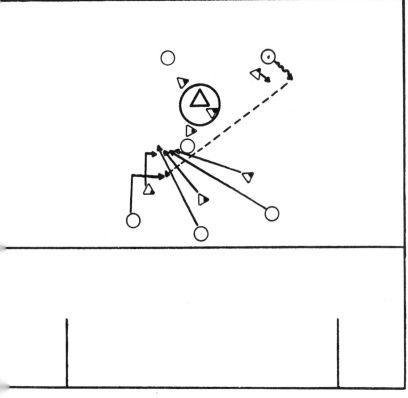

Figure 97. Three Man Midfield Brush.

soon as possible, since there is no man left deep enough to back up the play.

After any cut there is a temptation for a midfielder to linger in the area just in front of the cage. To brush off the crease man is acceptable, or to set up a post for the crease man to brush upon is also good, but to stay in the area merely waiting for an opening clogs up the middle of the crease area so that no one gets open. Midfielders should make their cuts and then clear out back to the midfield, leaving the crease area free for others. The return to the midfield should be made by circling to the outside, never by retracing the path of the cut, for to do so also jams up the center area. Even if a midfielder in such a mess were open, the chances of getting the feed would be slim since the feeder with the ball probably will not be able to get it through without having it intercepted.

Some sort of signal can be arranged to call the cut to be used, but it is better if the cuts can be run spontaneously with private signals, such as a nodding of the head, arranged between the players involved. If the midfield unit plays together for an extended period, the players learn to think as a unit and make meaningful cuts and brushes.

One last word on the timing of the cuts should be added. Unless the feeder and the midfield are in time with each other, the cut is wasted, since the feeder is not ready to pass. The midfielders should watch their feeders and realize when they are ready to feed. A feeder does not have to have his stick cocked back ready to pass before the cut starts, but he does have to be watching and be able to throw soon after the play starts. A feeder bringing the ball in from out-of-bounds behind the cage is ready. Any feeder not hard pressed within 15 yards of the cage should be ready to feed if he is not in the process of a dodge or some other play that takes his full attention. He should be ready to feed if he is just moving loosely behind the cage no matter in what direction he is moving or whether he has one hand or two on the stick. Until the midfield and the attack get their timing coordinated, there are likely to be mumblings that the midfield never cuts at the right time from the attack side of the ledger, and that the attack never feeds from the midfield side. Both sections of the team must realize that they have to work together to score goals.

Midfield Play while Ball Remains in the Midfield

Some of the best attacking plays involve leaving the ball in the midfield. If the man with the ball sees the chance, there is no reason why he cannot dodge as successfully as a feeder. In fact he may have better success, for his defensive opponent is not likely to be as skilled at stopping the dodge as a close defense man. There is no particular dodge that should be used. The running dodge, the roll dodge, the face dodge, and the dip dodge are all just as useful in the midfield as they are on the attack. The same injunctions apply to the dodging midfielder as to the attack man: (1) isolate the defense player so that he works one-on-one; (2) do not draw the stick back after the dodge to make the shot or pass; the trailing defense man who was dodged will check it; and (3) expect to be picked up by another defense man, and look for the chance to pass off if picked up before a good shot presents itself. If the man with the ball wants to dodge, the other midfielders should do all they can to get their men out of the play by cutting away from the ball. Normally they should try to take their defensive men toward the crease and then out the other side away from the dodger.

Of course, if the defender does not follow, the cutter will be free for a pass, even though his teammate intended to dodge when the play started.

The midfielder with the ball can use another midfielder as a post on whom to brush his defensive player just like an attack man. If the pick works, he will then continue in for a shot. If he does not get free, the man on whom he picked may well be free after he goes by. The midfielder setting up the post should move into position to set up the brush and remain stationary as the brush occurs; to lean into or otherwise block the defender is an interference foul. It is up to the man with the ball to hang his defender up on the post. After the man with the ball goes by, the post man should then break for the cage. The other midfielder not in the play should get his defense man as much out of the way as possible, remembering that if the play goes awry, he is the man to back up the action or retrieve the ground ball.

Actually, the midfielder has a very intriguing move that a man behind the cage does not really have. He does not have to dodge or lose his man completely in order to have a good shot at the cage; all he needs do is bore in as close as possible to the goal, even if he does not shake the defensive player. From a range of 10 to 15 yards out, with a good angle on the cage, a hard bounce shot can cause the goalie real trouble, particularly if the crease attack does his screening job properly. The midfielder who can shoot with either hand poses as a particular problem for his defender. To bore his way in, the midfielder with the ball runs a zig-zag pattern pressing his defender closer to the cage with every reversal of direction. When close enough the midfielder makes one final change of direction, gets his stick ahead of his defender, and lets go his shot. Normally, for accuracy, the midfielder will shoot overhand. But for a midfielder with a good hard, accurate side arm shot, here is one good play on which to use it. To succeed the shooter must have good ball control, for he will meet stiff resistance as he bores in. Naturally he keeps his stick well protected with his body. He must use discretion before starting his maneuver and must be willing to quit if it is not succeeding. His teammates should be alert to his plan and should move their men out of the way, just as if he were dodging. They should position themselves so that if one of their defense men moves to help cover the shooter, he will be able to pass off to the open teammate as soon as a second defender comes to play him.

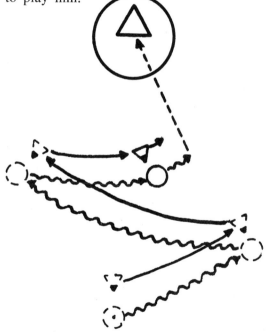

Figure 98. Zig-Zag Course Run by Boring Midfielder to Work Closer to Goal. With every change of direction, midfielder presses his man closer to the cage, protecting his stick with his body until he gets close enough to shoot.

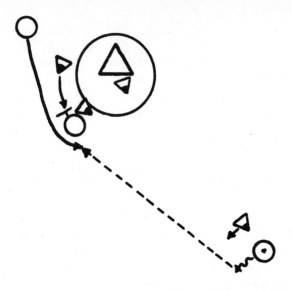

Figure 99. Feed From Midfield to Off-Side Feeder Brushing on Crease Attack.

A midfielder with the ball can also establish himself as a feeder. One possible play is to have the diagonally opposite close attack man to the rear of the cage brush his man on the crease attack man and take a feed from a midfielder. Another play is for the other two midfielders to brush on each other, and take a feed from their teammate. As with all midfield cuts, this brush will work best if the cutters have one change of direction during their cuts to set up the defensive players for the brush. A third play would be for the man with the ball to head toward a fellow midfielder who swings to his outside. As they pass, the ball is flipped to the outside man. The man who received the ball can try to bore in for the shot or can try to pass back to the man who gave him the ball, who continues to angle for the cage. This play can become more complex, like a basketball weave, when all three midfielders are involved. During the weave, the midfielder not

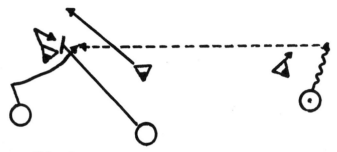

Figure 100. Two Man Brush in Midfield with Feed from Other Midfielder. Cutters should have one change of direction in their cuts to set up defenders for the brush. Feeding midfielder will help set up play if he fakes pass to rear of goal before making feed.

immediately concerned should be aware of his responsibility to back up the play.

One of the most usual midfield plays is the "give-and-go," where the man with the ball passes off to a teammate and then breaks immediately for the cage. Refer again to Figure 90. The play works best against a defensive player who has been pressing hard until the moment the "give" is thrown. The player to whom the pass is thrown can of course be either a midfielder or an attack man. Whenever an attacking player receives a pass he should look first to the crease area to see if there is an open man near the cage. Then he should look back at the man who threw the ball to see if the "give-and-go" has been set up.

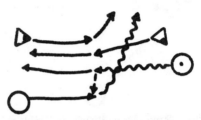

Figure 101. Flip Pass Between Midfielders. Receiver passes to the outside of man carrying the ball.

Figure 102. Flip Pass Between Midfielders with Return Feed. After flip, midfielder who made the flip cuts toward the cage to take a return pass from the midfielder to whom he flipped the ball.

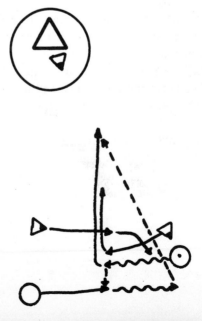

One of the reasons for playing the midfielders in units is that they become familiar with each other's moves. One member of an established unit should be able to tell what his teammates are going to do and how he should try to help them. All the basic midfield moves can be turned into drills, working three on three, and they should be practiced as such. Just to mention the possibilities open to the midfielders and then expect them to use them in scrimmage and game situations is a bit utopian in concept.

BALL CONTROL BY MIDFIELD

Aside from the attacking responsibilities of the midfield, the midfielders are vitally concerned with controlling the ball in the attacking half of the field. Not only will the opposition be unable to score if they do not have the ball, but the midfield itself will be rested if they do not have to move continually up and down the field.

To control the ball, it is vital that at least one member of the midfield unit concern himself with backing up the play so that when passes and plays go awry, the ball will not be lost. This is especially true when the ball is worked from the rear of the goal.

The control of ground balls in the attacking half of the field constitutes a good part of the backing up job. A midfielder should be on every loose ball in front of the cage. Either an attack man or another midfielder should join him immediately. The remaining midfielders should move to help out by positioning themselves on the defensive side of the fight to control a ball that might roll out of the scrap.

These are the basic offensive and defensive duties of

the midfielders. They may have more specific duties under particular offensive and defensive patterns. However, again it is worthwhile to emphasize that a midfielder is only as valuable as the caliber of his defensive play. If he contributes offensively, he is an even greater asset.

7. Attack Patterns

The six men on the attacking half of the field have been considered in earlier chapters as individuals, or in groups of three representing the close attack and the midfield. However, the whole attack should have an overall attacking pattern. Within this pattern are certain basic maneuvers that an individual, a pair of players, or a group can execute to initiate a scoring play. These have been mentioned, but no real effort has been made to bring all six players together as a unit.

It is intended that there be a difference between a "pattern" and a "play." A pattern is the general offensive philosophy that the team uses, while a play is a specific maneuver in that pattern designed to get off a shot at the goal. Before the play can be selected, the pattern for the attack will have to be specified.

After a pattern is selected, someone will have to decide how much emphasis to put on formal plays. Lacrosse is a fluid game. Most experienced teams do not have set plays, thus, given a set of circumstances, most of the moves made by the players are spontaneous. However, for the beginning team there may be merit in organizing and executing set plays so that each member of the attack will know exactly what is expected of him. One member of the attack, usually a feeder, can be designated as the "quarterback" whose job is to designate the play, either verbally, by gesture, or by field position. On signal from the quarterback, the entire attack starts into the play. Since each man knows his job, each should move in the proper direction.

This may be a good way to start a team of novices. The coach will have to make the decision. Without plays it takes beginners a long time to organize into a team. The feeder does not look while the midfielders are cutting; players trying to get free for a pass take their defense men down on top of the man with the ball who is dodging. Examples of inexperienced players not working as a unit are too numerous. Set plays bring order out of confusion. On the other hand, set plays are slow to develop; before starting, the signal caller has to wait until all his teammates are in position. Often the necessity of executing a set play does not allow a player to take advantage of a defensive mistake. If the defense diagnoses the play, it can overplay that move without fear that it will be caught short in the process.

The attack's job is not only to score, but also to control the ball. Every play will not end with a shot; nor will every shot score; and if the attack loses the ball after every play, it will not have too many opportunities to score. In every pattern, therefore, there must be at least one player responsible for backing up the cage, particularly since a shot going out-of-bounds belongs to the player on either team closest to it when it went over the line. There must be someone about 20 yards in front of the goal to retrieve balls that get deflected in that direction. These do not have to be specific players. The responsibilities can rotate depending on player position, but certainly all six men cannot be committed to one spot leaving no one available for these jobs.

Each of the following patterns involves a different alignment of attacking players or a different attacking philosophy. In each pattern every player, or group of players, has different options that can be executed; but everything cannot be done at once. Moves must be correctly timed and coordinated. Some teams have several patterns available for a particular game and alter their basic pattern as the game progresses. Others employ a single pattern throughout the entire contest. How many patterns a team has and how many it employs depends on the philosophy of that team, but with beginners it is wiser to employ a single pattern until the players have that formation mastered.

BASIC 2 - 1 - 3

This attack formation is the most common pattern; and even if a team does not plan to use it, it should be practiced, since the defense will have to play against it frequently. There are two close attack men behind the cage as feeders. Another close attack man plays the crease. He is likely to be assigned to this area, though the three close attack men can rotate so that each plays the crease on occasions. The three midfielders are stationed in an arc about 20 yards from the goal. This formation was used in the earlier chapters discussing individual and group play; the basic moves have thus been outlined.

Briefly then, the man with the ball has several options: (1) dodging, (2) feeding a teammate, (3) working a give-and-go, or (4) passing off to another teammate on the outside of the circle formation. The normal pattern is to work the ball from the rear of the cage a majority of the time, but there is no reason to assume the ball should always be returned to the rear of the cage before a new play starts. Some teams with strong midfields prefer to keep the ball in the midfield a reasonable amount of the time.

Figure 103.   Alignment of Players for Basic 2 - 1 - 3.

With the ball in possession of a feeder, every other player has an option. The other feeder can elect to brush on the crease man (see again Figures 53 and 54), set up a pick for the man with the ball (see again Figure 46), or remain ready for a pass, remembering that he is the one responsible for backing the cage. The crease man should draw to the far side of the cage, and then try to work himself free (see again Figures 51 and 52), or set up a brush with the other feeder or a midfielder (see again Figures 53 and 54). The midfielders can cut singly (see Figures 92, 93, 94, and 95), in pairs (see Figure 96), or in a group (see Figure 97). However, one midfielder should be alert to back up the middle of the field. This is the center man, if he is not involved in the cut; the remaining midfielder, if his partners cut; or the first man through setting up the brush, if all three go at once. Sometimes the feeder with the ball just wants to pass the ball out to the midfield to take pressure off himself or set up a new situation. The midfielder closest to him is his "relief man." This midfielder would also be responsible for getting his defense man out of the way if the feeder wanted to dodge.

With the ball in the midfield, each player also has several options he can exercise. The feeder closest to the ball is the relief man if the midfielder wants to pass off (see Figure 91). This feeder is also responsible for backing up the cage. The crease man pulls away from the ball and can either work himself clear for a feed or set up a brush for the offside feeder (see again Figure 99). He is also responsible for screening any long shots. The other two midfielders can cut singly or paired (see again Figure 100). The nearest midfielder is the relief man if the man with the ball wants to pass off. He is also the player with whom to work a flip pass, if desired (see again Figures 101 and 102). He must also remember to get his defense man out of the area if the man with the ball wants to dodge or bore in for a shot. The midfielder farthest from the ball is most likely to be the back-up man on ground balls, though this job will belong to whichever midfielder happens to be closest to the ball when it is free.

CIRCLE PATTERN

The circle pattern demands only slight adjustments from the basic 2-1-3, but it offers intriguing possibilities. The crease man ceases to exist, and the six attacking players space themselves roughly in a circle formation around the goal. The two feeders remain behind the cage and two midfielders remain approximately on the restraining line 20 yards out. The crease man pulls to one side of the field, while the third midfielder completes the circle on the other side.

The departure of the crease man from his normal position offers some interesting possibilities for the attack. To have an attacking player directly in front of the goal has certain advantages, but unfortunately he is invariably accompanied by a defense man. Removing the attack man removes the defense man also, leaving the middle free. If the attack is predicated on dodging, this is particularly desirable, since there is no defense man in good position to pick up a dodger.

Figure 104.   Alignment of Players for Circle Formation.

At the same time the middle is open for any normal brush between two players, as well as for any cut by a single player. Any two adjacent players can brush on each other to take a feed from the player with the ball (it makes no real difference whether he is behind the cage or not). This formation has an obvious advantage for the receiver of the feed, in that there is probably no defensive player between him and the cage after he breaks free.

The pattern has the disadvantage, however, of having no player left in front of the goal to screen shots, push in rebounds, or prevent the goalie from moving straight down the field on his clear. Thus, as is always the case before selecting a pattern, it is necessary to consider the personnel available. The circle is quite useful if a crease man must be played who is not particularly adept at getting free, screening, or covering rebounds. If he is valuable because of his ability to retrieve ground balls or set up brushes, would he not be just as valuable to the side where he could keep his defense man out of the center?

Plays for this pattern are like those for 2-1-3 so they will not be repeated. The only play missing is one in which the crease man acts as a post for another player cutting past him. But this option can be added by having a player come in and occupy the crease area for a brief time and then move out. While he is there, he can be used as a post by any other attacking player. Of course, by staying on the crease, he converts the pattern into a 2-1-3. Often, such a player is accompanied by a midfielder or a defense man unfamiliar with playing crease defense who will be easier to evade than would a man who plays the crease all the time. Because various attacking players can become crease men momentarily, each must be able to play the position, though none can be expected to be as proficient as a man who plays there permanently.

Figure 105.   Alignment of Players for 1 - 2 - 3 Double Crease.

DOUBLE CREASE OR 1 - 2 - 3

The other extreme from a circle offense is the double crease. Instead of eliminating the crease man, the double crease puts two men into the position. There are two good ways to add the extra crease man: one, the 1-2-3, and the other, a 2-2-2; the difference being that in the first, the extra crease man is nominally a feeder, while in the second he is a midfielder.

The choice of method again depends somewhat on the personnel available plus the style of play used by the opposition. The 1-2-3 is only feasible if one superior feeder is available and the opposition plays him in such a manner that he can control the ball alone behind the cage and get close enough to get off good feeds.

In the 1-2-3, as the ball moves down the field into a settled position on the attack, the team should probably start in a 2-1-3 until control of the ball is well established either in the midfield or behind the cage. At such time the feeder designated to play the second crease man should move into position in front of the goal to join his teammate already there.

Play of the Lone Feeder

Without the ball, the feeder plays loosely behind the cage, favoring the side where the ball is located and ready to back up the cage on a shot. He should move to the outside as his midfielders pass in to him, rather than staying behind the goal where there is danger of an interception by a defense man or goalie in front of the cage. He should not break in front of the goal, unless there is a perfect opening, for to do so would congest the crease area and leave no one to back up. In the rare cases when he does cut in front, one of the present crease men should be alerted to fade behind to assume his position.

When he has the ball, the man behind the cage becomes the feeder. If presented with an opening, though, he should not be afraid to dodge. He must remember, however, that there are two defense men playing the crease now, and the chances are that he will be picked up before he gets close enough to take a shot. He should be alert to spot one of his crease men for the pass as soon as he loses his own man.

Essentially, however, he watches for an open man to feed. The crease men should brush on each other by moving laterally across the crease to free themselves. He should first look at the crease man coming toward him in whatever maneuver is being tried, and then at the crease man going away from the play. The third target is the midfielder on the same side of the field as the feeder; the fourth is the mid-fielder in the center; the last, the far-side midfielder. These midfielders should try to brush on each other to free them-selves while he is in feeding territory. If he is pressured too much and wants to pass the ball off, his relief man is the midfielder on his side of the field, or one of the crease men can slide off the crease to the rear of the cage to help.

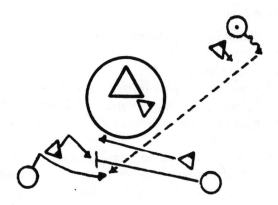

Figure 106. Basic Brush for Crease Men on 1 - 2 - 3.

As the players in front seek to free themselves, the feeder should move freely across the back of the cage keeping himself in feeding territory as much as possible. He should work first from one side of the rear of the goal, and then if nothing worthwhile develops, move across the back of the cage to the other side. In so doing, the defense must shift its coverage of the men in front, perhaps making an error. The feeder should, however, not move flittingly back and forth, for to do so only confuses his own attack men who must also adjust to his new position.

Play of the Double Crease

As the ball settles down on the attack, the lone crease man should pull to the edge of the crease farthest from the ball be it in possession of a midfielder or the lone feeder. The player from the rear of the cage coming in to play the crease with him then has the chance to brush off the post he has created and take an immediate feed. If the cutter is covered successfully, the crease man can himself then break toward the ball for the pass.

Figure 107. Initial Brush Made by Feeder on Crease Man as 1 - 2 - 3 Is Started.

After two men are on the crease, they can then set up a two-man brush pattern. Each should start on opposite sides of the crease, so that they brush while each is coming toward the center of the goal. Refer to Figure 106. The spot of the brush should be opposite the pipe of the goal farthest from the ball, for the man coming toward the ball is the primary target and should have time to catch the ball and get off his shot while still moving across the crease before he takes himself off the angle. The secondary target is the man going away from the ball. He should keep his eye on the feeder, for he may be the open man.

After their initial cut, the basic pattern for the two crease men is to continue such cuts across the mouth of the cage, making sure that as they brush on each other, the point of the brush is located on the side of the crease away from the ball, approximately in front of the pipe of the cage on this far side and about 3 to 5 yards out from the crease itself. See again Figure 106. In order to be effective, their brush should bring them as close together as possible. The man breaking from the feeder should run a straight path, while the man going toward the ball should adjust his course to pass as close as possible to the outside of his teammate so that the defense man is brushed off. The logical first move of the primary receiver should be toward the cage to take his defense man in, and then back toward his teammate to set up the pick. If he does not make such an initial move, the defense man will probably force his way between the two crease men without losing a step.

In learning to play the crease pattern, both men should be completely able to handle a ball thrown to either side of them. If they cannot change hands, they should be able to handle the ball backhanded with skill, for the feed will normally be thrown to their outside, and they alternate in their directions of cutting across the crease.

Soon the defense will start to adjust to prevent the pick. One possible defense is to anticipate the brush and lead the attack man across the crease. In this case, the attack men should start their cuts as normal, but when they reach the point of the brush, they should stop, pivot directly around, and go back in the direction from which they came. The defense men anticipating the pick will be ahead of their men and will be left out of position when the direction of the cut is reversed.

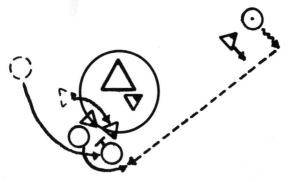

Figure 108.   Crease Man Brushes on Arriving Feeder Who Stops After Initial Cut at Start of 1 - 2 - 3.

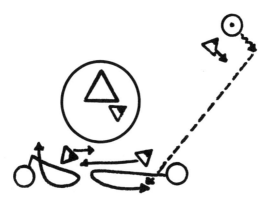

Figure 109.   Crease Men Reverse Direction Against Defense Men Leading Across Crease.

Another normal defensive reaction is to zone the sides of the crease so that a switch is called every time the brush occurs. Now the attack men should plan to flood one side of the crease—probably the side where the feeder is located. The man going away from the ball stops and goes back to where he started, while the man coming toward the ball veers to the same side, but deeper from the cage. The two will end up on the same side of the goal, but far enough apart so that no single defense man can cover both.

Other patterns will come to mind as the two crease men become familiar with each other and the reactions of their defense men. The same kind of pattern can easily be adjusted to feeds from the midfield, and there is no reason why the play should not start with the ball in the midfield, though the plan is to move it behind the cage.

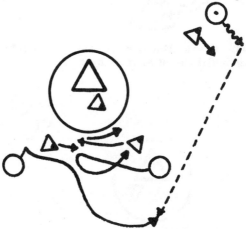

Figure 110. Both Crease Men Break to Feeder's Side of Cage Against Defenders Who Zone the Double Crease.

The crease men should practice with the feeder so that each knows what the other is going to do. The crease men must learn when their feeder is ready to throw; there is no point in brushing if he is not in a position to throw.

The feeder judges when to throw to either man. All either man needs to have free is his stick. Even though his body may be covered, he is still open. Each crease man should be prepared to move toward the feeder as he throws so that a defense man does not step in front and intercept the pass in the air. Therefore, each must keep his eye on the feeder at all times since the crease men do not know when or to whom the feeder will throw.

If the feeder dodges, the crease men must pull their men out of his way to the far side of the cage as soon as possible. Since there are two defense men in front of the cage, there is a good chance that at least one of the two defense men will not follow and will move to pick up the dodger before he gets close enough to shoot. The crease men must make sure they are spread so that no one man can cover both of them. At the same time they must realize that there is now no one behind the cage to back up a shot. As a shot is taken, the man closest to the back line should back up if the shot misses, while his partner, farther from the cage, should move in for the rebound.

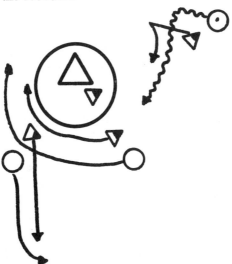

Figure 111. Crease Men Separate as Feeder Dodges. If a defender moves to pick up a dodger, he should pass off to one of the crease men in front of the cage. If no one picks him up, he moves in to shoot. Crease man closest to back line moves to back up while other crease man moves in for the rebound.

Play in the Midfield

A midfielder with the ball should always look in to the crease once the double crease pattern has been set up to see if one of the crease men might be free. Otherwise the midfield is free to work the ball as in the 2-1-3 formation.

With the ball behind the cage, the midfield can operate any of the cut patterns used in the 2-1-3 formation. They should, however, try to stay out of the area just in front of the goal, for to cut through this area causes congestion. Their shots in this pattern will probably come from 10 to 15 yards out, and few opportunities will be found for a point-blank shot by a midfielder. One more duty for the midfielder closest to the feeder is to act as relief man.

The pattern has intriguing possibilities, but should not be used unless the lone feeder is able to control the ball behind the cage. He must be sufficiently adept at finding open men to allow the burden of feeding to rest on his shoulders alone. The two crease men must have quick sticks and the ability to handle the ball well on short feeds.

2 - 2 - 2 DOUBLE CREASE

The play of the 2-2-2 is virtually the same for the two crease men as before, but the second crease man, this time, is a midfielder rather than an attack man. The pattern provides for the normal two feeders rather than one. If the double crease is to be used, this formation should be employed, rather than the 1-2-3, if a single feeder cannot control the ball alone, or if the defensive pressure on him is such that he cannot devote a majority of his attention to feeding.

A midfielder coming in to play the crease brings with him a defensive midfielder, who is probably not as well versed in playing the crease as a close defense man. However, there are two problems inherent in this pattern. First, the midfielder playing the crease will be slow getting back downfield when his team loses the ball, thus forcing his teammates to cover for him until he checks back. Second, since midfielders must be rested frequently during the game, there must be several people trained to play this position. These two problems must be considered before putting in the pattern. Naturally, if the midfield personnel needed to play the position are not available, the formation will be worthless.

Figure 112. Alignment of Players for 2 - 2 - 2 Double Crease.

Play of the Feeders

The feeders play as they would in a 2-1-3, adjusting to the requirements noted in the 1-2-3 for feeding the open men on the crease. They help each other, and rather than having a single man move from one side of the cage to the other, the ball is passed back and forth between the feeders. Should one of the feeders dodge, the remaining feeder can back up. This reduces the responsibility of the crease men. Naturally the feeders can work any brush, dodge, or pick-off play as in any other formation.

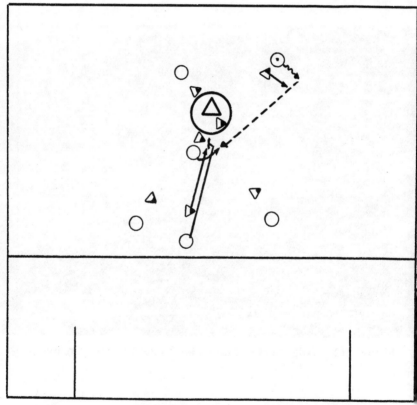

Figure 113. Arriving Midfield Crease Man Sets Up Post for Crease Attack to Start 2 - 2 - 2.

Play of the Crease Men

Since the second crease man comes from the midfield, there are two possible ways for him to enter the play. The first method involves the crease attack man taking station on the side of the crease away from the man with the ball. After the ball is settled down, the midfielder cuts right toward him and sets up a brush. The crease man breaks toward the man with the ball, around the cutting midfielder. Their subsequent pattern is as described for the 1-2-3.

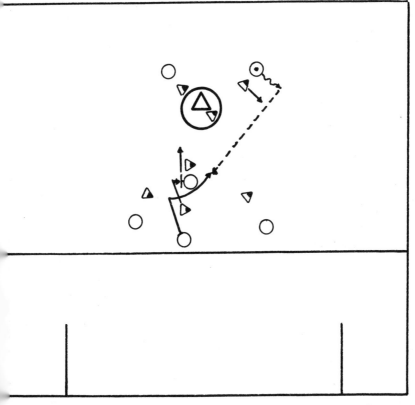

Figure 114. Crease Attack Moves Out to Set Up Post for Midfield Crease to Start 2 - 2 - 2.

The second method of starting the play is only practical once the ball has moved behind the cage to the feeders. The crease man moves off his crease about 10 yards, opposite the post of the cage most distant from the feeder. He takes station here, facing the feeder while the midfielder cuts past him, going to either side as his defense man dictates, heading toward the feeder. After the midfielder goes past, the crease man breaks for the opposite side of the cage. They can then start their cuts across the mouth of the goal as before if the feeder decides not to throw to either on the initial cut. The direction of the crease man's cut, after the midfielder goes past, may have to be adjusted if the defense starts zoning immediately; and it may be better for him to flood the zone by cutting toward the feeder also, but staying deep enough so as not to get in the way of the midfielder.

Play of the Deep Midfielders

Since only two midfielders remain deep, their play needs to be adjusted slightly. Their cuts will have to be single or two-man brushes. On a single cut, the other midfielder should remain deep to back up the play. If the cut is unsuccessful it is vital that the cutter get out of the area in front of the cage as soon as is practical, for even if he gets free eventually, the area is so congested that the feeder will have trouble getting the ball to him.

If a double brush is used, it should occur deep, again so that personnel are available to back up the play, and so that the cut does not cause the area in front of the cage to become too crowded. Normally the midfield shot will come from 10 yards out using this pattern. One of the crease men should be ready to screen any such shot.

The deep midfielders should realize that they have strong

defensive responsibilities, not only for backing up the play, but also for covering for their third man who is committed into the crease area and who, therefore, will be late getting back to ride a clear.

The key to the 2-2-2 pattern is the availability of several midfielders who can play the crease position. Without them the pattern has few advantages and some defensive weaknesses. To make it easy for the crease attack to work with the crease midfielder, there should be a definite member of each midfield unit assigned to play this position.

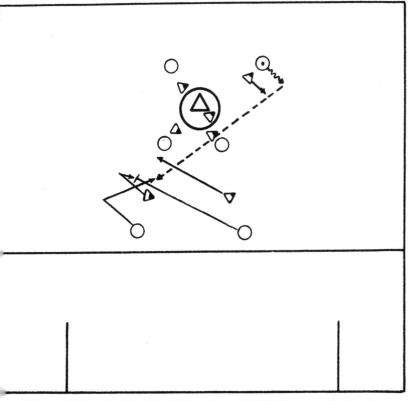

Figure 115.   Double Brush by Deep Midfielders m 2 - 2 - 2.

CREASE POST

Frequently, beginning midfielders have trouble coordinating their cuts with the readiness of the feeder. Either their brush pattern is run while the feeder is out of position or too preoccupied with other matters to take advantage of the play, or the feeder readies himself and finds no one cutting for him. The midfielders may also have difficulty getting organized to work an adequate brush spontaneously. Some teams, therefore, run their brushes or plays on signal. However, using the crease man as a post on whom the brushes can be run provides a formation where it is not as difficult to get the brush patterns run successfully.

The pattern is simple. The crease man moves out in front of the crease 10 to 12 yards, favoring the side opposite that on which the ball is located. He turns to face the ball, keeping his back to the midfield. Then the various midfielders use him as a post on whom to brush. The best play is a single brush on the stationary post, although two midfielders can brush simultaneously. The cutter can pass on either side of the post, depending on which is better for losing his man. The better brushes will probably be those in which the cutter passes on the side of the post where the ball is located. Occasionally, after the cutter has gone by, the crease attack may find that the attention of his defense man has been diverted either because a switch has been called or because the defense man is worrying about this cutter. The crease man should then break to an open area in front of the cage. The exact area into which he will break depends upon where the cutting midfielder went, and where the defensive coverage is weakest.

Although the pattern removes the crease man from in front of the goal, this may not be a serious loss, especially

Figure 116.   Alignment of Players for Crease Post.

if that crease man does not excel when close to the cage but rather needs a longer cut in order to get off an effective shot. Again the decision to use the pattern depends on the available personnel.

If a midfielder takes his cut and does not receive a feed, he should circle to the outside and return to the midfield area so as not to clog the crease area by loitering in front of the cage. He should remain only if he finds himself completely open.

As on any brush play, the responsibility for hanging the defense man on the post rests with the cutter. The post man cannot move into the defender without committing a foul. The cutter, therefore, should probably not run a true course past the post, but rather try to convince his defense man that he is going to pass the post on one side and then change direction at the last moment to pass on the opposite side.

MIDFIELD POST OR 2 - 1 - 1 - 2

A midfield post provides a pattern to use if the crease man is most valuable to the attack while remaining on his crease, even though the midfielders still have trouble getting their cuts timed with the feeders.

Again this pattern is quite simple. The crease man remains in his usual position, as in the 2-1-3, and works alone to get free. If the off-side feeder is inclined to brush on him, this possibility remains as an option (see again Figures 53 and 54).

Meanwhile one of the midfielders stations himself 12 to 15 yards from the cage favoring the side away from the ball. He faces the cage or feeder and keeps his back to the midfield and remains stationary waiting for his teammates to use him as a post. Cuts on this pattern should be single cuts, for to cut both the remaining midfielders at once leaves no one to back up.

Figure 117. Alignment of Players for Midfield Post.

The cutting midfielder should stay about 5 yards out from the crease after his cut and should cut wide of the cage to keep out of the way of the crease defense man. The post midfielder, like the crease post, makes his cut after his teammate has gone past and has attracted the attention of his defense man. He then cuts to an open section of the field.

The cutter who fails to draw a feed has two options after finishing his cut. Most of the time he should circle back to the midfield and open the area in front of the goal for another cutting teammate. But occasionally he may want to swing in to the crease so that he and the crease attack can brush on each other before circling out.

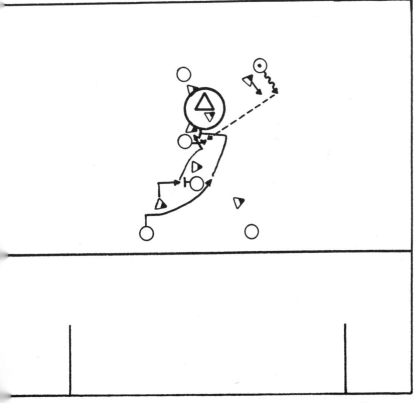

Figure 118. Cutting Midfielder on Midfield Post Can Set Up Brush for Crease Attack after Initial Cut Fails to Produce a Feed.

This pattern and the crease post pattern assume that the ball is being worked from the feeders to the rear of the cage. Both patterns work best against a tight man-to-man defense since it is easier to gain an advantage using the brushes on such a defense. A sagging defense can make it difficult to run these patterns since the defense is likely to pick off the feeds before they reach their target. This is particularly true if the defense man on the post man sags toward the goal. Since it is possible to effectively block these patterns, they should be secondary patterns used in spot situations only until the defense starts sagging to break it up.

MIDFIELD FEED OR 1 - 4 - 1

It can be advantageous in some situations to work the ball in the midfield looking for the feed or dodge. But each of the previous patterns was designed primarily for the ball to be worked behind the cage most of the time. The 1-4-1 is, on the other hand, designed as a feeding and dodging offense with the ball in the center midfield.

After the ball settles down on the attacking half of the field, the players take positions indicated in Figure 119. The center midfielder, in possession of the ball, moves laterally in front of the cage along the restraining line, and controls the ball most of the time. The other two midfielders move to one of the positions nearer the cage and are joined by one of the feeders and the crease man to form a wall of four men across the front of the goal. The position each man assumes makes little difference, since during the course of play each man will be moving from one position to another. The two men playing the inside slots should be about 5 yards apart and about 3 yards out from the crease, spaced equally from the center of the goal. The wing men should be about 5 yards farther out and slightly deeper, about 6 yards in front of the crease line.

The center midfielder must have all the capabilities of a feeder behind the cage to make the formation possible. He must control the ball a large part of the time and be alert to the feeding possibilities to his teammates. At the same time, he has a very advantageous position from which to dodge or bore in to the cage for a long shot, since he has his defense man isolated directly in front of the goal. The number of his teammates in the vicinity of the mouth of the goal provides him with an excellent screen for the long shot and the personnel to handle any rebounds.

Figure 119.   Alignment of Players for 1 - 4 - 1 Midfield Feed.

The lone feeder, remaining behind the cage, backs up the play. His job is made difficult by the fact that he must intercept any erratic feeds before they go out-of-bounds, since unlike a shot, they will belong to the opposition. He should remain in the rear except for the rare cases when he has an opening that is irresistible. Should he come in front of the goal, one of the other attack men should drop back to assume his position and back-up responsibilities. This feeder can also be the one to control the ball in the pattern, if preferred; the play of the four inside men is much the same. If the center midfielder wants relief, the feeder is the one to whom the ball should be worked.

The first good opening off this pattern comes as the personnel start to assemble in front of the cage. The feeder coming in from the rear of the cage has a ready made post in the crease man, who should have stationed himself on the edge of the crease away from the ball as the play was being set up. As the feeder goes past the crease man, he may be open, or the crease man may find himself open after the cutter has gone by.

If the center midfielder decides to dodge or bore toward the cage for his own shot, he should be alert to spot open teammates in the crease area, since the defense man who will have to come out to pick him up as he dodges will probably have to leave a man momentarily open in front of the goal to make the play.

With the center midfielder in position to feed, the basic brush pattern for the inside four is a brush play done in pairs. The combinations that can be run are numerous. For instance, one outside man can start laterally across the field having the others brush on him as he goes by or using them as posts for his own brush. Patterns will have to be worked out, however, so that the men are not all moving at the

3

same time. There must be enough cooperation to prevent
the crease area from becoming a confused mess and allowing each defense man to cover more than one man.

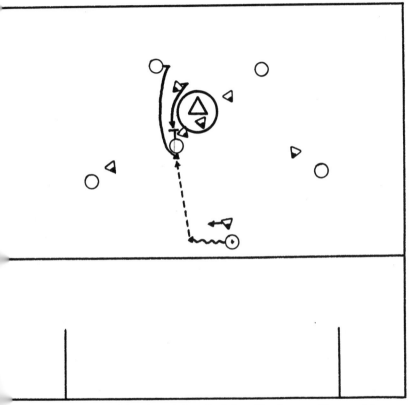

**Figure 120. Initial Brush by Arriving Feeder on Crease At-
tack at Start of 1 - 4 - 1.**

Probably the best simple play is the brush run by the
pair of players on either side of the cage. If the inside man
cuts to the outside, his outside partner can take a step or

two as though going behind the cage, and then cut back slightly diagonally across the front of the goal brushing on the inside man. The feed comes to him from the center midfielder while he is in position to get off a good shot right in front of the goal. Other simple patterns can be worked out where only two men at once are involved, and these will probably be more successful than if all four men are involved in the same play. There will be a good deal of switching of positions among these four players, so all should be familiar with play from all locations.

Should the ball move to the feeder behind the cage, the same possibilities exist, though the best single cut is probably the reverse of the previous one; that is, the outside man cuts toward the crease first and the inside man brushes on him, taking the feed going away from the goal.

When either the center midfielder or the man behind the cage controls the ball, the outside man of the four man wall closest to the ball is the relief man should the man with the ball want to pass off. He should be ready for the pass, and should move farther out and toward the man with the ball in such cases. He provides the link which makes it possible to move the ball from the center midfielder to his counterpart behind the cage without throwing the dangerous high looping pass over the top of the cage.

FEEDING FROM THE SIDE

Another pattern that changes the normal position from which the ball is fed and controlled involves working the ball to the side of the cage rather than from the front or rear. The basic pattern becomes something on the order of a 1-3-2 formation. The general field alignment would be like that in Figure 122. One feeder goes to the side about 15

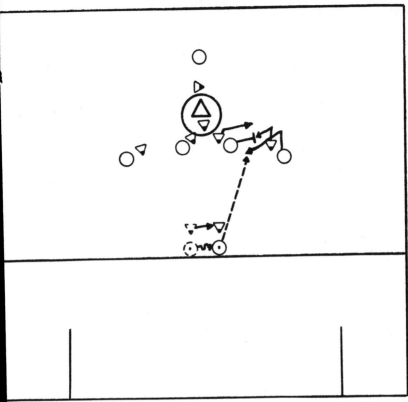

Figure 121. Cut by Inside Crease Man to Brush for Outside Man on 1 - 4 - 1.

yards from the center of the goal, moving parallel to the side line roughly between the goal line and the restraining line. A position 10 to 15 yards inside the restraining line is best for feeding. The remaining feeder plays behind the cage to back up the play. The crease man pulls away from the feeder to the far side of the crease. One midfielder drops in closer than normal to the cage, directly opposite the feeder, while the other two midfielders widen their spacing, but remain along the restraining line.

Figure 122.   Alignment of Players for Feeding from the Side.

This side feeding pattern is particularly advantageous when all cutters in front of the cage play the same way. If they are all right-handed, the feeder should take station on the left side of the goal; if they are all left-handed, he should feed from the right. In such an arrangement all cuts will be run so that the ball is passed to the stick side of the receiver, and no primary receiver will have to turn prior to getting off his shot.

Players will alter their positions on the field, but the station of the midfielder opposite the feeder should be filled at all times to back up missed feeds before they go out-of-bounds. If the man who first assumes this position makes a cut, which he will do often, one of the other midfielders should immediately slide over to fill the vacancy. Similarly, if the man behind the goal cuts, he should be replaced by another player, for he not only has the job of backing up the shot, but is also the feeder's relief.

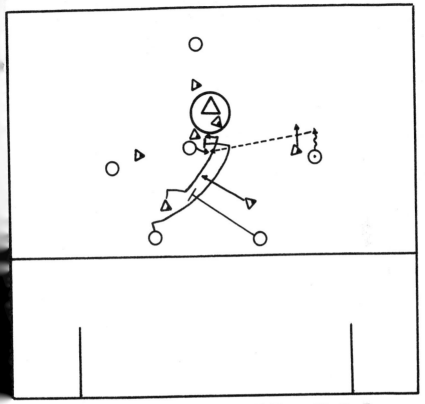

Figure 123. Brush Play by Deep Midfielders while Feeding from the Side. Either midfielder may continue in to crease to set up brush with crease attack.

One simple cut involves the two deep midfielders. The man closest to the feeder cuts diagonally away from the ball to set up the brush for his partner, who comes off the brush headed toward the feeder. After the brush, if no feed is thrown, one or the other, but not both, of the midfielders can continue on into the vicinity of the crease either to brush on the crease man or set up a pick for him.

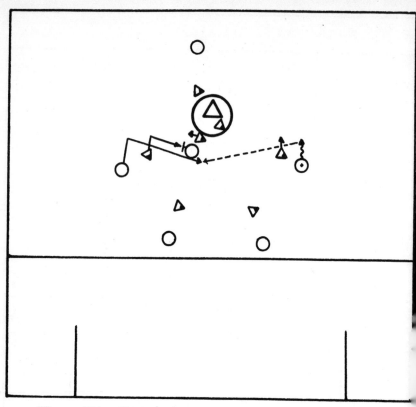

Figure 124. Side Midfielder Brushing on Crease Attack while Feeding from the Side.

Another play involves the midfielder opposite the feeder and the crease man, as the midfielder tries to pick off his defender on the crease man. In addition, this midfielder may brush on one of the other midfielders who has headed toward the cage to set up the play for him. Or, the man behind the goal can come around brushing on the crease attack man.

The man with the ball has the option of throwing to any of these cutters, but he is also in good position himself to dodge, or work a give-and-go with one of the neighboring players.

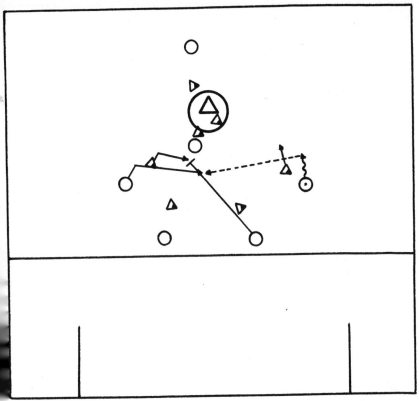

Figure 125. Side Midfielder Can Brush on Either Deep Midfielder while Feeding from the Side.

The possibilities available in this pattern are many, but it must be remembered that backing up is harder than in many other formations since the attack can easily lose a ball over the side line after a missed feed.

SLOW PATTERNS

All previous offensive patterns were based on the assumption that the attacking group was going to press the defense and make their opening as a result of aggressive actions, by dodging and cutting. Another approach makes the defense come to the attack, and forces the defense, thereby, to make their own mistakes.

For a slow attacking pattern, probably the 2-1-3 or the circle pattern is best, but any other can be developed with the same philosophy. The attack lays back 20 to 25 yards from the cage content to pass the ball back and forth, forcing the defense, in their anxiety to get the ball, to come farther out from the goal to make their plays. Instead of operating in a rough circle 15 yards from the cage, they are soon working 20 to 25 yards out. As a result they are spread farther over the field and less able to assist each other.

Meanwhile the attack tries to work a give-and-go. Soon, if this does not work, an attack man has his defense man isolated and can start to work his dodge. If the dodge succeeds, the other attack men start to converge on the cage. It is hard for the defense to recover and shift in order to pick up the dodger. When they do, however, because of the distance between members of the attack, another man is left wide open, and a pass should be thrown to him.

The pattern is slow. On the attack a man must be content to hold the ball for a while without making a serious move toward the cage until he draws a defender; then he should either pass off, try a give-and-go, or dodge if he has his man isolated. If one man does not hold the ball for a while, the attack must deliberately work the ball around the outside of their pattern until the defense is drawn out. Passes should be deliberate, accurate, and thrown before too much pressure is put on the man with the ball.

This pattern can be interpreted as a stalling offense unless it leads to a definite attack on the cage. However, if the attack takes care once the ball is moved over the restraining line in their attacking half of the field to keep it in this area,

no stalling penalty can be assessed. Should a stalling warn-
ing be given by the referee, the attack must be careful to
keep the ball inside this restraining line.

The basic formation used makes little difference. Until
the opening occurs, the ball is probably far enough from
the cage so that feeding men in front will not be very successful unless they are completely free. Cuts and brushes
should be worked around the outside of the pattern to
search for openings as the defense becomes worried about
their inability to get control of the ball. But scoring opportunities are most often the result of either a dodge or the
give-and-go. So the pattern is particularly intriguing if there
is reasonable speed on the attack to work the give-and-go
successfully, or if the attack has a good dodger or two
who need only to isolate their men in order to go past.

AGAINST A ZONE DEFENSE

Each of the previous patterns has been outlined against
a man-to-man defense in which each defensive player covers
a particular offensive player unless definite switches are
made. Even after such shifts, there is still one-on-one coverage. Since a majority of teams play such a defense, the
offense should be planned to meet such conditions. A brush
is predicated on the theory that a defense man responsible
for the attacker must be eliminated or slowed down if the
attack man is to get clear for a pass.

If pre-game information indicates that the opposition is
going to play a zone defense, it is possible to form a complete attacking strategy to meet this condition. However, if
suddenly it appears that the zone is being played, the
attack must adjust. It is useless to put in a completely new
attacking pattern in the face of such a problem during a time-

out or even during half time. Therefore the attack should have been drilled in a few simple theories to use against the zone, when and if needed. Plans should be simple and within the framework of the existing attacking pattern.

Since each defensive player in a zone is assigned an area to cover, the offensive counter is to put two players into the zone of a single man so that he cannot cover both. The attack need not know the limits of the zone of a defender; they will be discovered after the system is encountered. All the attack really needs is the theory of flooding a zone.

Zone patterns differ slightly in how hard they press the man with the ball. The attack should find this out quickly. Usually a man receiving the ball has a reasonable time to work a play before he is picked up, since most zones sag toward the center when no one in that zone has the ball. If the attack pattern has two men behind the cage, the man without the ball can often move to the front of the goal because his partner has plenty of time and does not need a relief man.

It is normally poor strategy to dodge into a zone. If properly set up, there will be another defense man assigned to pick up the dodger as soon as he enters a new zone. Since the players on defense sag toward the center when the ball is not in their zone, even if the first dodge succeeds, the man will not have an open teammate near the cage to whom he can pass.

If the attack plays their normal pattern, even though the defense is in a zone, they must adjust to flooding a zone rather than brushing off a defense man. Cuts should still be run, but the objective is now to get two attackers into one defender's zone.

With the ball behind the cage, an easy cut is to have the center midfielder arc behind one of the wing midfielders.

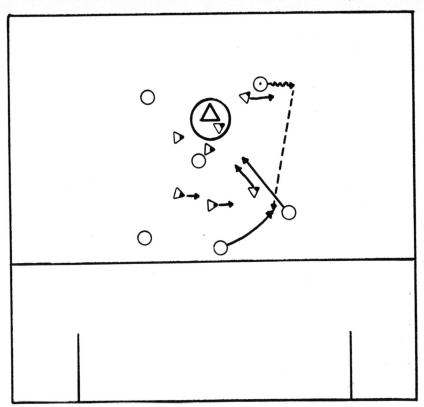

Figure 126. Wing Midfielder Moves Toward Cage as Center Midfielder Arcs Behind Him to Flood a Zone.

The wing midfielder moves toward the goal, but stays in his area while the center joins him a little deeper. The plan is that the defender will follow the wing who is already in his zone and will not be able to cover the center who has just entered the zone. Having the feeder without the ball arc around the crease man creates a similar situation.

There are many other ways of creating the two-on-one, but the basic premise is to flood a zone by moving a second man into a zone already occupied by a teammate and having the two spread wide enough so that one defender cannot cover them. To practice against a zone occasionally will make the possibilities obvious to the ingenious attack. Perhaps the situation will become clearer if first defensive zone play is studied as outlined in Chapter 8.

If prior plans are laid to meet a particular zone, the basic attacking pattern might be changed to best counter the expected defense. It might be worthwhile considering some of the formations discussed in the section on Extra Man Attacking Plays in Chapter 12, for when a team is down a man they will invariably play a zone, and extra man plays are designed to operate against such zones by moving two men into the zone of one man. They can be used when teams are all even as well as with an extra man.

Any attack pattern against a zone is a passing game. If the attack cannot control and move the ball effectively, the zone will cause great trouble. A dodging offense will probably not be effective, nor will a give-and-go offense (assuming the zone is played correctly). The attack must be willing to move the ball, flood zones, and take long shots to succeed. A good number of shots taken against a zone are likely to be relatively long—from 15 to 20 yards out. An attack willing to take such shots is likely either to score or draw out the defense. If the defense is drawn out, it becomes easier to flood a zone close to the cage and get a closer shot.

ATTACK PHILOSOPHY

The above patterns represent only a very small segment of the possible attacking patterns, but no matter what pattern is selected or invented, it must be tailored to fit the players who must execute it. With a group of excellent dodgers, it is not a good idea to base the attack on a feeding pattern. With good feeders, the pattern should allow them to exercise their talents. The pattern for beginners, at least, should be relatively simple. Even for advanced players, the simple system is often the most successful. Each player should know the possibilities that exist for him in the pattern selected.

The more advanced the players become, and the more familiar they are with each other's play, the more they will be able to invent or appreciate possibilities that exist in a given situation.

Whether plays, as such, are to be used or not depends upon the philosophy of the attack. There are arguments on both sides. The more experienced the team, the less likely it is to employ specific plays, but the beginner may need such plays.

While the pattern selected may contribute to the team's success, an alert attack scores many of its goals by taking advantage of defensive mistakes. All the play or pattern can do is offer the opportunity for the defense to make mistakes. It is then up to the attack to capitalize on these mistakes.

8. Defensive Patterns

Essentially the defense operates on either a man-to-man or a zone philosophy. Variations of each are used because of a team's personnel or the personnel of the opposition.

The play of the close defense was covered in Chapter 4, the role of the goalie in Chapter 5, and that of the midfield in Chapter 6. All three merge to play either a man-to-man or a zone pattern.

Goalie Play

No matter what pattern is selected, the goalie's role is always the same. He should still be the "field general" for the defense. He keeps his defense informed about the location of the ball. He directs his defense in how to play their men or zones and how to help each other. He makes sure his men are far enough from the goal—or near enough. He lets the defense men in the hole know when to check sticks on a feed into that area and orders shifts when a dodger must be picked up. He must know his own personnel well; their faults and capabilities; and he must know the opposition at the same time. While he must know the pattern being

268

played in order to be effective in his direction, the pattern affects the rest of the defense much more than it affects the goalie's own individual play.

MAN-TO-MAN

A man-to-man defense is the most common pattern. There are variations in how tightly individuals are played, and in fact how tightly the whole defense plays their men; but the basic theory remains the same.

Each man picks up one of the opponents and covers him as long as the opposition has the ball. The crease defense man makes an effort to play the attack man who is on the crease most often, while the other two close defense men play the remaining attack men, who may or may not play behind the cage as feeders. It is usual to assign a defense man to a particular attack man by name or number and to have him stay with that attack man. If enough is known about the opposition, these assignments can be made before game time. If this is not possible, adjustments can be made if needed after the game starts; but since each defense man covers his attack man even when the ball is at the other end of the field, it is easy to assign each to a particular opponent and have him stay with that man throughout the game.

Midfield coverage is more fluid. Midfielders can be assigned to specific men at the initial face off, but such rigid assignment has disadvantages. In the process of the clear it is difficult for a midfielder to always pick up a particular man—though it can be arranged. Because both the offensive and defensive midfielders have roles to play in the clear and the ride of the clear, individuals are likely to arrive in their attacking or defending positions at varying times. It is also probable that the offensive midfielders are willing to play any of the three offensive midfield positions—center or either wing—and it is therefore hard to predict where a particular man will be found during or after a clear.

A more fluid arrangement is to instruct the defensive midfield to head for the area in front of the cage as soon as the clear has succeeded, without regard for the midfielder each is covering. After each defensive midfielder has checked back as quickly as he can to a position about 15 yards directly in front of his own goal, each defensive midfielder turns to take an offensive midfielder coming down the field. The first defensive player to arrive takes the first or most dangerous offensive player to arrive, and so on. As each picks up a man, the defense should call the number of the man he has picked up to avoid having two men covering the same opponent. There can be moments when one or two defensive midfielders are back and must cover an extra man or two until their teammates check back. In this case those in position will have to zone the offensive midfield for a while before picking up a particular man. They should play a midfielder with the ball loosely and should offer only loose zone coverage of the other midfielders until all their unit checks back. Of course if the man with the ball poses a serious scoring threat, he will have to be played aggressively or closely, and any men close to the goal in the hole will have to be played more closely than midfielders farther out. This situation should last only a few moments until all defensive midfielders have checked back and picked up a man. There is no place in a midfield unit for the man who loafs when checking back and forces his teammates to zone the offense for any period of time. Once each picks up a man, a defender stays with his man unless a switch is called. If substitutions are made on the midfield while the ball is in the defensive half of the field, each replacement should be certain who his man will be before play starts again.

The man-to-man pattern can be played loosely or tight-ly depending on the theory of the defense, or there can be variations to fit the situation.

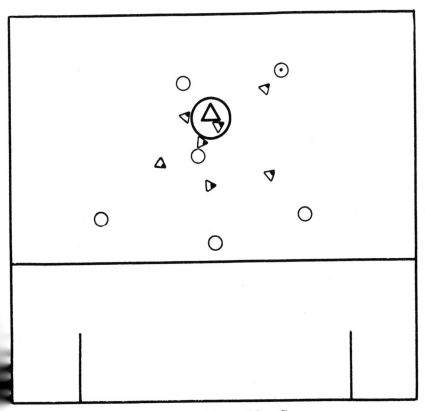

Figure 127.   Loose Man-to-Man Coverage.

Loose Man-to-Man

In loose man-to-man coverage the defense allows the attack freedom to move the ball outside of scoring territory but tries to prevent them from finding an open man in the hole. The defense man covering the ball picks up his man relatively slowly while definitely keeping himself under control. He should not press as long as his man is not in scoring territory. He moves between his man and the cage, maintaining proper field position, and bothering his man with pokes and chops without pressing to take the ball away. He is willing to allow the attack man to have the ball and feed some distance from the goal; but he avoids overplaying the man, thus forcing him to dodge. If the man with the ball insists on driving toward the goal, he should be played more aggressively, but as long as he stays a reasonable distance from the cage, he can be allowed to pass off to a teammate equally far from the goal without much interference.

The other defense men sag off their men toward the goal to varying depths depending on how close the ball is to their men and how serious a scoring threat their men are because of their field position. An attack man in front of the goal should be played tightly. A cutter who comes through the hole should be picked up more closely as he nears the goal, but a man who stays a reasonable distance from the cage should not be bothered. In these positions the defense can allow their opponents to receive a pass without much interference—assuming that they are far enough from the cage so as not to have shots. The attack will probably be able to shoot from 20 yards out—on the theory that the goalie will stop such a long shot—but shots closer in will be much harder to obtain.

The theory of the loose man-to-man is that eventually the attack will make a mistake; drop the ball; throw an erratic pass; or otherwise give the defense a good chance to gain possession. At the same time because the defense sags toward the cage when their men do not have the ball, the hole is somewhat clogged, and the defense men in this area will be able to pick off a number of feeds, even when they are not thrown specifically to the men they are covering. The pattern allows the attack to control the ball, and it may take a while before they make the mistake that gives the defense the ball, but this is to be expected.

Tight Man-to-Man

While still maintaining proper field position on each attacker, in a tight man-to-man the defense reduces the freedom of the attack to move the ball; this includes the outside area.

The man playing the ball tries to take the ball away from his man or to force him to throw a poor pass to a teammate. He does not go so far as to over-extend himself, and he must learn how hard he can press his man before turning him into a dodger.

The other players all tighten up on their men to such a distance that if the ball is thrown to them, no matter where they may be, the defender will reach his man just ahead of the ball. The theory is that it will therefore be much harder for the attack to control the ball and will have to put their full attention on just trying to hold the ball rather than scoring goals.

There is some danger that the defense in this pattern will become too aggressive in their coverage and play and commit fouls or make mistakes which might create attack openings. There are several weapons available to the attack. If the defense is fully alerted to them, the tight man-to-man is much more likely to succeed.

The first danger is the dodge. If the man with the ball is pressed hard, he may be forced to dodge, even though he had not really planned to do so. It is easier to dodge a pressing defense man than one who plays cautiously. Also, once the dodge is made, support from other defenders is not so easy to obtain since each defender covers his own man closely, making him less handy for backing up the dodge.

The give-and-go is a second strong attack weapon. As an attack man passes off, his defense man looks to follow the ball, and at that instant the attack man cuts past him to take a return pass. (Refer to Figure 90.) This play is easier to work against a defense man who sags only a little—or not at all—as the first pass is thrown.

Finally, with close coverage on each man, it is easier for two attacking players to brush off one or both of their defenders than if they are played loosely.

Whether a team plans to use a tight man-to-man as their general defensive pattern or not, there are likely to be times when it is absolutely necessary to play such a pattern. The most obvious, of course, is the situation late in a game when the defending team is behind a goal or two and finds it absolutely imperative to get the ball if it is going to score. Therefore a defense should be trained to press when necessary.

In normal circumstances, probably the best man-to-man pattern is a combination of loose and tight patterns.

Playing a Team with One Superior Dodger

Frequently the opposition has one star dodger on whom they rely. The man playing this attacker has a difficult assignment, but his job can be made easier if he has help from his teammates.

The man playing the dodger should bother the dodger

Figure 128. Play Against a Superior Dodger. Teammates sag off their men to back up defender playing the ball. If first dodge succeeds, nearest teammate picks up the dodger. If he fails, crease defense moves to make the play, and off-side defense man slides onto crease.

with pokes and chops but give ground with him as he nears the cage area making sure not to overplay him in the process. He will reach a point, however, where he must make a stand; here he should start playing the dodger with his hands.

Meanwhile the rest of his teammates should sag off their men to back him up. If the defender playing the ball can stop the dodger, the mission is accomplished. If he cannot do this, he should force the dodger to circle around him where he will then run into another defender who is backing up on that side. If the dodger avoids his own man plus the man who was backing up on the side to which he moved, the logical man left to stop him is now the crease defense man, who should move to do so—playing the dodger's body as he comes while covering his stick at the same time.

When he has gone past his own man and evaded the defender beside him who was trying to back up the play, the really good dodger will either try to shoot or pass off to a teammate in scoring territory before the crease man gets to him. If the crease defense makes his move soon enough, the dodger will have only a poor shot at the cage at best. Therefore he will look for a pass. The logical person for him to feed is the crease attack. To prevent a successful feed, the off-side defense man must sag off his man as the dodge starts and be ready to step in to pick up the crease attack when his defense man leaves. There must be a coordinated team effort to make the shift perfectly. The defensive midfielders who are not directly involved in the play should also sag toward the middle to be available should they be able to lend any additional assistance.

Playing a Team with One Superior Feeder

Playing an exceptionally good feeder requires almost the opposite approach. The man covering him now has a difficult but different task. First he should try to keep this feeder from getting the ball at all. Therefore he should play his man tightly all over the field when he does not have the ball. The other defense men should play more loosely in order to make the attack pass to these men to whom it is easier to get the ball than to the tightly covered superior feeder.

However, when the feeder does get the ball, his defense man continues to play him tightly keeping him as far from the goal as possible. The defense man makes his play 15 yards from the cage and can afford to give ground only to about 10 yards from the cage. He should be prepared to block the feed if possible. The other defense men should tighten up on all the men who are in or near the hole to give the feeder few good receivers. Defense men playing other attack men outside the hole should continue their loose coverage to invite passes from the superior feeder to another player not as able. In particular the other feeder should be played loosely so that he can receive a pass from his partner.

ZONE DEFENSE

The second basic defensive pattern is the zone. Essentially each player is assigned an area of the defensive half of the field; he covers any player who comes into that zone. If the ball is in his zone, the defender plays the ball. Otherwise he sags to the edge of his zone closest to the ball, keeping in mind his location with respect to the goal, and offers assistance to players in neighboring zones. However, unless a real emergency exists, he stays in the zone assigned to him.

Under most conditions this pattern concentrates a number of defense men in front of the goal. Therefore one of the first weapons of the zone defense is the ability to intercept passes or feeds thrown through or over the zone. Players should keep their sticks up, trying for the interception, while still covering their areas.

Meanwhile the attack will probably be able to move the

ball around the outside of the zone with ease—as in the loose man-to-man.

The exact areas assigned to the defensive players can be varied, but the usual defensive zone is a 2-1-3 zone with the areas of coverage overlapping slightly as shown in Figure 129. The crease defense man in the middle zone will cover the crease attack more or less man-to-man since he will be in this zone most of the time. The other two close defense men will sag to the front edges of the crease unless a man in their zone has the ball. They will go out to play a feeder in their area who has the ball, but will leave the other feeder relatively open. The midfielders cover men with the ball in their zones but otherwise sag to the inside edges of their zones so that the hole area is pretty well clogged.

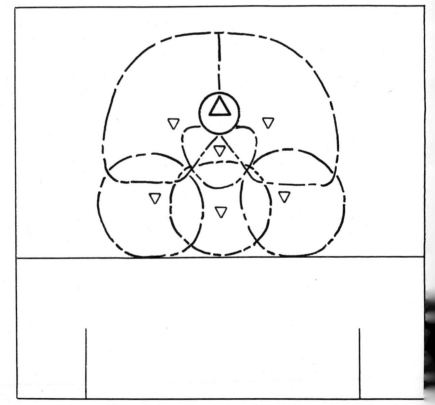

Figure 129.   Areas for 2 - 1 - 3 Zone Defense.

In the pure zone a player covers the man with the ball as long as he is in the defender's zone. If the player runs with the ball from zone to zone, each defender will pick him up in turn. For instance a midfielder with the ball running in an arc in front of the cage will be turned over to each successive midfielder as he moves from zone to zone. A feeder with the ball who slides across the back of the cage keeping the ball will be turned over to the other corner close defense man as he passes the back point of the cage.

Sliding Zone

Trading men, as the man with the ball moves from zone to zone, can create a situation that has two defenders momentarily covering the same man. If this switch causes difficulty, and it seems advisable to try to avoid what amounts to double coverage at the moment of exchange, a sliding zone can be instituted. It is a little more difficult to learn, but solves the double coverage problem.

In a sliding zone the man who first picks up a particular player with the ball stays with him until he passes off. As a result this defender may move out of the zone in which he started into another zone as he follows his man. The other defenders slide over to occupy new zones to cover the zone vacated by the defense man now covering the man with the ball. If a sliding zone is to be played, the defensive half of the field should be divided into a close defense area and a midfield area so that a midfielder does not end up playing close defense and vice versa. Therefore as a player moves from the midfield to the close attack area, he will still be passed from a midfielder to a close defense man as in a pure zone; but while he is in one half of the attacking area or the other, he will be covered by the same defender.

For instance, if a feeder gains possession of the ball, the

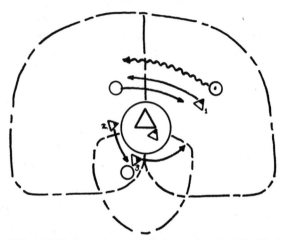

Figure 130. Sliding Zone as Feeder Carries Ball Behind Cage. Defender playing the ball stays with his man. Off-side corner defense man slides to crease zone, and crease defense man slides to the now vacant corner zone.

defense man who picks him up will stay with him if he moves across the back of the cage. The corner defense man, into whose zone he moves as a result of staying with that feeder, rotates into the crease zone, and the crease defense man rotates into the corner zone just vacated. In the midfield players just switch zones as the ball moves from one zone to another. The only time the man with the ball is passed from one player to another is when he moves from a midfield zone to a close defense zone, or vice versa.

Partial Zone

Rather than playing a pure zone or even a sliding zone, the defense may elect to play a partial zone which involves playing man-to-man on part of the field and playing a zone on another part. A partial zone can be set up in any manner desired, and the possibilities are many.

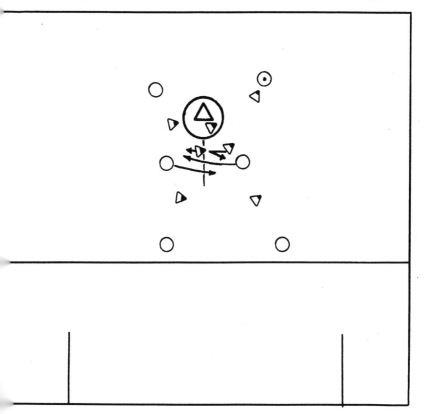

Figure 131. Two Man Partial Zone Against Crease Men in Double Crease Pattern.

It is possible to play the attack man-to-man while zoning the midfield. Another possibility involves reversing the procedure.

Partial zones can be used to combat certain specific offensive patterns. The double crease can be partially zoned by playing the crease men with a two-man zone while playing the remaining men man-to-man. Each man in the zone

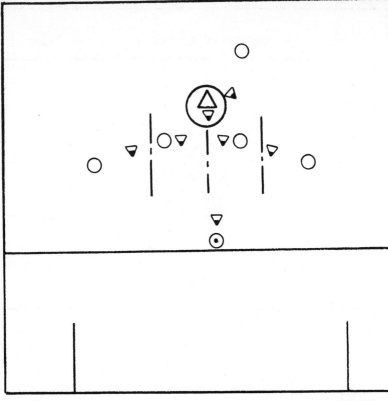

Figure 132. Partial Zone Areas Against Four Man Wall in 1 - 4 - 1 Pattern.

plays a side of the crease, covering the man who happens to be in his area favoring the side of his zone closest to the ball. Each defender can cover his zone until the attack realizes that they must flood one zone in which case the defense man in the unoccupied zone must slide into his teammate's zone to help cover that area.

The 1-4-1 offense can be zoned by covering the man with the ball man-to-man and zoning the four man wall in front of the crease. The defender on the feeder, or center midfielder,who does not have the ball at the moment sags toward the center of the goal prepared to pick up his man if needed.

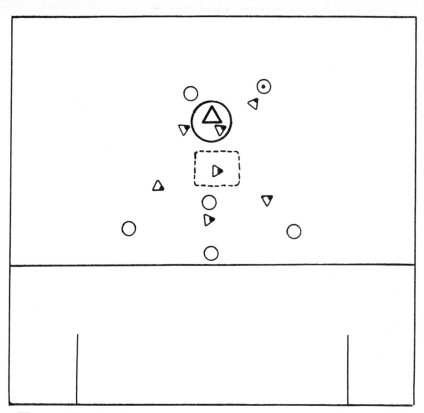

Figure 133. Partial Zone by Defender Covering Post Man in Any Post Pattern.

One of the post offenses can be zoned by having the defender on the post man drop off his man favoring the side of the field where the ball is located. He can then block feeds to anyone cutting past the post and can pick up the post man as soon as he makes a move toward the goal himself.

The partial zone can be set up as a result of prior planning, knowing what to expect of the opponents; or it can be developed spontaneously during the game when the defense realizes the kind of pattern being played by the opponents.

Rover Zone

Another possible zone to be used particularly against an opposition which does a great deal of dodging is the rover zone. One man is assigned to follow the ball and back up the man who is playing the ball at all times. The remaining defenders establish a five-man zone. The five-man zone must be flexible to adjust to different positions in which the ball might be located. The zone rotates to leave most open the man on the attacking team farthest from the ball. As a result when the ball is in the midfield the five-man zone is a 2-3 zone, while as soon as the ball moves to the close attack the zone is a 3-2 zone. At all times the rover backs up the defender playing the ball.

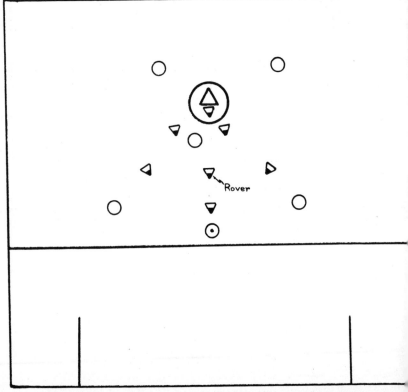

Figure 134. Rover Zone, Ball in Center Midfield. Five-man zone plays a 2 - 3 zone.

This zone will probably be most simple to learn if the rover is a designated player, while the other defenders establish the zone. In Figure 134 the ball is located in the center midfield. The five-man zone is a 2-3 zone and the rover backs up the man playing the ball. As the ball moves to the wing midfielder, as in Figure 135, the rover slides to back up the man now playing the ball. The rest of the zone defense slides to the side where the ball is located leaving most open the feeder diagonally opposite the ball. As the ball moves behind the cage, as in Figure 136, the rover again slides to back up, and the five-man zone slides into a 3-2 zone leaving most open the midfielder farthest from the ball.

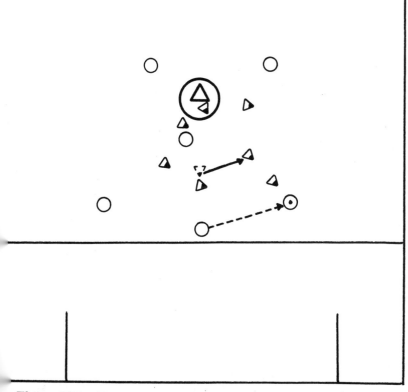

Figure 135. Rover Zone, Ball is Passed from Center Midfielder to Wing Midfielder. Rover moves to back up play. Five-man zone plays a 2 - 3 zone leaving most open the off-side feeder.

If played correctly the rover zone will be almost impossible for a dodging attack to play, for even when the attacker passes his own defender, the rover will be in his path. Since, however, there is one open man on the attack, an opponent whose offense is based on ball control and feeding will eventually find the open man. If they can figure how to get the ball to him without having it intercepted by a defender, the zone can be broken. It is surprising to find that it is difficult to get the ball to this free man, however. The rover zone will work best against an attack that always sets up plays from the rear of the cage. It is most susceptible to an attack that operates with the ball in the midfield.

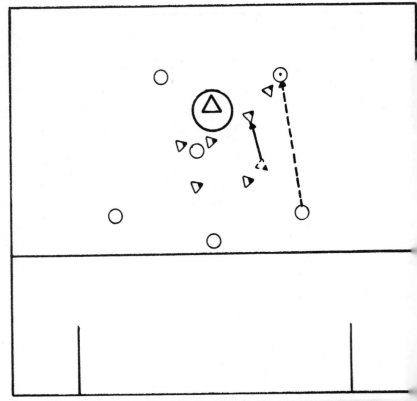

Figure 136. Rover Zone, Ball Is Passed from Wing Midfielder to Feeder. Rover moves to back up play. Five-man zone plays a 3 - 2 zone leaving most open the off-side midfielder.

Five-Point Zone

A more complicated zone designed to provide the back-up man of the rover zone without running some of the dangers of incomplete coverage of other areas is the five-point zone. Instead of dividing the defensive area into six zones, the five-point zone designates five areas which are always occupied, leaving one extra player to be used to back up the man playing the ball. The five-point zone differs from the rover in that no single man becomes the back-up man, making the shifts more complex, but at the same time providing more rapid and closer coverage.

There are two zones on the corners of the crease extending behind the cage, one zone in the area directly in front of the crease, and two midfield zones on either side of the goal and roughly 8 to 10 yards out from the cage.

The interior zones are always covered by the close defense men while the two outside zones are occupied by midfielders, leaving the spare midfielder as the extra man assigned to provide the additional coverage on the ball.

The two corner defense men sag toward the front of the cage when the ball is being played in some other zone, but go out immediately to play the ball aggressively as soon as it is carried or passed into their zones. The center or crease defense man roams in his middle zone playing the ball rather than any man and trying to line himself so that there will be three defenders in line with the ball—the man playing the ball, the back-up man (who will always be a midfielder), and finally the man in the center zone. In extreme emergency, if the attack works the ball past the first two defenders, this crease defense man will go forward to play the ball, but he usually concentrates on picking off feeds and passes thrown into his zone.

The midfielders occupy the two outside zones and pro-

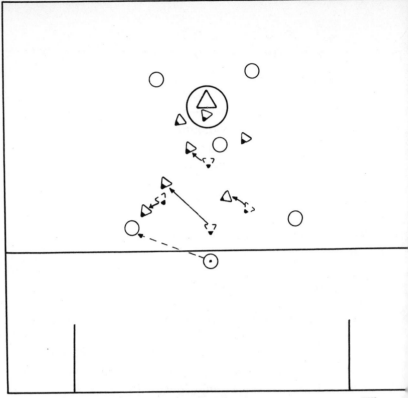

Figure 137. Five Point Zone; Ball Moves from Center to Wing Midfielder. Defender in wing zone picks up ball; defender in center occupies wing zone; crease defender lines himself with ball.

vide the back-up man behind the man playing the ball. As the ball comes down the center of the field the center midfielder picks up the ball ragging the man in possession hard while his two wing men occupy the two outside midfield zones. As the ball is passed to one of the offensive wing midfielders, the midfield defender into whose zone the ball was passed moves to pick up the ball, while the midfielder who was ragging the passer drops in behind him, becomes the back-up man on the ball, and now occupies the zone which the man ragging the ball previously owned.

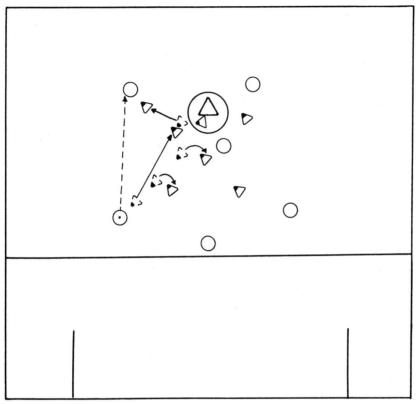

Figure 138. Five-Point Zone; Ball Moves from Wing Midfielder to Feeder. Defender in inside corner zone picks up ball; midfielder who previously was ragging the ball occupies inside corner zone; crease defender lines himself with ball.

As the ball is passed behind the cage to a feeder, the close defense man in that corner takes the ball, and the midfielder who had been ragging the passer moves into the back-up spot on the corner of the crease. He now owns one of the interior zones off the corner of the crease which he will hold as long as the close defense man on that corner is out playing the ball.

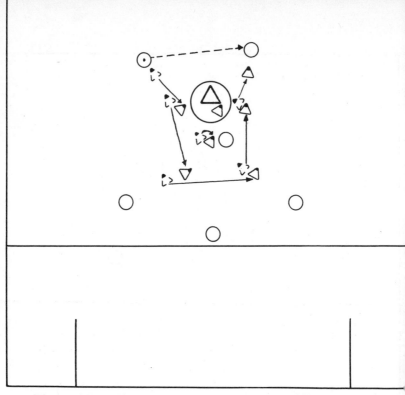

**Figure 139.   Five-Point Zone; Ball Moves Between Feeders.
Defender on new feeder's corner picks up the ball; entire midfield rotates in opposite direction to that of the ball; off-corner
defense man re-occupies his zone; crease defender lines himself with ball.**

In order to keep the close defense men in the zones to
which they were initially assigned, the most complicated
midfield shift occurs when the ball moves from one side of
the field to the other between the feeders or from a feeder
to the diagonally opposite midfielder. The midfield rotates on
such a pass in a circular direction opposite that of the ball.
On the simple pass between the feeders the corner defense
man into whose zone the ball has now been passed moves
to pick up the ball. The midfielder who previously owned
the outside zone on the side where the ball has now moved

slips in behind the defense man on the ball in order to back up. The midfielder who had the outside zone now farthest from the ball slides to the outside zone on the ball side of the field, and the midfielder who had been the back-up man slides back out to the farthest outside zone. (For an alternate method of shifting to adjust to passes between the feeders, see Figure 141 in the following discussion of the midfield zone.)

One of the intriguing features of the five-point zone is the opportunity for creating a fast break as soon as the defense gains possession of the ball. If the midfielders playing the two outside zones will break downfield immediately, the chances of finding one or both of them open for a quick pass are quite good. Under a man-to-man defensive pattern the midfielders are likely to be drawn in close to the cage while following their individual men on cuts and brushes making it hard for them to break downfield quickly enough to be free. In this zone neither outside midfielder can be drawn in this far, and both should be ready to break as soon as a teammate gets the ball. The crease defense man is quite likely to be the player to intercept the ball, and he should be thoroughly trained to spot one of these breaking midfielders.

The major difficulty of this zone is teaching position play quickly, for the slides employed must be practiced often so they become second nature. Once mastered, it takes a team with exceptionally fine stickwork to penetrate the area directly in front of the cage with any consistency.

Midfield Zone

A midfield zone is a mixture of a man-to-man defense when an opposing midfielder has the ball and a rover zone when the opponent's close attack controls the ball. It

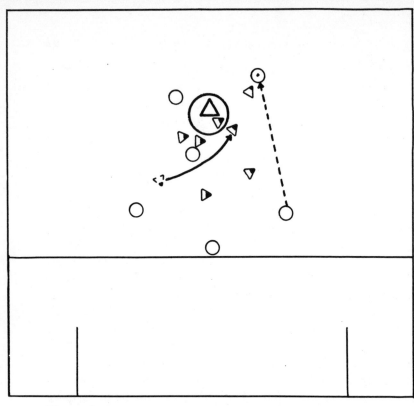

Figure 140. Midfield Zone with Ball Behind Cage. Rover from midfield comes in to corner of crease. Remaining midfielders zone the outside area. One corner defense man picks up the ball while the others zone.

avoids the weaknesses of the pure rover zone while providing excellent defensive possibilities when operating against a strong close attack. In order for this defense to be most useful the opposition should control the ball behind the cage a large majority of the time and their close attack should be so strong as to cause trouble were they to be played man-to-man. The defensive team should have an able goalie, for he will be called on to stop a number of long shots; one midfielder in each unit with good reflexes, so that he will be able to intercept feeds; and there should be some doubt about the ability of the defense to play the opposition attack man-to-man.

When the ball is in the midfield, the defense plays man-to-man—either loosely or tightly as desired.

As the ball moves to one of the feeders, the designated member of the midfield, who is to play the rover, drops in to the corner of the crease on the ball side of the cage. The other two midfielders zone the offensive midfield. The midfielder on the ball side of the field positions himself as though he were playing the wing midfielder on the ball side quite loosely. The other midfielder positions himself directly in front of the cage about half way in from the restraining line. They allow the opposing midfield to cut, moving out of these positions only a step or two as the cutters go by. It is most important that these midfielders not get sucked out of position. The close defense man playing the ball covers his man tightly trying to keep him as far from the cage as possible. The crease defense zones the crease area, though if the crease attack stays in front of the goal, the coverage will be almost man-to-man. If the crease attack slides off the crease, the crease defense does not follow. The off-side defense man slides in to zone the far side of the crease. He will cover the off-side feeder if he tries to cut in front of the cage, and he is responsible for the off-side offensive midfielder should he try to sneak into scoring position on the far side of the goal. Since he is playing a zone, he will not follow a cutter across the crease.

The defense plays to intercept any feeds thrown into the area in front of the goal. The rover in particular keeps his stick up and the entire defense focuses its attention on the

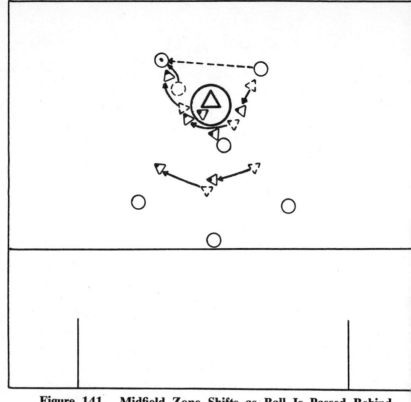

Figure 141. Midfield Zone Shifts as Ball Is Passed Behind Cage. Rover slides to other side of crease. Corner defense man picks up ball, and off-side defense man drops in to take his zone. Midfield zone slides across.

ball, trying to intercept. The defense man on the ball tries to keep his man far from the cage to make the feeds longer and therefore easier to intercept.

As the ball is passed to the other feeder behind the cage, the defense slides as in Figure 141. The feeder is picked up by the defense man on his side. The rover slides to the side of the crease where the ball is located. The defense man who was playing the ball before the pass was thrown retreats to the corner of the crease. The two deep midfielders slide across the field.

When the ball is passed out to the midfield, the defense reverts to a man-to-man. To make the transition, the midfielder into whose zone the ball is passed picks up the man with the ball. The other zoning midfielder picks up the closest attacking midfielder, and the rover, coming back out from the crease, picks up the midfielder farthest from the man who received the ball.

Figure 142. Goalie and Defense Man Driving Feeder off Back Point of Cage. Goalie makes first move to drive feeder toward defense man.

Feeder Standing on Back of Crease

In playing a zone it sometimes happens that a feeder stationed behind the back point of the cage receives a pass from a teammate before a defender picks him up. While it is possible for an attack man to achieve this position against a man-to-man defense, it is less likely.

A feeder would like such an advantage. It is an excellent feeding station, although the feeder will not want to try to throw through the goalie who is turned to block feeds over the goal. The position also has great dodging possibilities. A defense man coming after the attack man must circle the goal one way or another, even though he is allowed to pass through the crease. Therefore, as he starts after the attack man, the feeder merely circles the cage going the opposite way; someone else will have to pick him up. Two defense men have then been committed to him, and there is probably an open man to whom he can pass in front of the goal. To deliberately commit two defense men to the task of driving him off creates the same situation.

The standard method of forcing such a feeder off the point is to have the goalie round his cage to drive the feeder off the point so that he will be picked up by his defense man who should be rounding the other side of the goal. The goalie should make the first move so that the feeder is driven to the defense man's side. This leaves the goal uncovered for a moment, but if there is no one open in front to whom the attack man can pass, he cannot create a score.

9. Clears

The defense has accomplished only part of its job once it gains possession of the ball. In order to score, and incidentally to prevent the oppositon from returning to the attack immediately, the ball must be moved safely to the other end of the field. The defense must be able to clear the ball with skill and confidence.

By having the goalie come out of his crease to become an integral part of the clearing pattern, the defense has the advantage of having seven players against the six attacking players of the opposition; and full advantage should be taken of their numerical superiority. All clearing patterns involve spreading the seven defenders in such a manner that their six opponents cannot cover them successfully.

The defense man who first gains possession of the ball should immediately alert his teammates by calling "clear" to start them into their pattern. In many cases the clear starts as the result of a blocked shot by the goalie; so he is often the man to call "clear." In any event, he should instruct his defense to move into their pattern should the man who picks up the ball fail to do so.

In order to capitalize on superior numbers, the goalie should not hesitate to move as far downfield as the situation demands. It is not unusual for the goalie to move to the midline in the process of the clear, and the better clearing goalies sometimes find themselves going over that line.

Because the goal is virtually unguarded during the clear the pattern of the defense should include injunctions to the defense: (1) to clear by passing rather than trying to dodge and (2) never throw to a teammate in front of the goal, open though he may be. If either the dodge or the pass in front of the cage goes awry, an attack man who scoops up the loose ball or intercepts the pass will probably have only a short distance to go to an open cage and a cheap goal.

No matter what clearing pattern is employed, the quickest and most effortless clear is for the man with the ball to pass to an obviously open teammate downfield. If there is no open receiver, the man with the ball should move downfield as far as possible until picked up by an opponent. At this point he should pass to an open teammate, who will then carry the ball forward as far as he can until he is picked up. It may be that there is no open teammate farther downfield than the man with the ball, and the defense men should be willing to pass back toward their own goal if the open man happens to be in that direction. It is not unusual for a defense to start moving the ball down one side of the field, find they are blocked in that direction, reverse direction, take the ball back behind their own goal, and then start up the other side.

Quick Clears

There are two ways to clear the ball out of the defensive area quickly, and the man who first gains possession of the ball should look for each of these methods before resorting to a slower more deliberate pattern.

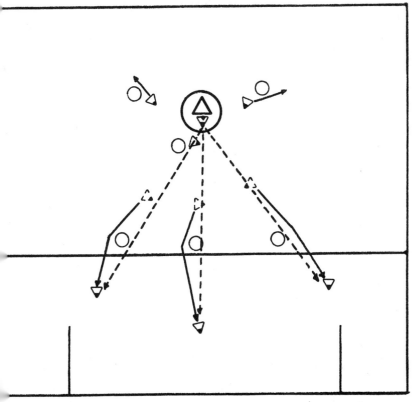

Figure 143. Quick Clear to Breaking Midfielders. On verbal command of "Clear," midfielders break for opposing goal and take lead pass from goalie, or defense man who retrieved the ball.

First, the man who retrieves the ball for his team may be able to run the ball downfield himself. This kind of clear is open most frequently to midfielders who retrieve loose balls in their area. Less frequently is the goalie or a close defense man in a position where his path to the attacking half of the field is wide open.

Second, as soon as the man who picks up the ball calls "clear," the midfielders should break toward the other end of the field, spreading out as they go so that no single man can cover two or three of them. At the same time they should be looking back over their shoulders at the man with the ball. The man with the ball, finding his path blocked by an opponent, may well be able to throw a lead pass to one of these breaking midfielders. The goalie in particular should be alert to this possibility. While he may find that he cannot run the ball directly downfield from the crease, he has a 4-second immunity in the crease where no attack man can molest him. As a result, even though surrounded by opponents, he can take a moment to look downfield and try to spot one of his midfielders breaking out.

Basic Clearing Pattern

If a quick clear cannot be accomplished, the defense should move into their clearing pattern. The standard clearing pattern from which various moves can be made is shown in Figure 144. The goalie circles out of his crease to the rear of the cage. The crease defense man remains in the vicinity of the front of the crease both for insurance and to wait to see what his role should be. The two corner close defense men head for the back corners of the field. The three midfielders break rapidly downfield to the midfield line where they spread as widely apart as possible.

The subsequent pattern depends somewhat on the ride used by the attack to counter the clear, but the attack cannot cover everyone, and there must be an open man somewhere in the defensive half of the field. The possible attack rides will be covered in Chapter 10. Special clears can be invented to combat specific rides, but basically the attack either zones the close defense and rides the midfield man-to-man, or they ride the defense man-to-man and zone the midfield. If the defense realizes which system is being used by the attack, this is all they need to know to select their proper basic clearing patterns.

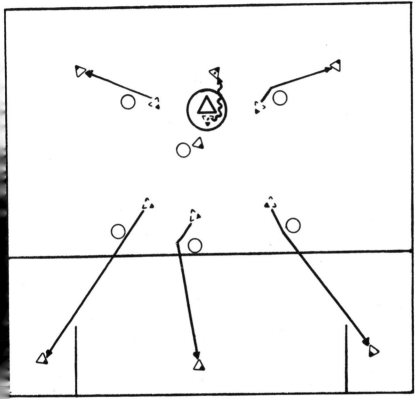

Figure 144. Basic Clearing Pattern. Defense men on feeders head for back corners of field. Goalie takes ball out to rear of cage. Crease defense man holds. Midfielders break for midline.

Clearing against a Zone on the Close Defense

Assuming their positions in the basic clearing pattern of Figure 144, the ball is worked to one of the corner defense

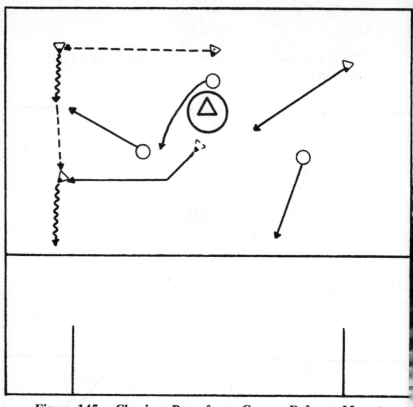

Figure 145. Clearing Pass from Corner Defense Man to Crease Defense Man Breaking for Sideline.

men—the more open one. As he moves down the field, an attack man will have to move in front of him to pick him up. The crease defense man then breaks to this side of the field ahead of the man with the ball and behind the attack man picking him up. A pass is thrown to him as he makes his cut. After receiving the ball, he turns downfield to stay ahead of the attack man who will be trailing him. If no one comes to pick him up, he runs the ball over the midfield line himself and gives off to one of his teammates in that area.

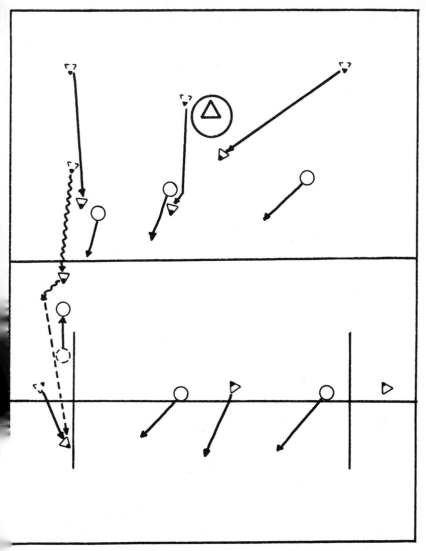

Figure 146. Subsequent Passes by Crease Defense Man Receiving Ball on Sidelines. Crease man runs ball down if unopposed, but passes to open midfielder if he is picked up.

As the crease defense man moved downfield one of his own midfielders was in front of him in the vicinity of the midfield line. If this midfielder's defensive opponent moves to pick up the crease defense man coming downfield, the midfielder moves into the attacking half of the field, and the crease defense man throws him a lead pass. If the midfielder's opponent does not go off on the crease defense man, he runs the ball over as planned. If the opposition midfield tries to slide another man over so that both men will be picked up, the crease defense looks toward his center midfielder who will be breaking toward the cage at the attacking end of the field. If the opposition also shifts to cover the center man, the far midfielder should be open. However, he should not break across the midfield line toward his attacking goal unless he is absolutely sure that none of the close defense men is going over the midfield line. In all clearing patterns the off-side midfielder is responsible for being sure that there are the required four men in the defensive half of the field, and no close defense man should have to be concerned about the off-side rule; this midfielder should always have this duty well in mind.

It is possible for the attack to shift well enough so that there is no one open ahead of the crease defense man to whom he can pass. As the play moves downfield, the corner defense man on the same side of the field should trail the play; and if the crease defense finds that he needs relief because he is under pressure and there is no one ahead to whom he can pass, his trailing defense man provides that relief. The goalie should also move downfield so that the attack will have to take his presence into account as they try to ride the clear. The off-side defense man should move cautiously downfield also and should slide toward the hole, for he is now the insurance defender should anything go wrong.

If it is necessary to move the ball back, the defense should retreat, bring the ball back, and take it up the other side of the field, looking for a similar opening as before.

As the clear starts there is the chance that the attack will immediately cover both the corner man in possession of the ball and the breaking crease defense coming to his side of the field. Under these conditions there will be only one attack man left to cover both the goalie and the off-side defense man. The ball should be passed immediately to one of these men by the corner defense man, and they should move the ball downfield, two against one, before the attack can slide over to even the odds.

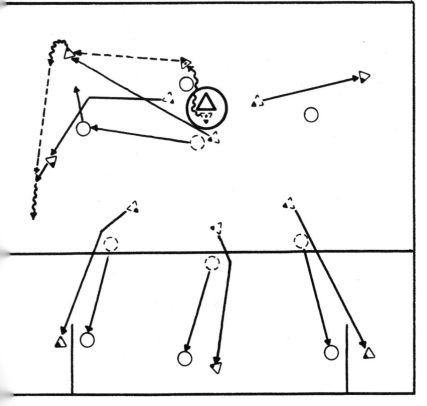

Figure 147. Crease Defense Breaks for Corner in Second Clearing Pattern. Corner defense man breaks downfield. Pass from goalie goes to crease man, or if he is too tightly covered, directly to corner man moving downfield.

If in the previous pattern the crease defense player finds himself covered tightly at all times, a second pattern should be employed. As the ball moves behind the goal, it will move slightly to one side or the other. When the crease defense decides which corner the ball is headed for, he cuts off his crease diagonally back into that corner. If he is free, the ball should be thrown to him. The defense man who was playing the corner, breaks down his sideline as soon as he sees the play start to develop. The pass goes to the crease defense man and then to this breaking corner man, or if the crease defense man is tightly covered, the pass goes directly to the breaking corner man. From there the previous down-field pattern is repeated.

The play of the other defense men is exactly the same as in the previous pattern. The goalie moves downfield with the play. The off-side defense man moves downfield sliding toward the hole as he does so. If, as the play starts, both the men intended to clear the ball are covered tightly then the goalie and the off-side defense man will take the ball down themselves.

Clearing against a Man-to-Man Ride on the Defense

If the attack rides so that there is a man covering each of the close defense men and the goalie, they must be zoning the midfield, two-on-three. Therefore the basic clearing pattern may need to be altered.

The open man is now in the midfield, and the ball should be passed out to the midfield as soon as possible. As the ball moves back and forth behind the goal, the two-man zone on the midfielders will slide from side to side. At least one of the midfielders will be open at a given moment. As the ball is thrown to the open man, he should move toward it to reduce interception possibilities. After receiving the pass, he should turn downfield. If there is a man on him, he should pass to one of the other midfielders cutting toward the opposite goal. One of them should be free since there is only one defender left to cover them.

It is probable that the open midfielder will be the one diagonally across the field from the position of the ball. This

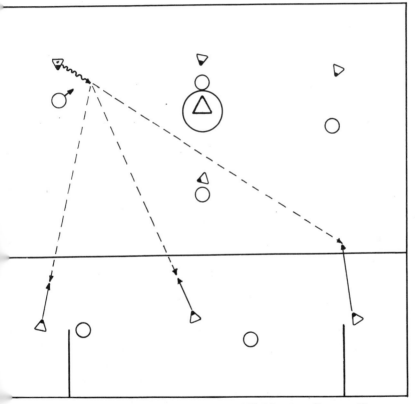

Figure 148. Long Pass to Open Midfielder by Corner Close Defense Man. Midfielder must move toward ball when pass is in the air.

is a long pass, obviously, but one of the reasons for insisting that the defense men use long sticks is so that they have the power to make this pass when needed. Care should be exercised, however, for the pass will be in the air a long time, offering a chance for an attacking player close at hand to get back and intercept the ball. One riding theory of the attack is to make the defense throw this long pass and try to intercept; so the defense must make sure that the midfielder is actually free before throwing, and the receiver must be sure to move toward the ball as it is thrown to him.

Against a hard ride the pressure on the defense is such that they cannot get set to throw the long pass out to the midfield. In this case there are two methods by which the midfielders can cut back toward the defense to help out by taking a shorter pass from a defense man.

First, after the midfield unit has spread itself between the midfield and restraining lines, the center man breaks back toward the defense heading straight toward the cage until he crosses the restraining line. He then breaks to the side of the field where the ball is located. Frequently no one will be covering him, so the clearing pass can be thrown to him. After he receives the pass from the defense, he turns back downfield so that no attack man can catch him and prevent the clear. If he then draws one of the zoning midfielders, he will pass to the more open of the two members of his own midfield who remained deep.

Second, again after the midfield drops back, both of the wing midfielders break back toward the defense leaving the center man deep this time. The zoning opposition midfielders cannot cover all three men, and the defense throws to the most open midfielder. From the point of view of the clear, the best play is the pass to the wing midfielder on the same side as the ball is worked. As he receives the ball and turns

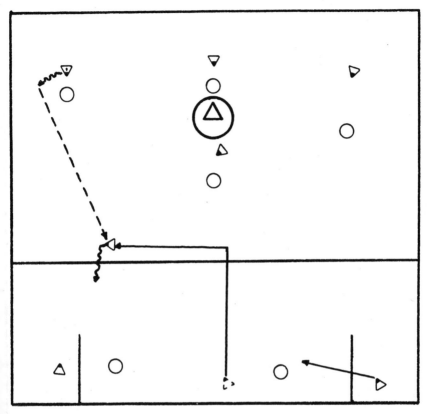

Figure 149. Breaking Center Midfielder Against Man-to-Man Ride on Defense.

downfield, the center breaks toward his side line to take the next pass. The other wing midfielder, seeing the clear in progress, breaks back toward the goal they are attacking trying to set up a fast break.

In operating against a man-to-man ride, the defense does not want too much of a spread since pressure can be put on the man with the ball, so it is imperative that he have a teammate nearby to whom he can pass. The defense also wants to hold the men riding them on the defensive side of the restraining line if the breaks just outlined for the midfield are to be effective. There is a good possibility for a fast break once the man-to-man ride on the defense is broken.

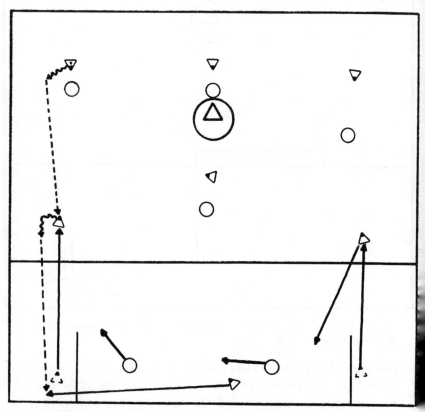

Figure 150.   Breaking Both Wing Midfielders Against Man-to-Man Ride on Defense. Pass goes to more open cutter.

Against the man-to-man ride the defense man trying to pass the ball may find that he is under great pressure while

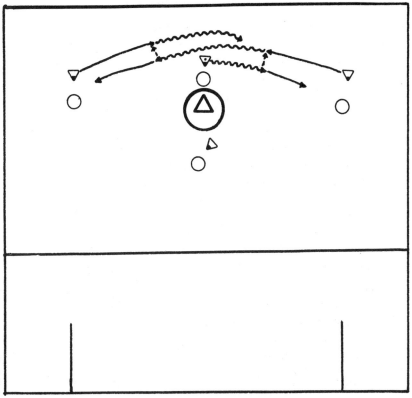

Figure 151. Weave Pattern Used by Close Defense When Tightly Covered. Pattern should be run 10 yards away from the back line, and flip passes to defense men should be thrown to their outside.

trying to find an open teammate. Under these conditions he has trouble getting set for the long pass, and it may take a few moments for the midfielders to start their relief cuts. The nearest defense man to the man with the ball being pressured should break back toward him to take a short pass. The defense should still be able to work the ball back and forth waiting for their midfielders to cut. If necessary the defense can use a weave pattern, similar to that which might be used by an attacking midfield, behind the cage to take the pressure off each other while waiting for midfield cuts. The man with the ball moves toward the passer, and passes him on the outside. They exchange the ball and continue on their courses each assuming the position the other just vacated. They should be careful not to allow themselves to be trapped on the back line where they can be forced out-of-bounds, so they should keep the weave ten yards from the back line to give themselves room to operate. Should the attack try to double team the man with the ball, a quick pass should be thrown to the man left open. The crease defense man probably does not become involved in the weave unless the opportunity of moving the ball forward presents itself. If needed he can cut to the rear corner to take a pass from a teammate, but one of the other defense men should then take his place on the crease. While working the weave under pressing coverage, the defense can employ a give-and-go—which will be particularly effective against attack men who are not accustomed to playing defense.

Long Pass Clear to the Attack (or "Gilman Clear")

In previous basic patterns the attack at the other end of the field has not been asked to play any role until the ball was brought to them. However, they could be used in several situations.

While waiting for the ball, the attack should have assumed predesignated positions. There are three possible ways of aligning the attack advantageously: (1) two up and one back; (2) one up and two back; (3) one or more attack men in the vicinity of the midfield line.

On the long pass clear (or "Gilman Clear"), a defense man throws the ball down his side line and over the heads of

Figure 152. Two Up and One Back by Attack with Ball at Other End of Field.

Figure 153. One Up and Two Back by Attack with Ball at Other End of Field.

Figure 154. One (or More) Attack Men in the Vicinity of the Midfield Line with Ball at Other End of Field.

the midfielders, not to a man, but to a spot, where the attack will pick up the ball. The pass will probably be on the ground when it gets into the attacking half of the field, but if thrown hard enough, it might be in the air. The attack man closest to the path of the ball moves out to intercept it. If this clear is to be used a great deal, the two up—one back formation is best for the attack, but the others can be adjusted to the play.

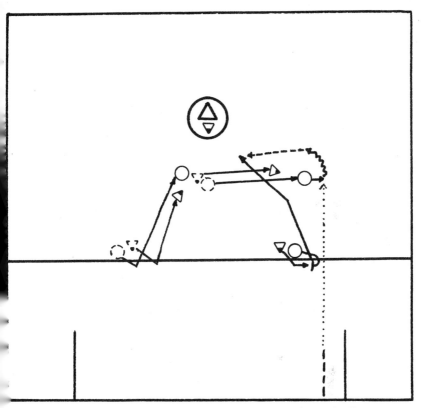

**Figure 155.   Attack Play on Long Pass (or "Gilman") Clear.
First attack man checks stick of defender, allowing ball to
roll past, and then heads for cage. Off-side attack heads for
cage. Rear attack man retrieves ground ball and looks for
teammate for give-and-go.**

The attack man moving toward the ball picks it up if he
can. If he is too closely covered, he checks the stick of his
defense man letting the ball roll past to a second attack man
behind him who backs him up. If this procedure is necessary,
and it will be if the play is used often, the attack will be

able to do a better job of gaining possession of the ball if the defense throws the ball on the ground rather than in the air. As soon as the ball rolls by, the first man turns and heads for the goal creating a give-and-go on the ground ball. Meanwhile, the off-side attack man also heads for the cage. If either is free, the man picking up the ball passes to the open man for a fast break. The off-side attack man is also ready to move in for the rebound if one of the other attack men gets a shot. He can also go behind the cage to back up if needed. If nothing develops in the way of a scoring play, the off-side attack man swings behind the cage to take a pass and settle the ball down in feeding position ready to start the normal attacking pattern.

Even if this clearing pattern is not used under normal conditions, it is often good to have available when the clearing team has a man or more in the penalty box and wants to get the ball down to their attack quickly.

Other Attack Assists to the Clear

As the ball starts downfield on the clear, the defense man carrying the ball looks ahead and passes to an open man in front of him. This open receiver might be one of the attack men. Since the attack man has a defender playing him, he should not break out to take the pass until his teammate is ready to throw. It would be better if he did not break at all until the ball was in the air. His teammate should anticipate the break and lead him with the pass. The attack man should be cautioned against breaking prematurely since at the end of the break, if the ball is not thrown, he will be hemmed in by the side line with a defender immediately behind him. He will be unable to get free without turning around, starting back toward the goal, thus taking his defender with him, and then breaking again. By the time he accomplishes all this, the play will have gone by.

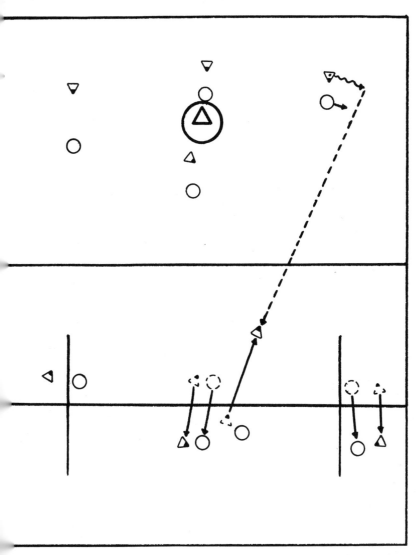

Figure 156. Attack Man Breaking Across Midfield Line to Help on Clear. One midfielder must remember to move on side for him.

Another attack play has the attack man going over the midfield line to actively help the defense men on their side of the field. One of the midfielders steps on-side, and the attack man breaks across the line to take a pass in the middle of the field just as though he were a midfielder on the clearing team. This play is particularly hard for the riding team to cover unless they are fully prepared for it. The defender playing this attack man will probably not follow over the midfield line since he will be going off-side, unless one of his own midfielders happens to be back for him. At the same time the riding midfielders will think they have the clearing midfielders covered and will not expect an attack man to take the place of a midfielder.

Starting Clear From Out-of-Bounds Ball

When the defense is awarded possession of an out-of-bounds ball behind the goal, the defender closest to the ball should assume possession. If possible, the goalie would prefer not to bring the ball into play, for should anything go wrong, he would rather be closer to his goal. Before stepping on the field with the ball, the defender should look downfield to decide what he wants to do. Should there be an open midfielder to whom he can pass immediately he should take advantage of this possibility.

If the attack is riding zoned on the close defense, the free close defense men should move downfield until picked up by attack men. By so doing the attack will probably sag off the man with the ball allowing him to move downfield before being picked up. When picked up, the nearest defender should cut toward him to take his pass. Otherwise the defense starts into their normal clearing pattern.

If the attack is riding man-to-man on the defense, there is a good chance that a long pass can be thrown immediately to a midfielder breaking back, and the midfield should be alert to start their play as soon as the referee's whistle is blown. The defense man has a chance to throw because the attack man playing him had to start 10 yards away as play began. The free defense men should move downfield until picked up, without going so far away that a pass to the nearest defense man is overly long. If the man with the ball is picked up as play starts, the nearest defense man breaks back toward him to provide relief. The crease defense man may want to break off his crease toward one of the back corners to provide this relief.

When the defensive team is awarded the out-of-bounds ball on the side line toward the middle of the field, a defense man should bring the ball in play releasing the midfielders to move downfield. Taking reasonable care not to leave the hole completely uncovered, the other defenders should move downfield. The attack will put pressure on the man awarded the ball—probably trying to double team him—and should he find no open man ahead of him and he, himself unable to run the ball forward, he should pass to a fellow defense man breaking toward the side lines behind him; the defense starts into its normal clearing pattern.

Drills

With these basic clearing patterns the defense is ready to move the ball downfield. Most clears involve long passes, and the defense in particular should be drilled on throwing and handling such long passes. Since they are invariably thrown to a moving man, the lead pass thrown to men going away from the passer should be practiced in various drill situations. Good practice on such passes is obtained by having the defense run through its clearing patterns throwing passes without any opposition.

Many specific clearing problems crop up because of the nature of the ride used by the attack. In Chapter 10, where specific attack rides are discussed, the defensive counters to these rides are also indicated.

10. Rides

One of the primary duties of the attack is to control the ball in its half of the field. It can probably do so effectively if no attempt is made to score, but it runs the risk of losing the ball in each attempt. Even if a play is perfectly executed, the goalie may stop the shot; sometimes other mistakes will be made which lose the ball.

Now the attack is faced with the problem of getting the ball back before the defense clears it. After losing the ball, an attack, which at one moment was quite offensively minded, suddenly must start playing defense and must cope with the problem of stopping seven men with its six.

Riding a clear successfully is difficult, but not impossible, though it takes good cooperation among the players involved to develop an effective ride.

The attack should do everything in its power to prevent the defense from recovering the ball in the first place. This means aggressively going after every ground ball, having two men on each such ball at all times, backing each other up, and regaining each ball that may be lost momentarily.

Even so, the defense does get the ball. The most unavoidable situation is a shot stopped by the goalie. No matter what the riding pattern may be, the first job is to prevent the goalie from clearing by himself. The crease attack man, if alert, should be able to keep the goalie from moving out of his crease straight downfield. He should force the goalie to turn and leave his crease to the rear. The feeders should try to prevent his exit and force him to pass. Naturally they cannot touch him while he has the protection of the crease. He has his 4-second period in which either to come out or pass the ball; so he must make a move in a reasonable length of time. In his rush to get out of the crease the feeders may be able to get the ball back. At the same time he should be prevented from clearing immediately to a breaking mid-fielder, and the midfielders should be alert to change from offense to defense after the shot.

If the goalie does get the ball out of the crease success-fully, or if the defense gets the ball elsewhere, the attack should drop into their ride. In planning their clear the de-fense probably wants to make the greatest use of their best stick handling defense men. In executing their ride the at-tack might well keep in mind any defense men who appear to be weak stick handlers and force the defense to make more use of such players than they wish. Playing the better defense men tightly and playing the inferior defense men loosely forces the defense to pass to their weaker men. Keep-ing this idea in mind often leads to a successful ride, regard-less of the pattern being played.

MARYLAND RIDE

The Maryland ride is a man-to-man ride on the mid-fielders with a 3-on-4 zone ride on the close defense and the goalie.

The midfielders move back immediately with their men and cover them tightly. They should play close enough to their men so they will definitely arrive at their men before the ball. They should sag off some distance when the ball is distant and tighten up as the ball gets closer. The attack has the major work load in the Maryland ride, and there is nothing so discouraging for them as to do their job well only to have the ball cleared to a midfielder who should have been adequately covered in this pattern.

The attack plays a zone against the close defense and goalie, operating on several rules. First, the farthest one of the four men from the midfield line is left open—even if he has the ball—while the other three men are covered. Second, if all four men are abreast, the man farthest from the ball is left open. After the attempt to take the ball from the goalie, the attack drops back into its ride. The attack men start to pick up the defense men about level with the face of the goal, though they will give ground back to the restraining line if necessary. They want to make the defense pass and must never allow themselves to be dodged. They can even give ground grudgingly all the way back to the midfield line if necessary to insure not being dodged.

If the defense leaves the goalie near his cage while the others move the ball downfield, the attack soon leaves the goalie alone, since he is now the back man on the field, and the attack is riding man-to-man and can afford to press harder since the open man to whom the defense can pass is now behind the ball. If the defense attempts to leave anyone in the hole, this man is left alone, and again there is man-to-man coverage, leaving the hole-man alone.

To avoid man-to-man coverage that will result if a defense man is left behind the ball, the close defense moves up the field four abreast. Now the attack tries to force the

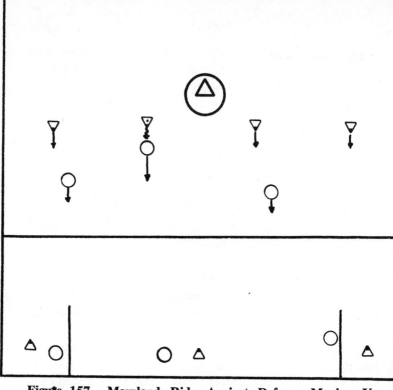

Figure 157. Maryland Ride Against Defense Moving Up Field Four Abreast. Midfield covers men tightly. Attack gives ground as defense moves up, leaving most open defense man farthest from the ball.

defense to throw a long pass. With the long pass, the attack expects to slide the zone across the field fast enough to get in front of the receiver before he can escape from the zone.

The attack will give as much ground as needed to maintain its coverage. It is vital for the other men on the field to cover their men closely, and the nearer the clear moves to the midfield, the more important is this close coverage. The riding team's defense men at the far end must cover their attack men tightly. The midfielders must do the same with their men. The closer the ball moves to the midfield line the less space the defense has to maneuver, and the easier it is to cover the men moving downfield, and the easier it is to step out and intercept a pass. If an interception can be made, the path to the goal is open, so there is the possibility of a good scoring chance.

Even if the attack does not plan to use this ride as its primary pattern, it should have the Maryland ride availabel to use in situations where it has a man in the penalty box and is not only trying to break the clear but also trying to delay its completion as long as possible. The only change from the above pattern will involve zoning the midfielders 2-on-3 in addition to zoning the close defense.

Breaking the Maryland Ride

If the defense will take its time and keep its composure it can break the Maryland ride. The more or less standard break to the ride has the defense move downfield four abreast. One of the two middle men should have the ball. The other middle man cuts diagonally downfield across the path of the man with the ball. The attack will have to cover him as well as the man with the ball and the man to the immediate outside of the ball, leaving the player on the far side of the field open. The man with the ball passes to the cutter, if free, otherwise to the man on the far side.

Attack Counter to Maryland Ride Break

The attack can counter the move, but will have to give ground quickly, dropping off the man next to the side line on the ball side of the field quickly to cover the cut while still covering the man on the far side. The midfield can help a little on the far defense man if their men have

not pulled them downfield farther than the midfield line. The
man who was playing the ball will have to drop back quickly and give more ground, for the man with the ball is now
the last man on the field.

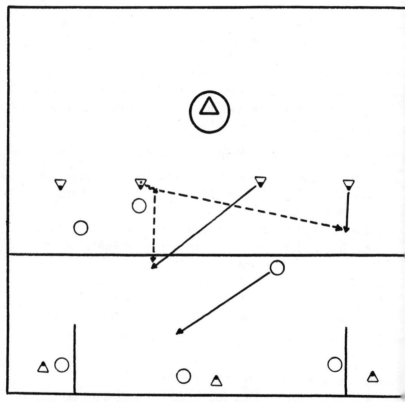

**Figure 158.   Breaking Maryland Ride by Cutting Center De-
fense Man. Cutter breaks across path of man with the ball and
takes pass if he is not covered. If attack slides to cover him, the
pass goes to most open side defense man.**

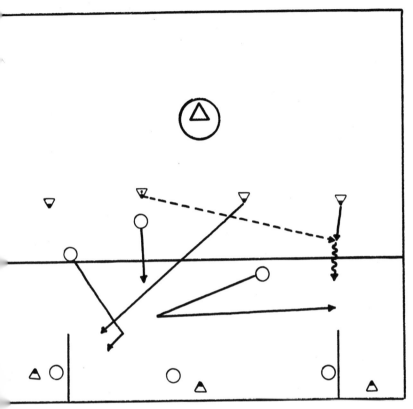

Figure 159. Attack Counter to Maryland Ride Break. When defense man breaks, attack man on his side covers him only to a position directly behind the ball, turns him over to the other side attack man, and breaks back to pick up far side defense man to whom pass is thrown.

Other Counters to Maryland Ride

If the attack counter to the 4-men-abreast break for the Maryland ride succeeds, or if it is known that an opponent is especially adept at using a Maryland ride, there are three slightly more complicated breaks to the ride. If they are to be used, however, it would be wise to practice each before game day.

(1) The defense moves up the field 4 abreast as before. The midfield drops far downfield, however, instead of waiting on the midfield line thereby opening much more territory in which the defense can operate. One attack man waits near the midfield line, however. The middle defense man who does not have the ball breaks across the path of the man with the ball as before. The lone attack man waiting near the midfield line steps over the line, and the pass is made to him if the breaking defense man is covered. The odds are that the man playing against this attack man will not follow.

(2) Another method of breaking the ride is to wait until the midfield line is approached and then clear to a defense man moving across the line. This is the best and simplest method against a ride that sags to the center line. The attack man covering the breaking defense man will probably not follow unless some arrangement is made for leaving a midfielder on-side. This is not particularly safe since if the clear succeeds, that midfielder will be late checking back on defense. To allow the defense man to make the cut, the far side midfielder should be aware of the play and remain on-sides. The other two midfielders, however, should retreat as the defense approaches so that the cutter has room to operate.

(3) A third break to the Maryland ride has the ball moved up the field by the goalie and the two corner defense men. The crease defense man breaks ahead of the ball to a position near the side line just short of the center line. One of the midfielders assumes a similar position on the opposite side of the field. The goalie moves downfield

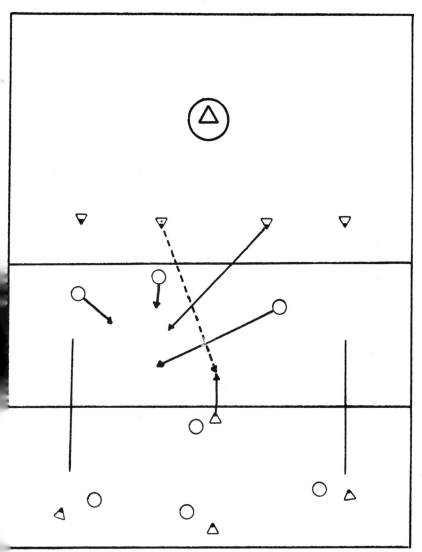

Figure 160. **Break to Maryland Ride Using Attack on Other End of Field.** Midfielders take their men away from midline leaving attack man near line to break across and take defense's pass.

with the ball as the center of the three-man wall. One of his two center midfielders, who have both moved over the center line to a position fairly close together near the center of the field, breaks back toward the goalie as he is

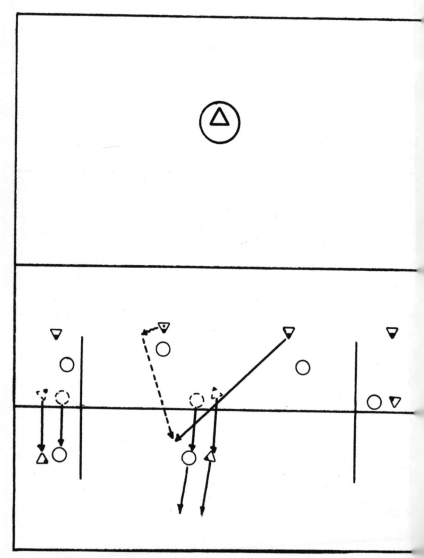

Figure 161. Break to Maryland Ride by Cutting a Defense Man Across Midline. Off-side midfielder must remember to stay on-sides.

picked up. If that midfielder is covered, the goalie throws over his head to the other deep midfielder. If he is open the pass goes to him. If both are covered, one of the other players must be open.

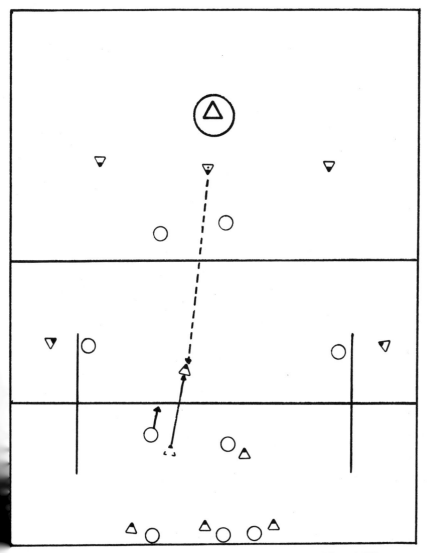

Figure 162. Break to Maryland Ride Using Breaking Mid-fielder. One midfielder and one defense man take positions on opposite sides of field. Other two midfielders go deep; one breaks back to receive clearing pass.

MAN-TO-MAN RIDE AGAINST THE DEFENSE

An alternate ride involves reversing the previous procedure and zoning the midfield 2-on-3 while playing the close defense and goalie man-to-man. To do this successfully a midfielder drops in to help the attack. The easiest assignment is to have the crease attack pick up the goalie; the two feeders pick up their close defense men; and the midfielder coming in pick up the crease defense man. Meanwhile the remaining midfielders will zone the three opposing midfielders as they take station near the center line in the normal clearing pattern. Their zone slides across the field leaving most open the midfielder farthest from the ball.

The man-to-man ride by the attack is a hard ride designed to panic the defense into throwing the ball away. The ride probably works best against an inexperienced defense. The logical defensive pass is to the most open midfielder. This is a long pass, and the attack plans that if it is thrown it will be able to pick it off. The man covering the ball rides hard; the others will sag to such a depth that they can get back to their own men before the ball reaches them.

If the long pass is well thrown, the midfielder closest to the receiver may still be able to get over for coverage. The attack man playing closest to this receiver may also be able to help out. The basic plan, however, is to try to get the ball before this pass can be thrown, or if it is thrown, to rush it enough so that it will miss its target.

It should be noted that in using this ride the riding team has committed one of their midfielders deep in the attacking half of the field. If the clear succeeds, he will be slow in checking back on defense, and the two remaining midfielders will have to be ready to zone the opposing midfield until he can check back to pick up his man.

Breaking the Man-to-Man Ride on the Defense

This ride can be broken by sagging one or two defensive midfielders into the restraining line instead of leaving all midfielders back at the midfield line where they would normally play. Refer again to Figures 149 and 150. As the ride starts, the cutter waits until the close defense men have all been picked up and then breaks toward the ball for the pass. If an opposing midfielder comes with the cutter, one of the deep men should be open. If not, the cutter should receive the ball. When, and if, he is picked up, there should be an open man nearby to whom he can pass.

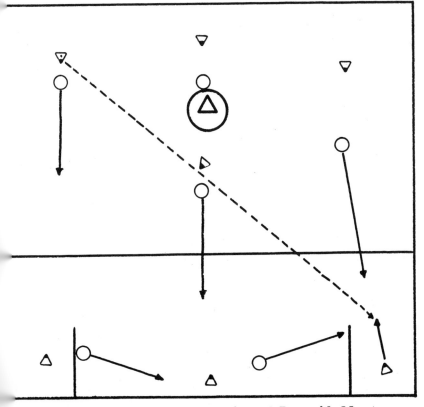

Figure 163. Coverage of Long Diagonal Pass with Man-to-Man Ride. Off-side attack man drops back quickly to cover midfielder receiving pass, while off-side midfielder also tries to make the play.

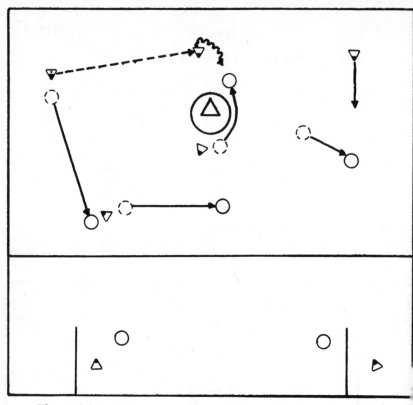

Figure 164. Attack Man Picking Up Ball After a Pass When Using Man-on-Ball Ride Does So Cautiously; Zone Must Slide at the Same Time.

MAN-ON-BALL RIDE

In the event that the opposition always sags a midfielder to break the man-to-man ride on the close defense, there is a third riding pattern that can be run with almost the same objective in mind. A midfielder remains deep with each clearing midfielder who remains near the center line. One man cannot cover two effectively when they have the width of the field in which to maneuver.

The attack man playing the man with the ball plays him

aggressively, while the other two attack men and the mid-fielder who joined them play man-to-man on the other close defense men and the goalie. This is done until the sagging opposing midfielder arrives, at which time they zone the men now in the area. Their zone will leave most open the man farthest back on the field, or the man farthest from the ball if all four of their men move up the field abreast.

When the man with the ball passes off to a teammate there will probably be some delay in picking him up since to move too rapidly may leave people open downfield. The attack will have to pick up the new man with the ball with some caution allowing the player who previously had that assignment time to check back and take his place in the zone.

In theory the defense should always clear. It has the extra manpower to succeed, but if the attack does a good job with its ride, whatever it may be, the attack can break the clear a good percentage of the time. If the attack men can hit fifty percent, they are ahead of the odds, but if they go after their job half-heartedly, they will not even come close to this percentage. It is sometimes hard to make the attack men realize that the success of their team is measured not only in the number of goals they contribute, but also the number they avert. If they can control the ball, even without scoring, and if they can prevent the opposition from moving the ball back against their own goal, they will be helping their defense reduce the number of goals scored on them. This makes each goal the attack scores that much more important.

11. Fast Breaks

A fast break is created anytime the attack men in the immediate vicinity of the goal outnumber the defense men who are close enough to make a play on the ball before a shot is taken. But this section concerns only the 4-on-3 fast break created as a result of an uncovered midfielder bringing the ball downfield.

Possibly the easiest clear leading directly to a fast break is an immediate pass by the man who retrieves the ball for his team in the defensive half of the field to a breaking midfielder headed downfield. But other situations can work out of the clearing patterns. Refer again to Figure 143.

The fast break pattern must be set up previously and should be simple in execution. The fast break develops rapidly, but also disappears rapidly. Probably there will be time for only two or at most three passes before enough defensive players are back to cover the attack men. The formation in which the attack men are aligned while the ball is at the other end of the field should be easily convertible into the pattern selected. The possible alignments of the attack men while waiting for the ball were illustrated in Figures 152, 153, and 154.

The fast break formation should be arranged so that each man is in position to shoot when he gets the ball. The players must be spread so that no two are in a straight line with the ball, and no two players should be so close that a single defender can cover both.

There are three basic fast break formations:

1 Up; 2 Back

Two attack men drop in near the cage, stationed so that they are 3 to 5 yards in front of the crease and 8 to 10 yards on either side of the center of the goal. The third attack man, or point man, waits roughly on the restraining line for the fast break. If possible the point man should be able to play both hands; if no such person is available, his major side makes little difference. The inside man to the right of the cage should be right-handed; the inside man to the left of the cage should be left-handed.

As the man carrying the ball nears, the point man pulls away from the ball, and when the ball arrives, a square, or rectangular, formation will be made with the three attack men and the midfielder bringing down the ball. If the man with the ball comes down the center of the field, the point man pulls to whichever side will be easier for him—if right-handed, he pulls to his right; if left-handed, he pulls to his left.

The point defense man will have to play the ball, or this man will continue on and shoot. If the midfielder continues in and shoots, the two attack men near the cage converge to play the rebound or to back up. If the defense man picks up the midfielder, as soon as the defense man commits himself, the midfielder passes off to the open attack man without waiting until the defender reaches him.

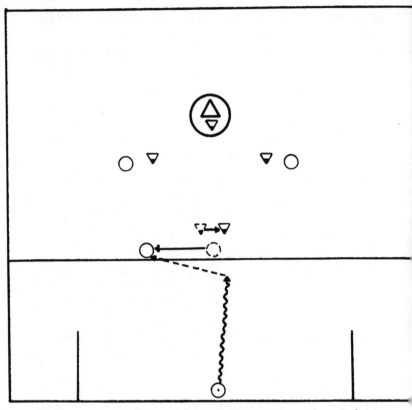

Figure 165.   1 Up; 2 Back Fast Break Formation. Point attack man pulls away from midfielder with ball and usually receives pass from midfielder.

The point attack man will receive the pass in a majority of fast breaks. He moves to meet the ball as it is thrown to him. If no one then picks him up, he bores in to shoot. However, one of the defenders covering a man close to the cage should be coming out on him. He should expect to pass to one of his other attack men. He looks first to the attack man on the same side of the cage as himself, secondly to the attack man diagonally opposite him (who is actually the most likely target), and if by some chance both of these are covered, back to the midfielder who passed him the ball. The point man will make his own job easier if he has some idea of the disposition of the defensive personnel before the ball is even thrown to him. Once the midfielder throws, all the point man's attention should be on the ball, but if he glances at the defense just prior to the pass, he will have a good idea which attack man will be most open for his own pass.

The attack man near the cage to whom the second pass is thrown should move toward the passer and to the front of the goal as soon as the ball is in the air. He must shoot with dispatch, for a defense man is probably bearing down on him. Occasionally he may want to pass off to the other inside attack man, who should now be moving across the mouth of the goal to look for the rebound. Any unnecessary pass merely adds an additional possibility of the ball being dropped.

The above play assumed that the midfielder passed off to the point man. Ninety percent of the time this is the logical play, but occasionally the defense shifts prematurely leaving one of the back attack men open. The midfielder should be alert to this possibility and make the appropriate pass. The back corner attack men react exactly as if the pass had come from the point attack man.

2 Up; 1 Back

In the second basic pattern one man drops back in front of the goal a yard or two in front of the crease. The other two men drop back inside the restraining line about 15 yards in front of the crease and 10 to 12 yards on either side of the center of the goal. The man with the ball heads directly for the goal making the fourth point of a diamond shaped figure. If no one picks him up, he will continue on to shoot. The man in front of the goal will screen for him and then play the rebound, if any.

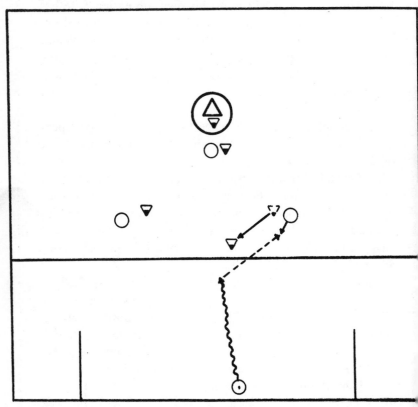

Figure 166. 2 Up; 1 Back Fast Break Formation. When mid-fielder is picked up, pass is thrown to open attack man.

If the midfielder is picked up, he passes to the open attack man. Again he passes as soon as the defense man has committed himself. Nine out of ten times one of the two outside men will be the free attack man.

As the pass is thrown to an attack man, he should move toward the ball. If uncovered, he should bore in and shoot. If picked up, he should pass to a teammate, looking first to the man in front of the goal, second to his partner across the way (who is the most likely target), and third back to the midfielder who gave him the ball.

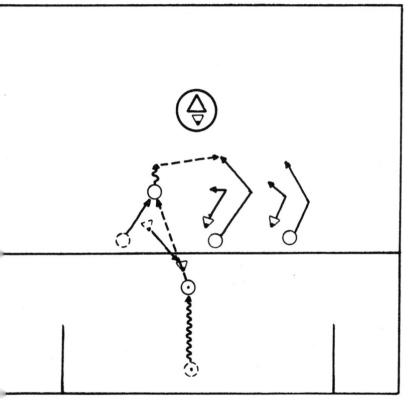

Figure 167. 3 Up Fast Break Formation.

3 Up

The three attack men should spread out along the re-straining line. As the midfielder approaches, one of the defense men will move to pick him up. The attack man who has been left open breaks for the cage to take a lead pass from the midfielder. The other two attack men move just enough to keep their defense men occupied. After the first pass is thrown, they break for the cage. If the defense shifts to pick up the first receiver, he will pass to one of the remaining attack men.

Variations on these basic patterns can be developed to confuse the defense, but the more complicated they become, the more chance there is for error.

Whatever pattern is selected, it should be practiced frequently; not only for the benefit of the attack, but also to train the defense in playing the 3-on-4 situation. There is considerable pressure on the attack in the fast break, and even without defense men causing a miscue, the attack may mess up the play from being over anxious unless it is completely familiar with the play and its possibilities. The major mistake made by inexperienced attack men is to stand still and wait for a pass. They must move toward the ball, concentrate completely on it, make the catch, turn quickly, appraise the situation, and pass or shoot as the situation demands. Failure to move invariably means that a defense man will intercept or check the stick of the receiver. This point cannot be emphasized enough.

DEFENSING THE FAST BREAK

Against the fast break, the defense tries to force the attack to pass a maximum number of times before getting a shot in the hope that the attack will lose the ball. It is also hoped that perhaps one the passes will be intercepted or deflected, one of the receivers will be checked before he gains control of the ball, or midfield help will arrive before it is too late.

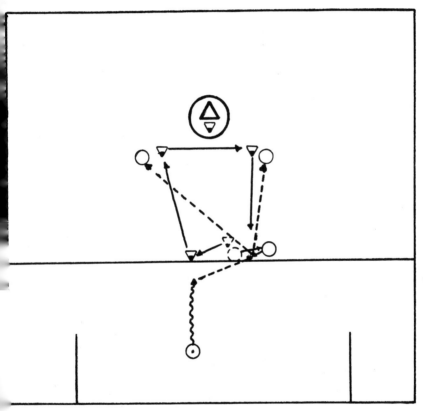

Figure 168. 1 Up; 2 Back Fast Break. Clockwise Rotation of Defense to Counter Counterclockwise Rotation of Ball by Attack.

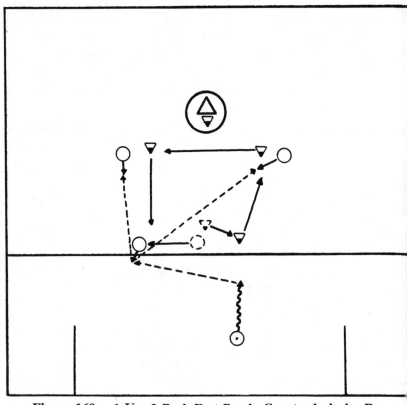

Figure 169. 1 Up; 2 Back Fast Break. Counterclockwise Rotation of Defense to Counter Clockwise Rotation of Ball by Attack.

As soon as the fast break is recognized, the defense pulls in toward the goal. (It is better too close to the goal than too far away from it.) The defender closest to the extra man coming in with the ball should meet him, play to force him to pass, and nothing more. Sometimes it is unclear which man should go, so the one who makes the move should announce loudly to his teammates "I've got the ball." He

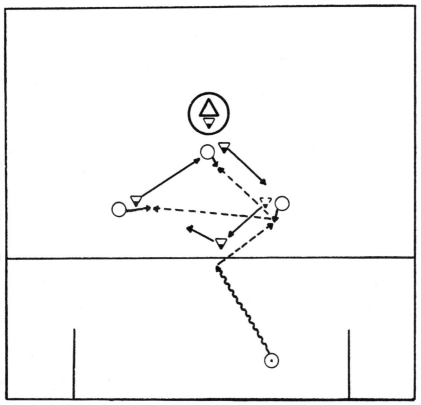

Figure 170.   2 Up; 1 Back Fast Break. Clockwise Rotation of Defense to Counter Counterclockwise Rotation of Ball by Attack.

should meet the midfielder just inside the restraining line and give ground toward the goal until between 10 and 15 yards out if the midfielder forces his way in. To move too soon takes the defense man out of further play; and his presence is needed. To move too late allows the midfielder to approach too close and shoot.

After the extra man is picked up and forced to pass, the

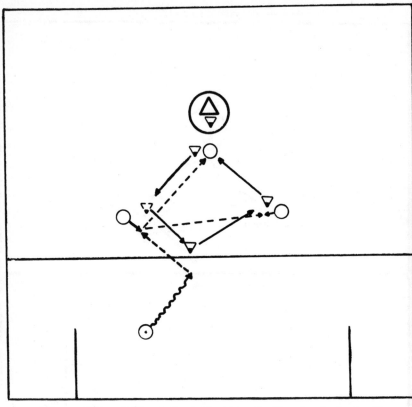

Figure 171. 2 Up; 1 Back Fast Break. Counterclockwise Rotation of Defense to Counter Clockwise Rotation of Ball by Attack.

defense rotates in the opposite direction to that of the ball. Assuming the ball moves around the outside of the attack formation in a clockwise direction, the defense moves in a counterclockwise direction, and vice versa. The defense can anticipate slightly the passes that will be made and so at least be ready to move as the ball is thrown.

When a defense man makes a play on a man near the

restraining line, as the point defense man does, as soon as the pass is thrown he turns immediately back to the crease to pick up a new man. In making the turn to the crease he should always turn to the inside of the field—never taking his eyes off the play by turning to the outside. He raises his stick to block subsequent passes as he heads for the pipe of the cage on his side. Only when close to the goal does he worry about picking up a man. Most other defense men will not have any problem which way to turn, but they too should keep their eyes on the ball at all times.

The defense is playing a zone, and no defense man should go behind the cage, even if an attack man does. Nor should a defense man follow an attack man outside the zone of immediate fast break danger.

Occasionally there is a situation where the goalie can help by checking a receiver. This is in addition to his normal duty of directing the defense. When a ball is thrown to an attack man uncovered near the crease, the goalie, if he believes he can reach this man before the ball, or just as the ball arrives, should come out of the crease to check the attack man, aiming for the attack man's body and checking his stick in the process. If he sees that he will arrive after the ball, it would be better for him to stay in the goal, fill as much of the cage as possible, cover the attack man's stick with his own, and provide a target with his stick and chest at which the attack man is likely to throw.

In theory the defense should not stop many fast breaks; in reality they stop a good number either through the excellence of their own play or through mistakes made by the attack. Both offensive and defensive plays on the fast break are hard to execute perfectly, and intensive practice is needed for both groups.

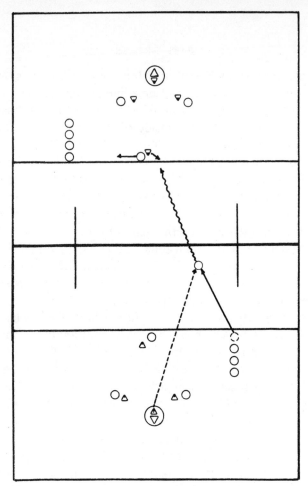

Figure 172.   Drill 30.   Full Field Fast Break Drill.

Drill 30—Full Field Fast Break Drill

Having midfielders bring the ball downfield on fast breaks provides rapid practice by creating a new situation as soon as the previous one is finished. Figure 172 diagrams a drill involving many players. With fast break patterns set up at either end of the field, the midfielders are arranged in two groups, one in the neighborhood of the restraining line at one end of the field, and the second in similar position at the other end. The goalie starts the ball in play and passes to a midfielder breaking downfield out of the group at his end of the field. The midfielder takes the lead pass and continues toward the other end of the field creating the fast break. As soon as that play is concluded, the defense man closest to the ball retrieves it and passes to a midfielder breaking out of the group at his end. It the ball goes out of play and cannot be retrieved quickly, the goalie puts another ball in play from a supply in his goal. While the fast break is run in the opposite direction, the first attack and defense against whom the play was run get back in position ready for another play.

For variation, a defense man can occasionally run the ball downfield creating a fast break rather than passing to a midfielder. After the attacks become fairly proficient, additional groups of defensive midfielders can be added so that there is a trailing defender in each fast break—making conditions closer to game situations.

12. Extra Man Attacking Plays

When an opponent draws a penalty of 30 seconds or longer, the attack is presented with one of its golden scoring opportunities. The number of such chances will obviously vary from game to game, but the team that profits most from such situations will very likely be the winner.

Extra man plays can be divided into two categories: (1) those which expect to locate an open member of the attack by passing the ball more rapidly than the undermanned defense can cover; and (2) those which move attacking players to create situations where a single defender is faced with the task of covering two attackers. No matter what type of play is developed, it should be relatively simple; the more complex the play becomes, the more chance there is for faulty execution in the stress of a game.

Even 30 seconds is a relatively long time in a lacrosse game; if the attacking team can settle the ball down in the designated extra man play quickly, there is no need to rush the execution of that play. The attack does not have to take the first opportunity available. It must take its time and wait for a really good scoring chance. If it knows its pattern well and does not throw the ball away, the odds are much in favor of the attack getting off at least one good shot at the goal.

The play used is not nearly as important as how well the offense knows how to operate it. One way to insure that the players know their assignments is to use one group of six players as an "extra man team" which is always on the field when an opponent is in the penalty box. The play selected should take into account the capabilities of the personnel designated as the extra man team and should be designed to take advantage of their strengths.

A play that fits readily into the normal attacking pattern is perhaps the easiest to learn. However, if the normal pattern involves a great deal of one man dodging, it might be altered. A dodger might succeed in an extra man situation, but because the defense will probably play a zone, he will be picked up more easily than in a man-to-man defense. Therefore it is poor theory to dodge with an extra man.

EXTRA MAN PLAYS FOR RAPID MOVEMENT OF THE BALL

Circle Pattern, with or without a Crease Man

As in Figure 173, the attack arranges itself in an arc in front of the goal, either leaving a crease man in position, or not as desired. The two normal feeders move to their sides of the goal and far enough to the front so that each is positioned for a shot. The ball, starting at any location, is moved around the arc with each receiver passing

off as he is picked up. The attackers should be spaced enough
apart so that no single defense man can cover two at once.
Each time the ball is passed the defense must move to counter. If the crease man is left in front of the cage, one defense man is almost completely occupied guarding him.
Naturally if he is free, the ball will be passed to him. If
he is covered all the time, the ball works its way around the
circle until an opening is found.

**Figure 173. Circle Extra Man. Attack passes ball around out-
side of circle, forcing defense to shift to cover, waiting for an
opening.**

The attack should be willing to pass the ball around the outside. To pass across the circle invites the interception. It will take a few passes before the defense gets itself out of normal position, and the attack must be willing to make the necessary number of passes.

The shot from this formation will probably be a relatively long shot—10 to 15 yards out from the goal—unless the shooter suddenly finds his path to the goal free. The two feeders should be ready to fade behind the goal to back up when needed. The crease man, if left in the center, should be ready to play a rebound.

2 - 2 - 2

As in Figure 174, the two feeders start behind the cage, and the crease man and a midfielder arrange themselves 2 to 4 yards in front of the crease and 7 or 8 yards to either side of the center of the goal. The two deep midfielders take station about the restraining line and slightly wider apart than the two crease men. The play starts after the ball is worked back to the feeders.

The feeder with the ball forces his side of the cage to draw a defense man. If no one responds, he continues on to the front of the goal to shoot. But having drawn a defense man, one of his teammates is open. In order he looks to (1) the crease man on his side, (2) the crease man farthest from him, (3) the midfielder on his side, (4) the midfielder on the opposite side, and (5) his fellow feeder. If none of the men in front of the goal is open he passes off quickly and hard to his other feeder, who repeats the process from his side.

If the first feeder had no open target in front of the goal, the second feeder must have been the uncovered man. He does not have a shot, but as soon as the ball is passed to

Figure 174. 2 - 2 - 2 Extra Man. Preferable strong stick sides for attack players as illustrated. Feeder with ball forces a defense man to play him, looking for an open man. If he finds none in front, he passes off to other feeder.

him the defense must rotate to pick him up, for if they fail to shift, he forces his side and comes around to shoot. It is on the probability that the defense cannot execute this rotation fast enough that the play is based. The feeders will probably have to pass the ball back and forth a few times before they get a good opening against an alert defense. One pass may be all that is needed against a slow moving or confused defense. The passes between the feeders must be hard and accurate so that the receiver can get off a feed immediately. The defense will be able to move faster than the ball if the pass is not thrown in this manner. When a feeder is waiting for the ball, he should be studying the defense. As each pass is thrown the feeder should watch to see where an open man will be by observing how the defense reacts.

The two crease men in front of the goal should be relatively stationary while waiting for the ball. The feeder must make up his mind in a split second whether to throw to them, and he often needs split vision in order to determine if they are open. If they are constantly in motion, it is hard for the feeder to locate them, and his pass may well be a poor one if they are not where he expected. The crease men have excellent scoring chances in close if the ball reaches them, but if the feed is slightly off target, they will not have time to react, since the feeding distance is so short. They should do all they can to make the feeder's job easier. They should move toward the ball only after it is in the air. There is probably a defense man barreling across the crease to pick them up. To stand still now invites his check. To move first toward the ball and then toward the cage, as little as a step, makes the defense man's job infinitely more difficult and reduces tremendously the power of his check.

The two outside midfielders should alter their positions slightly with each pass of the feeders. The man on the feeder's side of the goal should make it possible for a pass to reach him without passing over any defense man— the obvious one being the defender covering the crease man on his side. The off-side midfielder will find that near the center of the field there is an alley through which it is possible to receive a feed without having it pass over any defense man—though it will come close to several in its flight. The outside men need not be as stationary as the crease men, and it may be that one of the outside men will discover that he can sneak closer to the cage while the ball is being passed between the feeders without alerting a defender.

Since this play involves quick short passes, particularly by the feeders, it works best if some effort is made to position players to take advantage of their strong stick sides. It is unlikely that all members of the extra man team can play both sides equally well. In Figure 174 the feeder on the left rear of the cage should be right-handed; the feeder on the right rear should be left-handed. This is the reverse of the preferable alignment for normal play. The crease man on the left front should be right-handed; the one on the right front, left-handed. Cases can be built for playing the outside midfielders either way, but one should be right-handed and the other left. To start it is probably better if the one on the left front is right-handed, and his partner on the right front is left-handed. Game adjustments can be made after it is seen how the defense plays and which deep man is likely to have the shot.

1 - 3 - 2

Under some defensive systems no one will come out on the feeders, and they are left completely alone while behind the goal. The 1-3-2 takes advantage of a condition where a lone feeder is allowed to operate without pressure.

In Figure 175 the ball is worked back to the lone feeder. The other two attack men and a midfielder provide the three men on the crease. The normal crease man plays in front of the goal about 2 or 3 yards off the crease. The two side crease men play about 7 or 8 yards on either side of him and about 4 yards in front of the crease so that each has an angle on the cage. The two deep men play so that they have alleys to them from the feeder, and they will probably be less wide part than the two wide crease men.

Figure 175.   1 - 3 - 2 Extra Man. Lone feeder forces one side to make a defense man play him, looking for an open man. If none is found, he rolls around back of cage and repeats move on other side.

The feeder takes the ball and forces a side to draw a defense man to stop him from rounding the cage. After drawing such a man, the feeder looks (1) to the crease man on his side, (2) the middle crease man, (3) the off-side crease man, (4) the midfielder on his side, and (5) the off-side midfielder, in that order, passing to the open man. Of course the feeder will have to decide if the open man can get off a shot before being checked. If he elects not

Figure 176. 4 - 1 Zone by Defense against 2 - 2 - 2 Provides Opening for Attack to Move into 2 - 3 - 1.

to throw, he then rolls behind the cage and forces the other side of the goal. Since no defense man plays him permanently, the defense must shift to pick him up on this new side, and the play is based on the inability of the defense to make this shift.

The same instructions given to the crease men on the 2-2-2 apply to those on the 1-3-2 as do the observations on the optimum arrangements of stick sides for the players, though it makes no difference which is the strong side for either the feeder or the center crease man.

A combination extra man play can be made out of the 2-2-2 and the 1-3-2. The only needed adjustment to move from one to the other is to have the spare feeder slide to the front of the cage to become one of the crease men. The normal crease men slide away so that the three of them are properly spaced. In this way a play is provided if pressure is put on the feeders and another if pressure is not.

2 - 3 - 1

Against an extra man team that plays a 2-2-2, some defenses will play almost man-to-man on the crease men and feeders, leaving a single man to guard the two deep midfielders. Against such a defense the obvious feed is to one of these deep men. As he receives the ball, he looks for the opportunity to shoot, but if picked up immediately by the lone defender, he passes off to his partner on the outside

Figure 177. 2 - 3 - 1 Extra Man Arranged by Cutting Off-Side Midfielder to Crease. If he is uncovered, feed goes to him; if covered, lone deep midfielder is most likely open.

for the shot. These deep midfielders will have better success with their long shots if they shoot side arm. Since a defender coming out to play the shooter is probably in line with the cage, an overhand shot is likely to strike him, whereas the side arm stands a better chance of getting around him.

If the attack would rather shoot closer, however, they should go into the 2-3-1 by having one of these deep men cut into the center of the crease area. The two crease men, already present, slide slightly to the outside as the midfielder arrives. The cutting midfielder may be open on his cut, and a feed can be thrown to him as he arrives in front of the goal. He should time his cut so that he arrives while the feeder on his strong stick side has the ball. If he is right-handed, the feeder to the left rear of the cage should have the ball.

If the lone midfield defender comes with the cutter, there is no one left to defend against the remaining deep man. If no one comes with the cutter, the defense in front of the cage will now have to zone the three crease men, and the attack can create an opening by passing the ball back and forth behind the cage.

1 - 4 - 1

As in Figure 178 one midfielder remains deep on the restraining line, one feeder remains behind the cage, and four men arrange themselves across the front of the crease. The two inside crease men are about 3 to 4 yards in front of the crease and about 5 to 6 yards on either side of the center of the goal. The wing crease men are wider and farther off the crease.

The ball can be worked from the rear of the cage or from the center midfielder. If worked by the feeder, he first forces one side and then the other while searching for an

Figure 178. 1 - 4 - 1 Extra Man. Ball worked by lone feeder who forces a side looking for open man. Ball may also be worked by center midfielder.

open man. With each change of side the defense must slide to cover him. If the defense puts a man on him permanently (which is the best defense against this pattern), there is an open man in front of the goal. As he forces a side, the feeder looks at: (1) the inside crease man nearer to him; (2) the inside crease man who is farther from him; (3) the wing crease man on his side; (4) the center midfielder; and (5) the off-side wing crease man. The off-side crease man is the least inviting target, not because he has a poor shot from his position, but because to get the ball to him requires throwing through the defense.

To work the ball from the center midfielder, the feeder must make overtures of coming around the cage, even if he never does so, to cause the defense to worry about him. If he remains behind the cage, out of the play, the defense can cover the men in front man-to-man, but when he makes an apparent attempt to come around and brush on one of the inside crease men, the defense must sag to cover him, leaving someone open. The center midfielder looks first to the inside crease men and then to the wing crease men. His pass to any of them is equally good.

PATTERNS DESIGNED TO FLOOD A ZONE

The second kind of extra man play can be worked to flood the zone of a single defense man by cutting men in front of the crease and passing the ball to the man with the best opening in that defender's zone.

The attack may choose to stay in their normal offensive pattern and run plays from this alignment rather than going to a different formation for the extra man. Any pattern already outlined can be amended to provide for extra man plays, and the possibilities are many.

In the Circle

One of the easiest flooding plays to arrange in the circle is to start with the center midfielder and have him pass the ball to a midfielder on his wing. This forces the defense to shift to that side. Then have a return pass thrown back to the center immediately, as in Figure 179. The man to the other side of the center then cuts through the middle of the area, and the feeder on that corner of the circle moves into the void left by this cutter. There is probably only a single defense man covering the territory as a result of the initial pass, and if he goes with the cutter, the feeder moving into the area is open. Otherwise the cutter is uncovered.

Another cut that can be run off the circle pattern requires that the ball be started at one side of the circle and passed all the way around. When the ball reaches the feeder on the

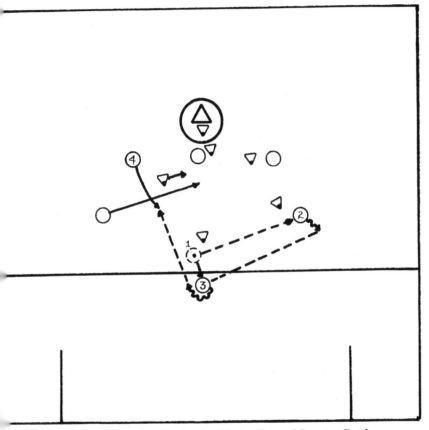

Figure 179. Feed by Center in Circle Extra Man to Cutting Feeder. Center passes first to one wing midfielder to force defense to cover, takes return pass, and feeds either cutting wing midfielder on other side, or feeder who breaks behind the wing.

corner opposite that where the ball started, an alert defense will have rotated to cover all players near the ball. At that instant one of the players on the far side of the circle should cut directly toward the man with the ball into the same zone as that already occupied by the crease attack man. One of these men—probably the cutter—should be free.

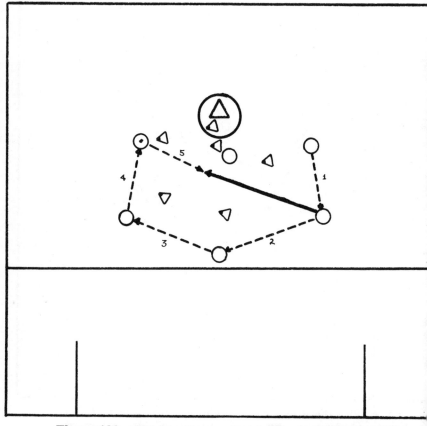

Figure 180.   Feed by Corner Attack Man in Circle Extra Man to Player Cutting to Crease Area from Far Side. Ball is first moved almost completely around circle to force defense to shift and set up opening for cut.

Circle Variation of 2-2-2

The two crease men on the 2-2-2 remain in front of the crease, thereby tying up two defenders. The four men on the outside, circle in one direction—counterclockwise in Figure 181—while the ball is moved in the opposite direction—clockwise in the illustration—until the defense becomes confused at the two-way rotation and loses a player in front of the goal.

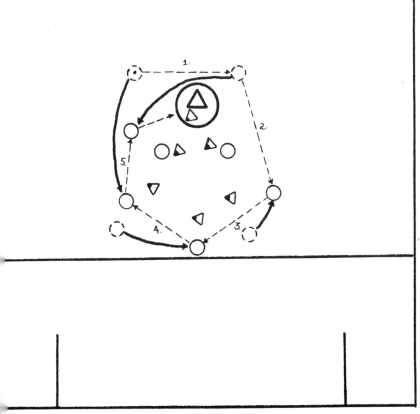

Figure 181. Circle Variation of 2 - 2 - 2. Ball starts with feeder on right rear. Ball moves in counterclockwise direction while four players on outside of 2 - 2 - 2 move in clockwise direction.

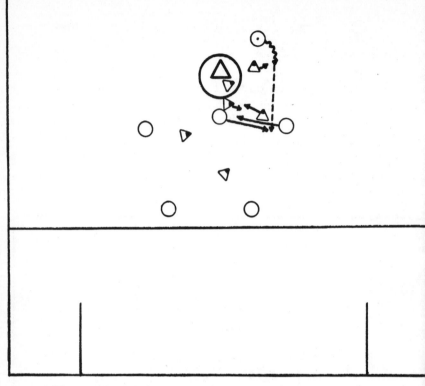

Figure 182. Brush by Crease Men in 1 - 3 - 2 Extra Man.

Flooding Cuts in Multiple Crease Patterns

Since the defense men in these patterns probably play
zones, the crease men can flood each other's zone. The outside crease man on the side the ball is located merely moves
toward the center as illustrated in Figure 182 for the 1-3-2,
but the same possibility exists in each of the other patterns.
As he moves toward the center, taking his defense man with
him, the crease man next to him cuts to the outside, and as
they pass, the lone defender is left with two men in his zone.
If the defender continues with his initial man, the man
coming to the outside will be open. If he switches men, the

man going toward the inside will be open briefly before he enters the territory of the next defender.

A simple brush of the two deep midfielders creates a similar defensive problem (in a formation where there are two deep men). The play amounts to a normal two-man midfield brush, though there need be no actual pick. The midfielder on the side where the ball is located cuts to the center of the field as illustrated in Figure 183 for the 2-2-2. His cut pulls the defense man in his zone toward the center of the field, and the other midfielder cuts into his territory by crossing behind him.

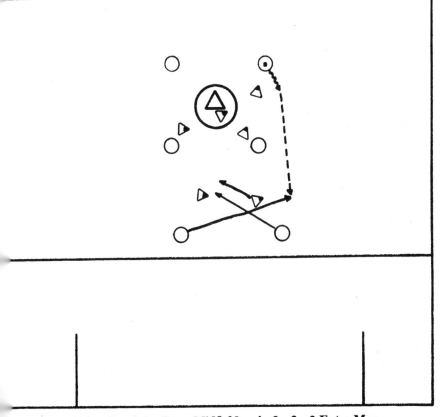

Figure 183.   Brush by Deep Midfielders in 2 - 2 - 2 Extra Man.

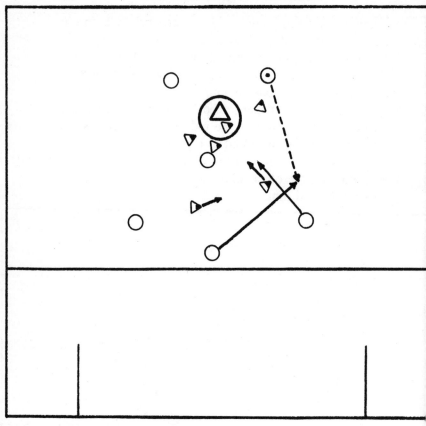

Figure 184. **Brush by Deep Midfielders in 2 - 1 - 3 Extra Man.**

In the 2-1-3

Staying in the conventional attacking pattern provides similar cutting possibilities. These cuts can be made by any two adjacent men. As in Figure 184, one of the easiest is again the brush of the two midfielders closest to the ball.

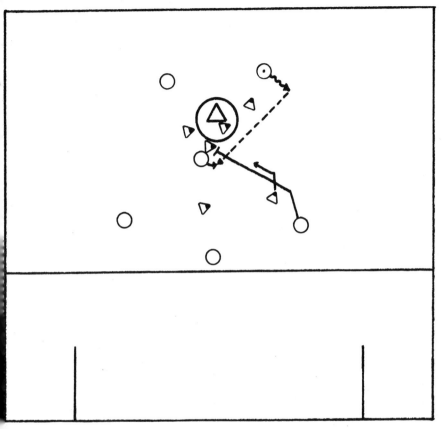

Figure 185.   Cut by Midfielder to Set Up Brush for Crease Man in 2 - 1 - 3 Extra Man.

In Figure 185, one of the midfielders cuts into the crease area, and the crease man brushes on him so that there are now two men in the crease area normally covered by one defense man.

With the ball in the midfield as in Figure 186, the brush
pattern for a feeder coming around the rear of the cage
working off the crease man can be used to advantage if the
ball is in the midfield.

**Figure 186.   Feed from Midfield to Cutting Feeder in 2 - 1 -
3 Extra Man.**

Figure 187. Extra Man Backs Up the Ball after Clear. If ball is passed off, which should be prevented by playing other men tightly, extra man slides over to back up new player with the ball.

RIDING THE CLEAR WITH AN EXTRA MAN

Some definite provision must be made in the plan of the extra man for retaining possession of the ball if the first shot misses or is deflected. Even if the defensive team gets the ball, a very hard man-to-man ride must be applied to try to regain the ball before the penalty expires. Some teams advocate riding the clear by putting two men on the defense man with the ball and zoning the rest of the defensive team, leaving most open the defense man farthest from the ball.

In spite of the hard man-to-man ride by the attack, there will be occasions when the defense will succeed in clearing the ball. The team that has the ball and is down a man in their attacking half of the field, will usually stall, waiting for their man in the penalty box to return. The team with the extra man should make every effort to regain the ball. Each player should cover his man very tightly. The man playing the ball should aggressively force his man and try to retake

Figure 188. Double Teaming Man with Ball after Clear. Normal defender plays stick side; extra man plays off-stick side.

the ball. The extra man, preferably a midfielder, should back up the ball. If the ball is passed off successfully, the extra man should slide to back up the new play. If the hard press forces a successful dodge, the extra man should pick up the dodger. The team with the extra man should be alert for the return of the penalized player. As soon as he appears on the field, the first man to see him should call "All even," and the midfielder who was backing the ball should slide over to pick him up, and the defense reverts to its normal pattern.

If desired the extra man team can take a slightly more dangerous gamble by sending two men after the ball. The normal defender approaches his man on his stick side, while the extra midfielder helps by playing the man on his off-stick side. If the ball is passed off to another player, the extra man then slides to help on this new opponent.

13. Extra Man Defense

The defense against the extra man will probably be a zone since the defense is missing a player. Without knowing specifically the play to be used by the offensive team, the defense should drop into a 3-2 zone. The crease defense man covers the center of the inner zone, his two other close defense men take the corners, and the remaining two midfielders cover the outer zones.

Since close defense men are more familiar with play near the goal, in the event that the penalty is assessed against a defense man, another is frequently substituted for one of the midfielders. Thus the midfield plays a man short rather than the defense. If the substitution is not made, one of the midfielders drops in to a corner close defense position.

Since the defense wants to protect against a shot taken close to the goal, it will allow the attack to move the ball outside of scoring territory. The defense tries to prevent the ball from moving into or through the hole by keeping sticks high and looking for the interception anytime such a pass is threatened.

The defensive team must decide how much pressure to

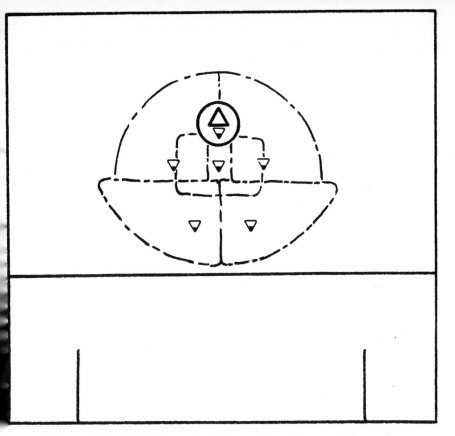

Figure 189.   3 - 2 Zone by Defense When Down a Man.

put on feeders behind the cage. There are three schools of thought: (1) The defense man on the feeder with the ball can wait just to the rear of the plane of the goal to prevent him from rounding the cage but allow him to control the ball behind the goal. (2) He can pick up the man with the ball at a reasonable distance from the goal and play him only a little more cautiously than if the teams were even. (3) He can play this feeder more aggressively than normal since most attack men are told not to dodge with an extra man. Under any system, however, the corner defense man whose attack man does not have the ball should drop into the area in front of the goal on his side of the field to await developments.

There are advantages, and disadvantages, to each system. The feeders, if not picked up, will be allowed to feed unmolested. But few, if any defense men, will be stranded behind the goal unable to get back to men in front when the ball changes from one man to another. Therefore the feeder will have fewer targets. If pressure is put on the feeder, he will have better targets; but he will not have the time to get off as good a pass.

As in any zone, a defense man covers the man with the ball only in his zone; the possible exception being a corner defense man instructed to allow a feeder to control the ball behind the goal. If the ball is not in a player's zone, he covers the man in his zone closest to the goal. If there is no one in his zone, he stations himself at the limit of his zone closest to the goal where he will be able to pick up any dangerous man and in an emergency help a neighbor in the adjacent zone.

The defense plans to leave most open any man behind the goal without the ball, or if there is no such man, the opponent farthest from the ball. In the event of any confusion among the defense men the simple instruction to move toward the side of the field where the ball is located and toward the ball will often put them in the correct position.

As long as there are two or more attacking midfielders remaining deep, the midfield defense men should remain deep. There are occasions when they can help in the immediate area of the goal, and the goalie should call for such help when needed. The three close defense men should remain in their zones except in rare cases when one man might be called upon to pick up an uncovered deep opponent. Again the goalie should be the one to dictate such a move.

If the pattern to be used by an opponent is known, the defensive system can be planned prior to the game, and during the game specific moves can be introduced to block specific plays. A few such defensive plays against specific patterns previously mentioned are:

PLAYING A CUTTING OFFENSE

Since possible cutting patterns designed to flood the zone of one defender are so numerous, it is impossible to diagram all of them. The defense should guard against being led out

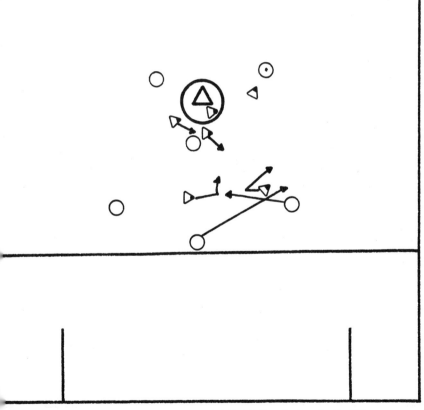

Figure 190.   Zone Coverage of Midfield Cut in 2 - 1 - 3. Wing defender turns first cutter over to center man and remains in zone to pick up center midfielder.

of their zones when playing against such a pattern. If the attacking team is working cuts in their midfield, the two midfield defenders must be careful to remain deep, not follow men out of their zones, and cooperate with each other by verbal warnings of the cuts being taken. One such play is diagrammed in Figure 190 for a midfield brush in a 2-1-3. As the wing midfielder starts his cut, the defender goes with him toward the center of the field. He turns the cutter over to his partner at the edge of his zone and moves back to pick up the second cutting midfielder. The third offensive midfielder is left relatively free.

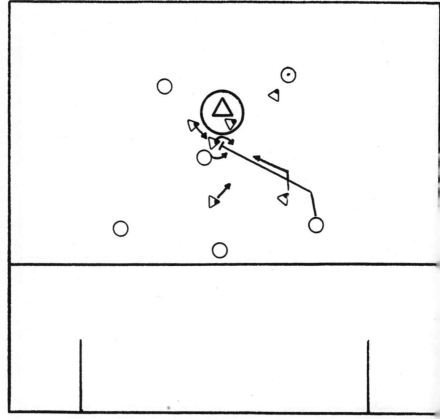

Figure 191. Zone Coverage of Midfield Cut to Crease in 2 - 1 - 3. Crease defense man picks up cutter, turns him over to corner defense man, and remains in zone to pick up breaking crease man.

On a cut that involves a brush close to the crease, the off-side corner defense man can help block the play. In Figure 191 such coverage is diagrammed for a cut by a midfielder to set up a post on the crease out of the 2-1-3. As the cutting midfielder starts, his outside defender sags with him and turns him over to the crease defense man who plays between the cutter and the ball. The corner defense man starts to slide into the center to help. The crease defense remains in his center zone, and as the crease attack brushes on the midfielder, picks up the crease attack, turning the cutting midfielder over to the corner defense man.

There are many possible cuts. As long as the defense is alert and covers its zones properly, it can pick up such plays and cover adequately. If any unusual situation occurs, the goalie should direct his defense to make the play he thinks appropriate.

AGAINST A BALL CONTROL PLAY

Offensive patterns that emphasize short quick passes by the attack to relatively stationary men are harder for the defense to cover. There are two important rules for playing such a pattern: (1) do not leave a man on the crease in order to pick up a feeder until someone relieves that defender; and (2) do not hesitate to leave a man on the crease for an open midfielder when the ball moves to the midfield. As the attack moves the ball, it hopes the defense will violate one of these rules, for in this manner are openings created. Defensive plays against ball control would include:

The Circle Extra Man

If the crease attack is left in front of the goal, the center defense man takes him. Otherwise as the play starts, the center defense shades to the side of his zone closest to the ball. The more numerous the passes in this pattern, the more likely will the defense be forced to employ a rotating zone. The defense rotates in the opposite direction from the ball. They cover the ball and the nearest man to each side of the ball. Most of all they must anticipate what their next move should be.

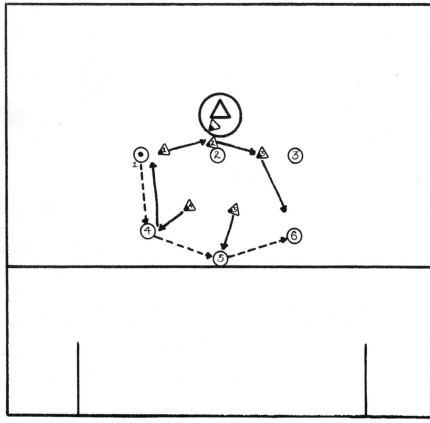

Figure 192. Sliding Zone Against Circle Extra Man. Defense rotates in opposite direction from the ball, covering the ball and the two men nearest to the ball.

In Figure 192, assuming the ball starts in possession of attack man No. 1, defense man No. 1 covers him. If the pass goes to No. 4, defense man No. 4 picks him up. A pass to No. 5 requires defense man No. 5 to cover. Now the pass to No. 6 forces No. 3 to come out of his corner position to pick him up. This would leave attack man No. 3 open if the slide were not employed. Defender No. 2 will have to slide off the crease to pick him up. As he moves, defense man No. 1 slides onto the crease, and defender No. 4 drops back on the corner defensive position. This slide has violated one of the basic defensive theories, for No. 4 is a midfielder who has been forced to slide in close to the cage. Now No. 5 and No. 3 are in the outside positions. When an opportunity presents itself, the defense will realign itself into its normal positions; but it can play as it is for a short while.

2-2-2

There are two ways to play the 2-2-2. One is to play the two deep men man-to-man, and play a sliding zone on the inside against the crease men and the feeders. The slide across the crease demands good teamwork. The feeder without the ball is left free. The corner defense man cautiously picks up the feeder who just received the ball to give his teammates as much time as possible to make the slide. The center defense man slides over to the crease man on the side where the ball is located, and the off-side corner defense man covers the crease man on his side. As the ball is passed back to the other feeder, the slide is reversed.

The second defensive alignment is to zone the two deep men with a single midfielder, having the off-side midfielder drop in to pick up a crease man. This will place four defense men on the crease men and feeders, more or less man-to-man. This is the safer pattern if the feeders are to be pres-

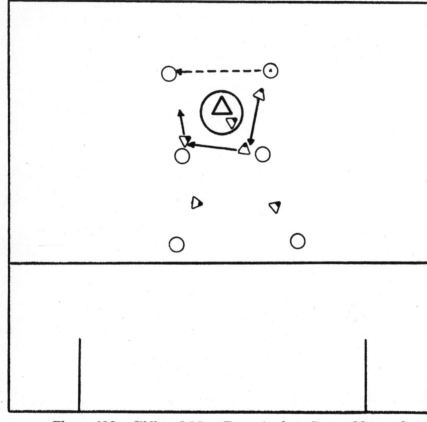

Figure 193. Sliding 3-Man Zone Against Crease Men and Feeders in 2 - 2 - 2. Corner defense man picks up feeder receiving ball cautiously allowing other defense men time to slide.

sured behind the cage. However, the midfielder coming in close to the cage should not make the move until the ball moves behind the cage.

After a pass from a feeder to one of the deep offensive midfielders, the lone deep defender will pick up the receiver,

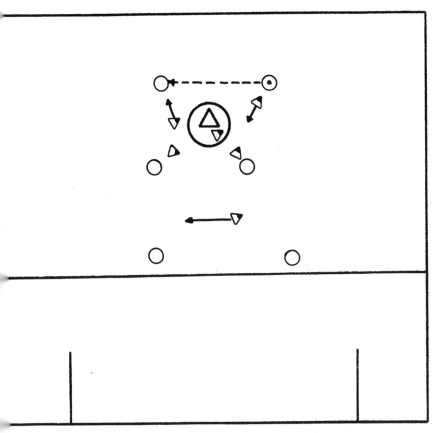

Figure 194. 4 - 1 Zone Against 2 - 2 - 2. Lone midfielder slides across as ball is passed behind cage.

and a man will have to go back out on the other midfielder. He should be the man playing the crease man on the side of the free midfielder. He may or may not be the midfielder who dropped in. But this situation can be tolerated for a brief period until there is an opportunity to switch back.

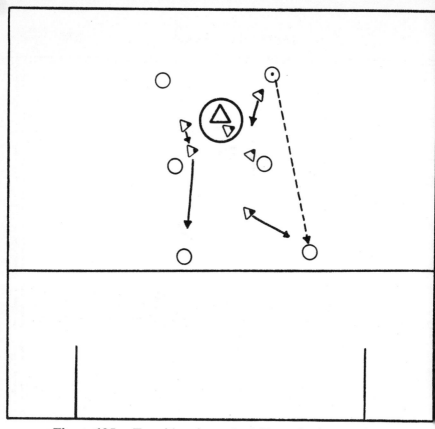

Figure 195. Transition from 4 - 1 Zone Against 2 - 2 - 2 to 3 - 2 Zone When Pass Is Made to Deep Midfielder. Off-side defender on crease comes to pick up remaining midfielder.

1-3-2

The best defense against a single feeder is to have the defense man who picks him up stay with him until he passes off, even though he slides across the back of the goal in the process. Before the play starts the defense should line up in their normal 3-2 zone. When the feeder receives the ball, the defense man playing his corner picks him up and stays with him.

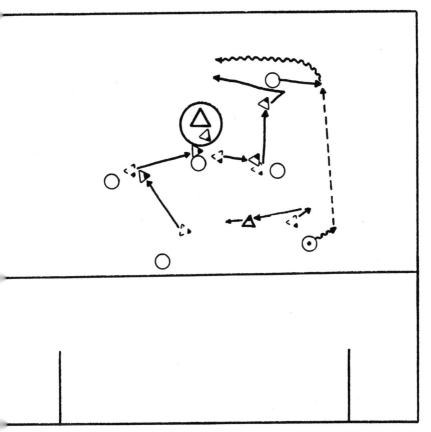

Figure 196. Transition from 3 - 2 Zone to 4 - 1 Zone When Ball Moves Behind in 1 - 3 - 2. Corner defense man picks up feeder and stays with him. Off-side midfielder drops in to pick up off-side crease man as close defense men slide.

Against the 1-3-2 the best coverage is now provided by dropping a midfielder in to cover the corner crease man farthest from the feeder. Then the inside men are covered man-to-man while one defender zones the two deep men.

Another method of setting up the same coverage is diagrammed in Figure 197. It should be employed when the corner defense man on the feeder's side is already covering the ball when the pass to the feeder is made. (It would be very hard for him to drop off the ball and pick up the feeder.) The crease defense man picks up the feeder while the midfielder who is dropping in takes the center of the crease area.

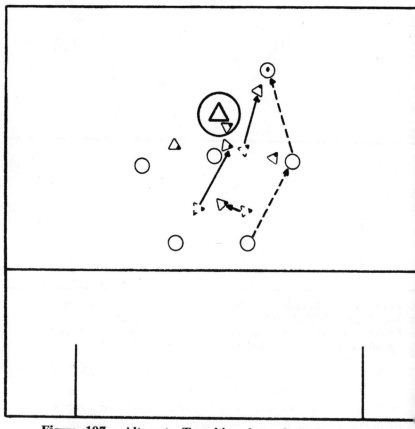

Figure 197. Alternate Transition from 3 - 2 Zone to 4 - 1 Zone When Ball Moves Behind on 1 - 3 - 2, If Corner Crease Attack Handles the Ball. Off-side midfielder drops to crease to relieve crease defense man who takes feeder behind the cage.

In either formation if the ball is passed out to the offensive midfield, the lone defender must pick up the ball, and whoever was playing the off-side corner crease man comes out to take the other offensive midfielder. This man may or may not be the midfielder who dropped in, but as before the situation can be tolerated for a few moments at least.

2-3-1

The 2-3-1 poses some difficult defensive plays if the opposition is able to handle the ball well. There are two ways to defense the play:

(1) As soon as the play is set up, one defensive midfielder remains deep playing man-to-man on the lone offensive midfielder. The other four defenders play the three crease men and the two feeders. They can either put a man on each feeder and play a two-man sliding zone on the crease men, or play a four-man sliding zone against all five attackers. To play the four-man zone, one defense man picks up the feeder with the ball, and the other three cover the crease men, leaving the off-side feeder open. When the ball is passed to this feeder, the corner defense man closest to him picks him up; the center defense man and the other corner defense man slide across the crease to cover the opening he left, and the defense man who was playing the old feeder drops in to become the off-side corner defense man.

This play will not be fast enough against a good attack. There is another defense which will better cover the play, but it should not be used without considerable practice. The defense men playing the corners stay on their men as the ball is passed between the feeders. The crease defense goes off on a feeder who has just received the ball, and the defense man who was playing the ball quickly sags to the crease.

Neither feeder should be played far from the cage, for these defenders must get back to cover the middle crease man as soon as their men pass off.

(2) Another approach to the play requires that both defensive midfielders drop in to cover the corner crease

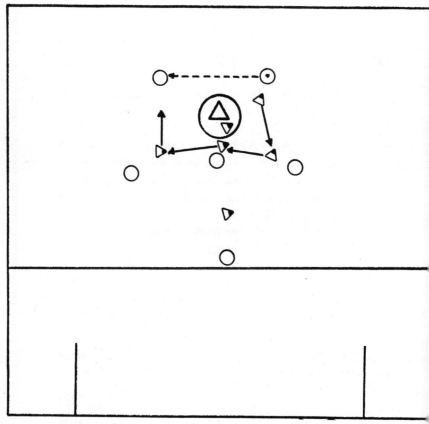

Figure 198. 4 Man Sliding Zone on Crease Men and Feeder in 2 - 3 - 1 As Ball Is Passed Behind Cage. Corner defense man picking up ball does so cautiously allowing time to slide.

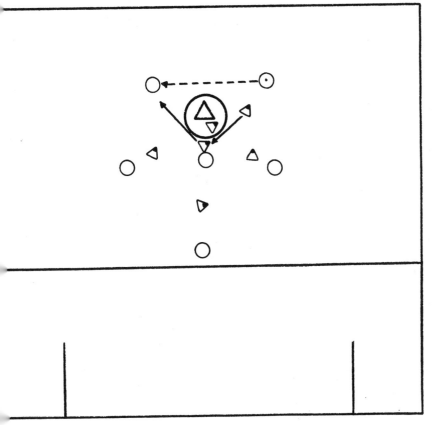

Figure 199. Sliding Zone on Center Crease Man in 2 - 3 - 1 As Ball Is Passed Behind Cage. Crease defense picks up ball very cautiously allowing defender playing feeder who passed off time to return to crease.

men—who are probably the offensive midfielders—leaving the lone deep man open. The five offensive players close to the cage are covered man-to-man, and the feeders can be pressured fairly hard. When the pass is thrown to the open deep man, the defender closest to him (who is likely to be

the center defender of the three covering the crease men)
turns and heads for the midfielder as fast as possible. If pressure is put on the feeders, and the defense men keep their
sticks up, the pass to the open midfielder must be looped,
and a big, fast defense man barreling down on the deep midfielder can discourage him from taking time for his shot—
if he gets it off at all.

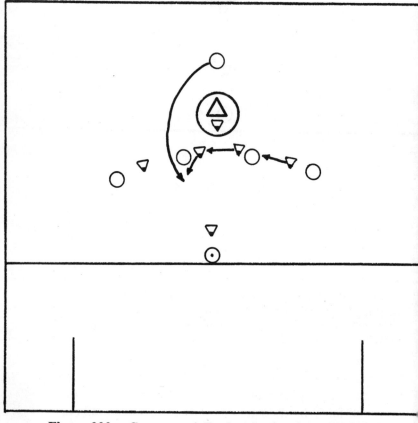

**Figure 200.   Coverage of Feeder Cutting from Behind Cage
on 1 - 4 - 1. Inside defender picks up cutter and off-side defense
men slide.**

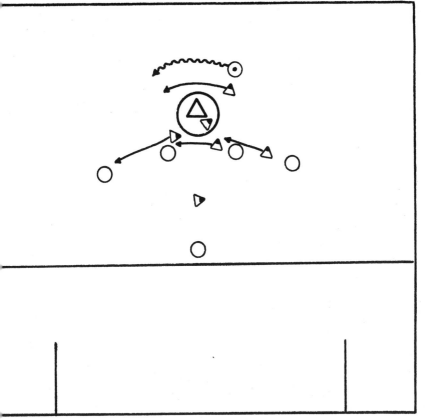

Figure 201. 4 - 1 Zone Against 1 - 4 - 1. Defense man play- ing lone feeder stays with him. Other 3 inside defenders slide as feeder changes sides of the cage.

1-4-1

With the center midfielder in possession of the ball, the coverage is almost man-to-man. The feeder behind the cage is left free, although if he threatens to come around, he must be considered. When it becomes clear on which side he is going to make his appearance, the corner defender on that side stays put. The defender on the inside crease man on that side picks up the feeder as he goes past. The inside crease man who was left is picked up by the other inside defender who slides across to do so. The off-side corner man now has two men to cover, of whom the inside man is the more dangerous.

When the feeder is in possession of the ball, one defense man should cover him, no matter to which side of the cage he goes. There are two ways to play the other men: (1) A midfielder stays deep with the center midfielder, although he can sag appreciably. The other three defenders slide across the crease leaving most open the corner crease man farthest from the ball. (2) The four inside men can be played man-to-man leaving open the deep midfielder. (See again the second method for playing the 2-3-1.)

Unless a specific play is to be defended, the 3-2 defensive alignment is the safest. The goalie and the crease defense man are invaluable in directing the defense to cope with a particular situation that may suddenly develop. Perhaps to make the defensive unit more cohesive, a 5-man group should be designated as the extra man defensive team to play whenever the team is down a man. This would usually mean designating a pair of midfielders to be added to the normal close defense. Substitutes familiar with their roles must be available since the player who drew the penalty possibly belongs to the defensive extra man team.

CLEARING WITH A MAN DOWN

Clearing when a team is down a man is obviously more difficult than when the teams are even. The defense can expect to be ridden hard. The ball must be moved quickly from man to man when the pressure is put on. To delay a pass usually results in loss of control, though a defender will hold the ball as long as possible if no pressure is put on him.

When it looks as though all teammates are covered, this is the time for the long pass (or "Gilman") clear aimed for the attack men at the opposite end of the field. (Refer to page 312.) Even if this clear fails, the offensive team loses valuable time in retrieving the ball and getting it back into its offensive half of the field.

OFFENSIVE PLAY WHEN DOWN A MAN

If the clear succeeds, the conservative close attack settles the ball down and stalls until their teammate returns. The rules specifically exempt this procedure from a stalling penalty. Probably the opposition will press hard for the ball.

Rather than risk the dodge and run into the back-up man, the team with the ball will do better to pass, keeping the team trying to regain possession continuously off balance. If possible the team short a man would prefer to have the ball behind the cage; for if lost there, the distance to the far end of the field would make it increasingly hard to generate an extra man play before the penalty expired.

If the ball is lost in the attacking half of the field, the attack that is down the man should go into a Maryland ride. The midfield will have to zone 2-on-3. If nothing else they hope to delay the clear long enough so that the penalty will be terminated before the ball moves back downfield.

A less conservative team may go into their normal offensive pattern when they get the ball. The defensive team will now be pressing so hard that they will make mistakes. Possibilities for the fast break, give-and-go, and the dodge are most likely to appear against a defense that is over anxious.

Figure 202.   2 - 2 Box When Down Two Men. Do not play men behind the cage. Try to prevent ball from entering or passing over hole area.

PLAYING DOWN TWO MEN

Occasionally two players will be out of the game at the same time, and the defense is faced with an even greater problem. Their best basic pattern is a 2-2 box. Another possibility is a 3-1, but the same defensive rules dictate the play of the defense as in any other extra man situation.

There should be no thought of playing a feeder behind

the goal; all efforts should be concentrated on men in front. In all extra man defenses the defenders should be trying for the interception of any pass thrown through the hole, and this is particularly important when down two men. The defense should try to cover the ball and those men most dangerous and closest to the ball. They cannot cover all men at once and should allow the attack to pass the ball around the outside of the pattern. If the defense gains possession of the ball, it may be wise to use the long clear immediately.

DOWN THREE OR MORE MEN

These situations are very rare. The best defense is a 2-1. Protect the middle of the crease first. If the defense is ever able to get hold of the ball, heave it the length of the field, and let the attack try to control it, or at least fight for it long enough so that the missing players can get back into the game.

14. Center Draw

The center draw is a specialized play. At the start of each period and after each goal the two centers face off in the middle of the field. The ability to control the ball on a majority of the draws gives a team a definite advantage. To control the draw almost every time gives that team a commanding position.

Preparing for the draw should involve both offensive and defensive planning. On the defensive half of the field each close defense man should start near his attack man, positioning himself between his man and the cage. Neither man can help immediately, for each must remain behind his restraining line 20 yards from the center of the field until a man on either team gains possession of the ball or until the ball passes over one of the restraining lines. But they quickly come into play once either event occurs.

The wing midfielders are released from their areas as soon as the referee blows his whistle to start play. They can, therefore, immediately be of help. After looking at the position assumed by the centers, it becomes clear that the ball cannot be moved by either center to his right front through any quick move. The only direction that the ball can go with force is to the left front of a center. Therefore the midfielder on the center's right can play no immediate offensive role in the face off, but he does play a most important defensive role. The teams align themselves roughly as shown in Figure 203. The exact position of each player is not particularly important except for that of the right wing midfielder who should start at the defensive end of his restraining line. On the whistle he should move as fast as possible to a spot on the defensive restraining line directly in front of his goal. If the opposition gains possession, he is the man responsible for preventing a fast break.

The left wing midfielder takes position behind his restraining line as far into the offensive area as possible and on the whistle moves into the offensive area to help his center. It is quite conceivable that, if the center gains only partial control of the ball, it will roll out to a position where the wing man can pick it up.

Though the draw should be approached with the positive attitude of gaining the ball, practical considerations may convince a team that it is losing the draw with regularity. In this case the left wing midfielder should take position on the defensive side of the midfield line and react to the whistle as does his teammate on the other wing.

The three attack men are restricted by their restraining line until the same conditions which release the defense men are met. There is little purpose in arranging them on the line since they, as a group, probably can be no more help than one man alone. Therefore on the draw they might as well align themselves close to their fast break formation with the expectation that their center will come out of the draw with the ball and create the fast break.

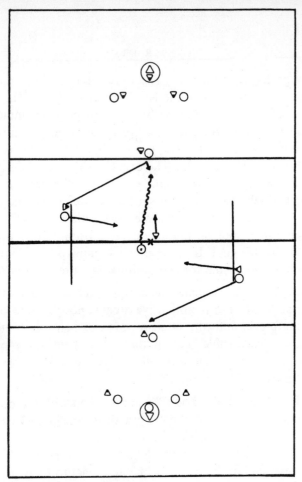

Figure 203. Proper Alignment of Players for Center Draw and Initial Moves for Midfielders.

Alignment When Down a Man

If a face off occurs while a team is down a man as a result of a penalty, the vacant position should either be on the attack or that of the left wing midfielder. If the team feels that its center can take the draw cleanly by himself and create the fast break, the open slot should be the left wing midfield position. If it is felt that the center will need help gaining the ball, one of the attack positions should be left open—though the player on the left wing will have to remain on the attacking side of the midfield line.

WINNING THE DRAW

The center's stick should have a relatively good pocket near the wood wall, and the webbing should be supple. Other than that the center's main key to success is not his equipment, but quick reactions. He who can move first on the whistle is most likely to win the draw. Perhaps if a new center must be trained, the coach should look for a midfielder with enough size so that an opponent cannot overpower him, but more important he should look for quick reactions at the sound of a whistle. Few other athletic maneuvers develop this kind of quickness. The only comparable situation is that encountered by a wrestler starting in the referee's position; a coach might well try men with wrestling experience as centers.

There are certain moves the center can make to try to prevent the opponent from taking the draw cleanly. But the center should always approach the draw with a positive attitude, and plan to take the ball himself, not just try to block the opponent.

The position from which he starts can help him get a good initial move. Both hands must be on the stick on the ground; the right hand high on the throat of the stick, and the left hand on the butt of the stick. His weight should be on the balls of his feet so that he is balanced without falling either forward or backward. The right arm should be bent at a comfortable angle so the elbow can rest against the knee of the right leg if the extra backing of that knee is needed to keep the opposing center from driving forward. The eyes should be on the ball at all times, and the back should be roughly parallel to the ground.

There are several possible offensive moves that can be employed to gain the draw cleanly:

The Rake

The center presses forward with the face of his stick and at the same time draws the stick to the left forcefully raking the ball out of the opponent's crosse so that it is propelled out to the left front where he or his wing midfielder can pick it up.

Figure 204.   The Rake.

The Clamp and Rake

On the whistle the center forcefully rotates his stick forward forcing his opponent's stick over backwards. The center will better be able to rotate his stick in this manner if he starts with his wrists bent way back. He then lifts the rear hand slightly and rakes the ball to the side.

Figure 205.   The Clamp and Rake.

Body Block and Rake

The center steps into his opponent with his right foot meeting him with his shoulder thereby screening him from the ball which can then be raked or kicked out to the left.

Figure 206.   The Body Block and Rake.

The Flip

The most graceful and advantageous of the draws is a flip by the center to throw the ball into the air in front of him where he can either catch it in the air or pick it up off the ground as he heads for the cage. The major advantage of a cleanly performed flip is the excellent possibility of creating a fast break. At the same time it is the most difficult draw maneuver to learn and demands the best reactions.

The referee places the ball between the two sticks resting evenly on the wood walls of the sticks which are no more than an inch apart. To provide a better chance for the ball to roll into his stick, the center should press down on the throat of his stick firmly with his right hand to straighten the bend in his stick and bring his wood wall closer to the ground.

On the whistle he drives forward with the lower wall of his stick to force the ball into his stick and rotates the stick backwards so that the ball falls into his pocket. This rotation will be easier if the center starts with his wrists pushed forward. He then lifts his stick upwards with his right hand, leaving his left hand on the ground slightly longer, and throws the ball over his opponent's crosse.

Figure 207. The Flip; Going Over Top.

The major counter for the flip is to clamp the center's stick immediately on the whistle. If this is done, the center cannot lift his stick as planned; so he drives forward with his right hand, keeping the face of his stick parallel to the ground until his stick—and the ball—pass underneath his opponent's stick. Then he flips.

If a center plans to use the flip, he should practice each day, but not for an extended period. After a short period, returns from extended time on the maneuver diminish rapidly.

Figure 208. The Flip; Going Underneath.

DEFENSIVE MANEUVERS

If the opposing center gains the draw repeatedly, it may, as a last resort, be necessary to have the center employ a defensive plan. Defensive maneuvers that might be tried include (1) clamping the opponent's crosse firmly and forcefully, (2) using the body block, and (3) drawing the stick backwards rapidly on the whistle allowing the ball to drop to the ground where each center has an equal chance to pick it up. If any of these measures is necessary, they might be accomplished best by replacing the normal center with a large defense man equipped with the larger defense stick.

15. Repair of Lacrosse Sticks

The life of a lacrosse stick depends on the amount of use it gets, the treatment it receives, and the quality of the repairs made on it. As a general rule, a stick, given reasonable care, should last two seasons.

Minor adjustments to prolong the life and serviceability of the stick were mentioned in Chapter 2. The thongs on the ends of the treated rawhide wall at the throat should be loosened when the stick is not in use to reduce unnecessary pressure on the head of the stick. The side wall should be straightened by interweaving tongue depressors or pencils into the wall when needed. If the wall becomes excessively warped, it can be wetted, reformed, and allowed to dry. Naturally the stick should be kept clean and dry, particularly after use in inclement weather. It is doubtful if the use of a leather oil will do anything to improve the stick or prolong its life.

Temporary repairs to the wall, bridge, or netting may be made during a game with string or shoe laces. In making such repairs an attempt should be made not to alter the pocket or basic characteristics of the stick.

More permanent repairs will occasionally have to be made. Someone close to the team—coach, manager, or equipment man—should be trained in making such repairs, although if materials are made available and instructions given, the players can be expected to make their own repairs. There are a few professional firms that offer to rebuild sticks. However, since this process may take some time, their services might be reserved for the off-season. Costs are generally reasonable, though the wood of the stick should be carefully inspected to ensure that rebuilding will be worthwhile.

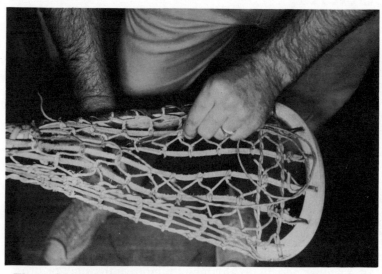

Figure 209. Replacing Clock Cord in Netting of Stick. Old pattern should be followed with replacement piece; needle nose pliers are quite useful in drawing clock cord through narrow openings.

Rawhide Replacement

Rawhide strips of the same width as in new sticks can usually be obtained from any sporting goods store. A sharp knife, razor blade, or biology scalpel should be available for cutting slits in the rawhide for splicing. For replacing rawhide strips in the netting of the stick, a pair of needle nose pliers is quite useful.

The pattern to be replaced can be traced by inspecting a stick in good condition. The old rawhide should be removed carefully so as not to distort the arrangement of other serviceable parts of the stick. The new piece of rawhide can then be threaded into place following the pattern of the nonserviceable piece.

Netting Replacement

The same material used in the original netting may be obtained from a dealer in lacrosse equipment. The job will be more permanent if identical material is used, though this is not absolutely necessary. To replace a worn out section of netting, the weaving pattern of a stick in good condition should be inspected and followed in making repair. The pattern becomes obvious with experience. Again a pair of needle nose pliers is invaluable in threading the new material through tight places. Joints, between material left in the stick and the new material, should be made so that they cannot possibly interfere with the smooth passage of the ball in or out of the pocket. The sections of material should be joined with knots that will not slip. A square knot or a sheet bend will work well on the cords. If the netting of the stick is made of rawhide, splices are made just like those used for the rawhide strips in the pocket.

Clock cord is the most difficult repair material to work with. In order to render it pliable so that it can be threaded

Figure 210. Splicing Treated Rawhide. Slits are made in the ends of two pieces to be joined. End of one piece is passed through slit in loose piece of rawhide and then free end of loose piece is passed back through slit in fixed piece.

into position it should be soaked in *cold* water. About 45 minutes is usually sufficient for most jobs. Clock cord is twisted. Prolonged soaking reduces the degree of twist, thus shortening the life of the replacement piece. To secure two lengths of clock cord, a water knot (or Englishman's knot or fisherman's knot) is probably preferable to any other.

Replacing Treated Rawhide

The bridge and sections of the treated rawhide wall of the stick may also be replaced. Again replacement joints

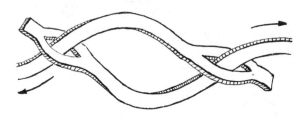

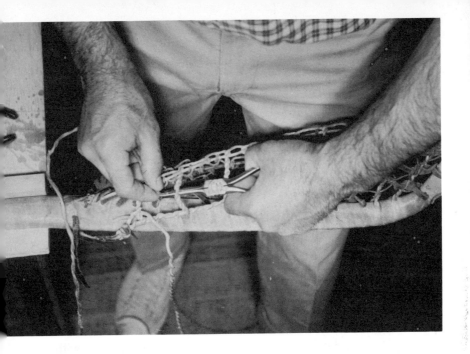

Figure 211. Replacing Treated Rawhide in Side Wall. Pattern of old piece should be followed. Needle nose pliers used to draw rawhide through tight places.

should be located so as not to hinder the free movement of the ball in the stick. Treated rawhide may be spliced in a manner similar to that of regular rawhide thongs. Sections of treated rawhide may be knotted together, though the knots will be quite bulky. Where possible, the splice makes a neater job.

Again, the pattern used in replacement should be determined by inspecting an undamaged stick. The piece to be replaced should be carefully removed from the stick so as not to disturb the pattern of sections that are to remain. A biology scalpel and a pair of needle nose pliers are again most valuable tools.

In order to make treated rawhide pliable enough to be workable, it must be soaked in *cold* water. Probably a 45-minute period will be sufficient for most purposes.

A relatively frequent problem is encountered with the bridge, or stop, in some sticks. It is subjected to more wear and tear than is the side wall and therefore breaks more frequently. The entire bridge can be replaced if needed. A bridge in good condition in another stick should definitely be inspected, for the pattern used to produce a smooth job is slightly complicated. Some new sticks need to have an addition made to the stop to prevent a ball from slipping past the bridge and becoming lodged in the throat. This should be done by adding either a vertical or horizontal twisted strand of treated rawhide to the existing bridge.

Cracked or Broken Sticks

With the advent of fiberglass tape it has become possible to repair the wooden part of almost any stick. Prior to the development of this product such repairs were made with adhesive tape, or some similar product, or the stick was abandoned as beyond repair.

Kits are available specifically to repair sticks, but the materials may be purchased just as easily from a local marine dealer.

Rawhide thongs, laced onto the side wall or head of the stick where repairs are to be made, should be removed. All varnish or other substance must be removed from the wood by scraping or sanding. A quarter-inch electric drill with a sanding disk attached will reduce the time of this operation considerably. Pressure should then be put on the stick to realign it, if the break caused any displacement. A vise, C-clamps, or any similar tool will help hold the stick in place. If the break is at the bend in the head of the stick, a metal rod, pointed at one end to fit into one of the holes used for the rawhide lacings along the wood wall, and firmly braced diagonally across the stick to the end of the head of the stick, will hold the broken stick in proper alignment.

Fiberglass tape in one-inch width is easier to work with on most parts of the stick, but wider tape may be used if desired. The fineness or coarseness of the weave of the tape is a matter of choice. A fine tape will produce a smooth job, but it is hard to wrap without wrinkles. Either an epoxy resin or a polyester resin may be used. Each is mixed with small quantities of a hardener to make it solidify. The epoxy resin produces a much harder coating, but it is more expensive and takes 24 hours to cure. The polyester will harden in less than eight hours. Both can be speeded by heat, such as supplied by any standard heat lamp. Mixing directions supplied by the manufacturer should be followed, though within limits the hardening can be speeded by adding slightly more catalyst. Care should be exercised, however, for appreciable heat is generated if too much catalyst is added. Either resin should be mixed in small quantities for immediate use. Each hardens and becomes unworkable in a short time. Either disposable paper cups or a glass bowl should be used for mixing, and care should be taken to prevent the resin from spilling onto other objects—it is very hard to remove. Brushes or tongue depressors may be used for applying the resin to the stick. Brushes must be soaked *immediately* in lacquer thinner if they are to be used again.

When the pieces of the stick have been aligned, the wood should be glued in place with any good furniture glue. Then a liberal coat of resin is applied to the wood. The fiberglass tape should be wrapped smoothly—wrinkles will cause air bubbles and weak spots in the job. The tape should be impregnated with resin; the pores of the tape must be completely filled with resin.

Figure 212.   Fiberglassing a Stick. Stick is sanded, re-aligned, glued, and coated with resin. Fiberglass is wrapped on smoothly and impregnated with resin.

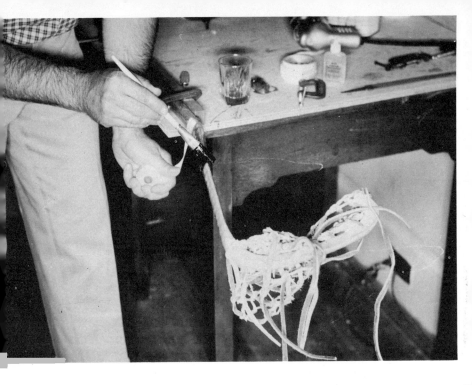

After the job dries, the holes used for rawhide lacings that have been covered should be redrilled. Then the repair should be smoothed by light sanding. Again an electric drill will save considerable time. The stick is then restrung, and it is ready for play again.

To fiberglass an unbroken stick is of little help and only adds to the weight. When an untreated stick breaks, the wood invariably splinters. Almost always the pieces can be fitted together, glued, and the stick fiberglassed. Once a stick has been fiberglassed, if it breaks again, the break tends to be complete and perpendicular to the grain of the wood. To repair such a break so that it will hold is extremely difficult. Occasionally it is necessary to re-fiberglass a stick that has been used a great deal, but most repairs, if smoothly done, will last the lifetime of the stick.

16. Coaching Techniques

Coaching lacrosse, in many respects, differs little from coaching any other field sport. However, the game does involve some specialized player training. Certainly the use of the stick is novel. The degree to which players are expected to think for themselves during the game is unusual. Therefore most coaches spend a great deal of practice time scrimmaging. Under controlled scrimmage conditions, players get as much chance as possible to experience various game situations.

PRACTICE ORGANIZATION

Obviously the coach's approach to his team will depend to a large degree on the individual experience and skill of his players. However, he should organize a planned practice. It is all too easy to get carried away working on one phase of the game to the boredom of the players and the neglect of other factors. In making a practice schedule, the coach must decide what is to be done to meet the following necessities and difficulties:

420

Conditioning

Lacrosse competitors must be in superior condition. There is probably no other game that involves as much running as lacrosse—no matter what position is played. Enough conditioning work must be provided so that players will not tire excessively during the game.

Such work can be approached by special conditioning exercises, particularly running exercises, such as wind sprints. Or similar progress can be made by using drills involving stick handling at full speed or by scrimmaging for an appreciable part of the practice.

Warm-Up Exercises

In order to avoid muscle injury early in the season, or at the beginning of a practice, calisthenics can be introduced at the start of each practice or game. Exercises to stretch the groin and hamstring muscles are of particular importance.

Another solution is to begin each practice or warm-up with basic drills in stick work techniques which also involve motion by the players. Such exercises would include ground ball drills, clearing drills, and shooting and cutting drills performed without contact until players are sufficiently warmed up so that possibilities for pulled muscles are reduced.

Not only should the goalies be physically warmed up, but their reactions should be warmed up as well. To put a "cold" goalie into the cage in a scrimmage situation is likely to make him ball shy very quickly.

Stick Work Drills

Stick work drills can be used as warm-up drills for experienced players. For the inexperienced player they should also be used to teach and perfect fundamental stick handling principles.

Specific abilities can be perfected more readily in drills than in scrimmages. This is particularly true of ground ball drills, and most coaches devote at least a few minutes each practice to such drills.

Shooting and dodging drills for attack men and midfielders should be run frequently for short periods of time. Clearing and defensive drills should be introduced for the defense men and midfielders at the same time. As many different drills as is reasonable should be employed so that practice does not become boring. The actual play of the game is challenging and exciting because situations are continually changing. The same should be true of the drills used. It is better to spend a few minutes on each of several drills in a practice than it is to run only one drill for an extended period.

Many specific drills have been outlined in previous chapters. Others can be invented. These drills should simulate actual game problems as closely as possible, and players should be aware of the skills they are expected to demonstrate as they work a particular drill. Beware of the tendency to invent too many complicated drills making it more effort to learn how to run the drill than to play the game. Drills should force the players involved to handle the ball frequently. It is better to run the same drill in several small groups at various places on the field rather than gathering the entire squad in one location to run the drill.

Contact Drills

After the players are warmed up, contact drills can be run; 1-on-1 and 2-on-1 ground ball drills are favorites. Dodging drills for the attack and defense may be employed if the attack intends to use the dodge as a strong weapon or the opposition is expected to dodge frequently.

Limited Play Situation Scrimmages

Certain plays can best be worked in controlled situations; where the play can be repeated over and over in a short period of time by starting play with the situation previously set up and stopping as soon as the situation being drilled has passed.

One situation involving a limited number of players and worth some practice time is 3-on-3 attack against defense play. The attack especially should be trained to play together as a unit; for each player should be thoroughly familiar with the moves of each of his teammates. Three-on-three dodging and feeding situations can be developed. At the same time 3-on-3 midfield plays should be practiced, if the midfield is expected to be able to control the ball and work it into scoring position.

The fast break is another play that should demand practice from both the offensive and the defensive points of view.

Both clearing and riding patterns should be practiced in limited scrimmage—both being worked on at the same time. The ball can be put in play by a shot at the cage and the play continued until the defense either clears across the midfield line or the attack gains control of the ball and is forced to settle it down, unable to find an immediate scoring opportunity.

Half Field Scrimmage

The half field scrimmage offers better coaching possibilities than does a game-like full field scrimmage, particularly when new offensive plays and patterns are introduced. If the squad is large enough several scrimmages can be held simultaneously.

By using the half field, less time is spent moving the ball

up and down the field so that more practice on a specific play can be obtained in a limited time. The coaching staff can also concentrate its attention on a smaller area and have better control of the play.

If there are players excluded from the scrimmage, care must be exercised to rotate them into the play. Perhaps if several attack, defense, and midfield units are available, they might be rotated so that each unit has the chance to play against each other—possibly on a timed schedule. If entire units are not available, players should be rotated regularly on an individual basis.

The extra man play is particularly well suited to this kind of half field scrimmage. This is especially true if a special group is designated to work the play. Both the offense and defense should practice their roles often, for the extra man is one of the very best scoring opportunities. To make the scrimmage more realistic perhaps the attack should be given the ball as though a foul had occurred and then be allowed 30 seconds or a minute in which to score. So important is this play, that some time should definitely be devoted to it prior to each game, even though the same players have been working the same play all season.

Scrimmage

One of the features that makes lacrosse so interesting for players is that a good deal of practice time is usually devoted to game-like scrimmage. As a result the game is being played not only on game days but also at every practice session. There is so much freedom for individual thinking and action in the game that if adequate training is to be provided, provision must be made for scrimmage. So important is this training that many coaches spend a majority of practice time in such a manner.

PRE-GAME PLANNING

The amount of pre-game planning done depends on the knowledge collected about the coming opponent. Obviously if certain offensive or defensive patterns are expected from the opponent, some practice against these patterns should be planned, and specific maneuvers to be used should be practiced. This would apply in particular to the expected extra man offensive pattern.

At the same time plans can be laid for coping with specific players on the opposition. As much information as possible should be supplied to players who will be assigned specific opponents, and insofar as possible these men should be trained for the kind of player expected. Perhaps the opposition will have a particularly strong dodger or an exceptional feeder who should be played in a particular manner.

Naturally it should be remembered that the opposition can alter their normal pattern for a particular game, and while a team can be prepared for the kind of play expected, it should be emphasized that preparations are being made only on the basis of the past. Lacrosse is so fluid that not all situations that will arise can be anticipated, and there is always room for uncertainty when trying to predict the play of an opponent—even with excellent scouting information.

GAME ORGANIZATION

Prior to game time plans should have been laid to provide for any special groups of players who should be together. If desired, extra man offensive and defensive teams should have been named and have practiced together. If midfielders are to be played as units, these units should be designated before preparations for the game are complete.

Game Warm-Up

A pattern for warm-up prior to the game should be announced. The calisthenics or warm-up drills to be used should be arranged. Provision should be made to allow the attack men and midfielders to have some shooting practice at the cage. The feeders should have the chance to sharpen their passes.

Adequate provision should be made in warm-up plans so that the goalies get the chance to become accustomed to their goal. A coach or carefully chosen player should be detailed to this job. Some teams warm-up their goalies as soon as they take the field; others leave this phase of the warm-up until just before game time. Some warm up the starting goalie first and his substitutes later; others reverse the procedure.

Substitutions

After the game gets under way care should be exercised to ensure that the midfields are alternated reasonably often. Each coach is of course the best judge of when such changes should be made. Some alternate midfields on a prearranged plan based on the time played by each. Others try to match the midfield of the opposing team with their own midfields. Care must be taken to ensure that there is going to be midfield strength in the latter stages of the game.

Statistics

Many coaches find it valuable to have someone keep game statistics over and above those normally kept on the official scoring record. Such items as dropped balls, missed scoops on ground balls, erratic passes, missed shots, successful and unsuccessful clears and rides, and similar information when carefully accumulated can sometimes reveal player strengths and weaknesses that were not readily apparent in the heat of the game.

BUILDING A PROGRAM

Lacrosse owes its spread to devoted ex-players who have experienced some of their greatest athletic pleasures on the lacrosse field. The attitude of the coach and his approach to the game can greatly influence the reactions of his players. Lacrosse is an amateur game; while no coach ever approaches a season with any idea other than producing a winning team; and no player should approach a season with any idea other than working hard to win, still lacrosse is a game, and players and coach alike should enjoy their season.

Neither lacrosse practices nor games are drudgery. Not only should the star players be able to play in practice, but also the least able member of the squad. If successful teams are to be built over a period of years, there must be adequate opportunity in the program for all boys who wish to play. When players become so numerous that it is not practical to handle all in a single unit, lower level teams should be introduced.

The sooner a boy can start playing lacrosse the better he is likely to become. The younger player should be encouraged to start by providing him with competition on his own level. Very few, if any, boys should be discouraged from playing. While the exceptional athlete may become the star of the team, almost any boy, with reasonable coordination, can learn to play lacrosse skillfully, if he will devote time to perfecting his stick work. An athlete does not have to be fast or big to play the game, if he will only learn to handle his stick. He has the opportunity to do so only if the lacrosse program accommodates anyone interested in playing.

Start players young; let everyone play; make practices interesting and enjoyable; nothing can stop the spread of the game. Lacrosse enthusiasm is contagious!

Index